Stony Ground

One Teacher's Fight
Against Juvenile Crime

To JANET —

WHO ALWAYS GIVES SO WILLINGLY
OF HERSELF AND CONTINUES TO TOUCH
LIVES.

LINDA WILLIAMS POST

WITH LOVE AND BEST WISHES,

Linda Williams Post

EAKIN PRESS ★   Austin, Texas

FIRST EDITION

Copyright © 1994
By Linda Williams Post

Published in the United States of America
By Eakin Press
An Imprint of Sunbelt Media, Inc.
P.O. Drawer 90159 ★ Austin, TX 78709-0159

ALL RIGHTS RESERVED. No part of this book may be reproduced in any form without written permission from the publisher, except for brief passages included in a review appearing in a newspaper or magazine.

ISBN 0-89015-918-1

Library of Congress Cataloging-in-Publication Data

Post, Linda Williams
    Stony ground : one teacher's fight against juvenile crime / by Linda Williams Post.
        p.   cm.
    ISBN 0-89015-918-1 : $16.95
    1. Problem youth — Education (Secondary) — Texas — Temple. 2. Problem youth — Behavior modification — Texas — Temple. 3. Juvenile delinquency — Texas — Temple — Prevention. 4. Educational counseling — Texas — Temple. 5. School discipline — Texas — Temple. 6. Temple High School (Temple, Texas) 7. Post, Linda Williams. I. Title.
    LC4802.5.T4P68   1994   93-9095
                                                                              CIP

**For my students
and Robert**

Contents

Contents

Preface

The events in this book are real. They are compiled from taped interviews with the principal characters and from more than three years of research. Although the narrative is based on memory and the conversations have been re-created, the book is told in the spirit of the truth as these people remember it.

The actual names of the juvenile offenders have appeared in newspaper accounts, court records, and police files. I have chosen to change their names and the names of other juvenile characters because I wish to protect their right to privacy. Four adult names (Luis Torres, Ricky Dominick, Von Taylor, and Carolyn Taylor) have also been changed. All other characters are real.

I am deeply indebted to Sheriff Dennis Walker and the Limestone County Sheriff's Department for assisting me in my research of the Brooks murder case; to the many friends of Chester Brooks for sharing their favorite anecdotes about the victim; and to attorneys Joe Cannon, James Kreimeyer, Jerry Secrest, and Gerald Brown for teaching me the basics of Texas criminal law.

I extend a special word of thanks to the central character and his family for allowing me to share their private pain in a very public way. And my eternal gratitude to the Dirty Dozen — who taught me everything I know about education.

Behold, a sower went forth to sow.
Some seeds fell by the wayside . . . and
some fell upon stony ground.

Matthew 13:3–5

CHAPTER ONE

The Dirty Dozen

Angry voices filled the teachers' lounge.

"He's got some nerve in blaming us," an irate colleague railed. She gripped the front-page section of the *Austin American-Statesman* and glared at the headlines:

Juvenile Crime Hits Unrivaled Highs
Breakdown of Societal Institutions Blamed

The article cited recent FBI statistics about the rise in juvenile crime. The number of murders, rapes, and assaults committed by juveniles had reached a twenty-five-year high. FBI Director William Sessions blamed "the breakdown of families, schools, and other institutions."

"What does he expect us to do about juvenile crime?" wailed a weary, frustrated teacher. "We have enough to do already."

"That's right. And we sure don't teach Murder 101 up here. What those kids are doing on the streets, they didn't learn at school. Try blaming the movies they watch and the music they listen to."

"Yeah. And whatever happened to the parents and the community? We can only work with what they send us."

My colleagues were clearly riled by this latest bout of teacher bashing. We had long been criticized because American students were considered inferior to the Japanese and Germans. Now we were being partly blamed for producing the most violent generation in modern history.

The teachers' lounge stirred with controversy as the juvenile crime article was hotly debated. By the next day, however, most teachers would have forgotten the furor. The FBI statistics would be buried somewhere beneath the myriad duties and mounds of paperwork.

But I would remember. I knew, firsthand, about violent juvenile crime and the responsibility of the public schools. The Dirty Dozen had taught me well.

I met the Dirty Dozen in the fall of 1976, during my first year at Temple High School in Temple, Texas. Their nickname came from a nervous colleague across the hall who had observed twelve hard-looking boys standing outside my classroom before school started. She was reminded of the rowdy, hell-raising hombres she'd seen in the WWII film *The Dirty Dozen,* and gave the boys their nickname. It seemed to fit.

Even before those surly, streetwise "troublemakers" set foot inside my English classroom, before their boisterous voices and feisty fisticuffs filled the room with mayhem, I knew about them. The vice-principal had tried to warn me, but I hadn't listened.

"They're mostly throwaway kids," the vice-principal had explained as he scanned the twelve names on my first-period class roster. "Many of these boys come from dysfunctional homes. They're either truants or discipline problems or juvenile offenders. I'd say you've got every troublemaker in the tenth grade."

He narrowed his eyes and studied my reaction, as if sizing me up for the job at hand. He was, no doubt, asking himself whether this little petite brunette in the tailored suit could ride roughshod over a class of rowdy renegades; she looked mighty young, despite her twenty-eight years. He seemed skeptical.

"Is there some reason for placing all these boys in the same class?" I asked, skimming the faceless names on the class roster.

He nodded. "They're enrolled in a special work/study program called CVAE — Coordinated Vocational and Academic Education. It's a new alternative program funded by the State of Texas to reduce the dropout rate. These boys attend academic classes in the morning and work in the afternoon. In addition to earning credit for English and math, they also receive credit for their work experience."

The vice-principal went on to explain that most of the boys

2

in the class were at least one grade level behind, hated school, and wanted to drop out. While the State hoped this program would curb the dropout problem, it had provided few guidelines for instruction and no books for kids who couldn't read. "You're supposed to coordinate your lessons with their work experience," he instructed. "Teach them to read paragraphs from training manuals and fill out job applications. Practical things like that."

"For an entire year?"

"Do the best you can," he said.

"Well, this class certainly sounds like a challenge, but I've had some experience with dropouts."

I explained that my last teaching assignment had been at the Army Education Center in Frankfurt, West Germany. I had followed my husband, an Army major, halfway around the world to discover I wasn't cut out for a life of tea parties and idle chitchat at the Officers' Wives Club. So, I'd committed the unpardonable breach of military decorum and found a job that allowed me an identity and life of my own.

The Department of Defense hired me to teach adult education classes to GIs who needed a high school diploma to advance in rank or to remain in the service. My Army Education Center classroom resembled the old one-room schoolhouse, with students ranging in age from eighteen to forty-eight and holding credits from the eighth grade through the twelfth grade. Young soldiers away from home for the first time mingled minds with hard-core veterans recently returned from the hell-holes of Vietnam. I taught the troops English and history and government, and they taught me about the shortcomings of public schools and why they'd left them. That on-the-job training had been invaluable.

"After working with the GIs for three years, I've learned about aggressive behaviors, survival skills, and creative strategies," I told the vice-principal. "Now I'd like to use some preventive measures and keep kids in school."

The administrator forced a half-smile, as if amused by my youthful enthusiasm. "When you've been in the trenches for as long as I have, Mrs. Post, you'll realize that some of these kids are lost before they get to us. Some are gonna drop out or end up in jail, no matter what we do." A look of sadness clouded his eyes as

3

he added, "Try to teach them something while they're here, and don't feel bad when you lose them."

"I don't intend to lose them," I said emphatically.

Looking back, I fear my words may have sounded egotistical, but I hadn't meant them to be. When I first entered the teaching profession, I discovered I had a special gift for working with troubled kids, a compassion and understanding that often allowed me to break through their barriers of anger and hostility and resentment. For five years, I had reached out to problem students and had witnessed positive behavioral changes in their lives. It never occurred to me that, someday, there might be a child I couldn't reach.

And so, I had disregarded the vice-principal's prophetic warning about the twelve boys entering my classroom the following morning. I believed that if I were faithful to sow my seeds of goodness, my efforts would be honored. I was soon to learn, however, the parable of seeds on stony ground.

For on that first day of classes, three future felons entered my room: a child molester, an armed robber, and a convicted murderer. One of these boys would change my life.

CHAPTER TWO

Like an Army Platoon

Rebels. That was my first impression of the Dirty Dozen as they burst through my doorway and scrambled for the desks at the back of the room, pushing and shoving as they jockeyed for position. The coveted seats were along the rear wall, where the boys could brace their heads upright, hide behind their mirrored sunglasses, and sleep without most teachers noticing.

I noticed. The GIs had taught me that trick, so I moved into a counteraction as soon as the tardy bell had sounded.

"Gentlemen," I said in an official voice, "something unpleasant is about to happen. You will undoubtedly hear moaning and groaning from the person seated next to you. Bodies may twist and writhe on the floor in terrible contortions. But please don't be alarmed; I've never lost a student. Ready?"

I paused a moment for dramatic effect and looked each boy in the eye. No one moved. Assuming the demeanor of a first sergeant, I gave the command. "All right, gentlemen, let us now begin with the alphabetical seating arrangement."

"Say what?" screeched a tall, skinny black kid at the back of the room.

"Aw, she's gonna tell us where to set," grumbled a blond boy, his foot shoving hard against the desk in front of him.

"Well, I ain't sittin' at the front," ranted a 230-pound bruiser in a muscle shirt. "I ain't movin'."

Having learned early in my teaching career that silence is the only argument that can't be refuted, I chose to say nothing further. I merely stood at the front of my classroom, looked the boys squarely in the eyes, and smiled.

5

It was the smile that caught them off-guard. Scowls, they knew. Anger, they knew. They were masters at provoking those reactions from teachers. But smiles? That was something else. They seemed puzzled.

I repeated my instructions. "Gentlemen, we will now begin the alphabetical seating arrangement. Mr. Bonner?"

"Huh?" grunted a lanky kid in a black satin jacket. His buddies laughed, and he glanced toward them, basking in the attention.

"Mr. Bonner, will you please move to the first desk on this row?"

"Why can't I stay here?" he asked, stiffening in his chair and glancing at his buddies for a sign of approval.

I was tempted to repeat the traditional "because I said so" routine, but I didn't want to provoke a confrontation of wills. Instead, I bridled my tongue, stared at him without blinking, and smiled.

Seconds passed. Finally, he rolled his eyes toward his friends, rose from his desk, and moved toward the desk I had indicated. His body managed to strike every chair along the way.

"Thank you for your cooperation, Mr. Bonner," I said as he slouched into the desk by the door. "You've got the best seat in the house. You'll be the first one out of here."

A broad smile creased his face as he considered his advantage. He adjusted his sunglasses and glanced at his buddies in haughty rivalry; he'd pulled off a real coup.

After that, the relocation of the Dozen went without incident, except for the one boy who requested to see the nurse.

"On the first day of school?" I asked.

He nodded and mumbled something about a headache.

"Well, I'm sorry," I said, "but Tuesdays are our Nurse Days."

"Huh?" he asked as his eyes widened.

"We've been assigned to see the nurse on Tuesdays. With 2,300 students in this school, we can't all go at the same time. I'm afraid you'll have to wait until Tuesday. Sorry."

My malingerer slumped back in his seat and heaved a weary sigh. It was going to be a long year. I stifled a grin.

While the boys filled out index cards with information concerning home, places of employment, and class schedule, I scanned their faces, trying to connect the twelve names. Being able to call

6

a student by name was important in maintaining discipline; in addition, it signaled that I thought them important enough to remember. I noticed the boys fell into three categories: the brothers, the ropers, and the hoods.

The five brothers wore long Afros, heavy gold chains, and shiny leather jackets. Clinton was the slick con artist with the engaging smile; Kenneth was the smooth ladies' man with the sweet talk; Kenny was the class clown with the endless repertoire of animal impressions. "Rabbit," nicknamed for his bunny-like movement and his nervous giggle, constantly chattered, while Ronald seldom spoke at all.

The ropers were Donny and Robert and Jim, the free-spirited cowboys dressed in faded Wranglers and scuffed boots. They drove pick-up trucks, chased girls, and raised hell — in the Old West tradition. The hoods were Johnny and Dennis and Danny and Rodrigo, clad in the traditional James Dean T-shirts and jeans. They were into fast cars, fast music, and fast living. (Johnny would die before his eighteenth birthday.)

The vice-principal had been right about the Dirty Dozen. They were the throwaway kids: boys with a history of failure, truants that no one wanted to teach, troublemakers nobody cared about.

I cared. They must have seen that from the first day, because they didn't challenge my authority despite their reputation of having "run off" their last teacher. Ignoring their long hair and defiant dress and surly looks, I began by chipping away at their "hood" image. I addressed them as "Mr." and referred to them as "gentlemen," trying to accord them the same measure of respect that I wanted in return.

Recognizing that many of the boys had problems in accepting authority figures, I tried to establish a non-threatening climate in my classroom without sacrificing good discipline. When I counseled them that first day concerning class rules, I handed out a paper entitled "Mrs. Post's Ten Commandments" and began reading:

> 1. Thou shalt arrive to class punctually and be seated in thy assigned chair when the tardy bell ringeth.
> 2. Thou shalt bring with thee daily thy quill and scroll.

7

3. Thou shalt refrain from conducting private conversations after class discussion begineth. .

4. Thou shalt refrain from the laying of hands upon the body of another student . . .

As I peered over the top of my paper, I saw the boys looking at each other and grinning. They had gotten the message about appropriate behavior without feeling brow-beaten or run over by the Gestapo. Experience had taught me that humor can be an effective tool in establishing discipline and correcting misbehavior, and I used it often to defuse potential problems.

Once the boys had a clear understanding of the behavior I expected, I began to work on raising their low self-esteem. I looked for opportunities to point out their unique abilities, hoping to reprogram the way they saw themselves. If I could convince them that they had self-worth, if I could prove to them that they could succeed, then perhaps they'd see themselves as something more than "losers."

I began by restructuring the curriculum to insure success. Although I had high expectations and insisted on challenging the boys with the classics, I changed my technique of presenting the material. I often allowed the boys to work in small groups, drawing on each other's strengths.

"You mean, we can copy off each other and you ain't gonna get mad?" asked the boy in the wire-rimmed glasses, his eyes brightening.

"You have to pull your weight, Mr. Hill. We're like an Army platoon; each man has a job to accomplish if we're to fulfill our mission."

"Far out," said the boy with the peace medal around his neck.

By the end of the first six weeks, this class of throwaway kids had mastered the required basic skills and had finished their work with A and B averages. For boys with a history of academic failure, their performance was impressive. Once the boys discovered they could succeed in my class, they began to take pride in their scholastic accomplishments. Learning became fun.

I also tried to reinforce their personal achievements and acceptable behaviors. Boys who had been belittled and berated in traditional classrooms began to feel good about themselves in our alternative class, where they received praise for their daily accomplishments, no matter how small or insignificant.

In addition to handing out occasional treats like chewing gum or candy bars, I also used intrinsic rewards to spur the boys on. Simple words like "Great job, Mr. Bonner, you were really on target with that answer," or "That's an interesting idea, Mr. Livingston, what makes you think so?" gave them a sense of security about themselves and stimulated their thinking. Our vocational English classroom became a place of learning and caring and accepting — a place where each individual was valued for his worth, no matter how "different" he might be.

As I came to know the boys that first semester, I also tried to set up a surrogate support system to compensate for many of their dysfunctional families. Trying to nurture them with love and patience and discipline, I baked brownies for their birthdays, gave hugs of encouragement, and offered counseling. In time, I came to think of them as my sons.

Although each member of the Dozen had a special need, I found that Jim Taylor troubled me most. Looking back on those early weeks of school, I've tried to recall what first attracted my attention to the quiet leader of the Dozen. Perhaps I'd noticed his gorgeous blue eyes, or his mischievous grin, or his striking resemblance to a young Paul Newman. Or maybe I'd singled him out because I felt he didn't belong in that class. He was different, somehow, from the other boys. He didn't fit the "throwaway" stereotype that the vice-principal had described. I checked into his background. The results, I found, were unsettling.

Two years earlier, Jim had been the all-American boy. He was a class favorite nominee, a talented football player, and an average student. He had been reared in a Christian home by parents who loved him. Jim's father had been an All-American football player in college, and had later played professional football for the Houston Oilers. Jim's mother held an important administrative position at a Temple hospital, in addition to rearing three other children in their middle-class home. This was not the pattern of a throwaway kid.

Yet Jim had recently run away from home, committed five church burglaries, and been sentenced to six months' probation by the juvenile court. The paradox puzzled me: Why would a boy with such potential get into so much trouble? I began searching for answers. The turning point, I found, came during his eighth-grade year at Lamar Middle School. That's when he dropped out of football.

Football, the great god of Central Texas, could make a difference in a young boy. Friday night football was king in Temple, Texas, a quiet and conservative community of some 40,000 residents located in northeastern Bell County. Dating back to 1880, when the Gulf, Colorado, and Santa Fe Railroad held the first sale of town lots, this progressive community had become known as a leading medical center in the Southwest.

But if a local resident were asked to describe the city of Temple, he probably wouldn't mention the historic Santa Fe Railroad or the prestigious Scott and White Hospital. Squaring back his shoulders and throwing out his chest, he'd proudly boast that Temple was "the home of the Wildcats." Having said that, no other explanation would be necessary. Folks around the state know about the Wildcats.

The Temple High School Wildcats ruled the throne in District 15-AAAA competition. Under the direction of head coach Bob McQueen, Temple's football program had become a powerhouse. Week after week, the town turned out en masse at Wildcat Stadium to cheer its blue-and-white gladiators, "the pride of Temple."

When the team advanced to district and regional playoffs, area merchants closed down stores on Saturdays, and half the town packed up and left. Christmas parades were rescheduled and civic events were canceled as the town "backed the Cats."

The town's mindset was probably best reflected in a large mural painted on the gym wall at Bonham Middle School. The half-dozen middle school players, clad in basketball and track uniforms, looked with awed reverence toward the colossal Temple High School football player towering above them. Overhead, the words read:

THINK BIG. BE A WILDCAT.

From the moment Jim Taylor put on his first pair of shoulder pads at the Ralph Wilson Boys Club, he had wanted to be a

10

Wildcat. He, like so many other ten-year-old youngsters, had been caught up in the ritual that transformed Texas boys into powerful young Adonises. As if anointed and set apart, Jim played the game of football with passion, intensity, and skill.

He had undoubtedly inherited his love of the game from his dad and granddad, both of whom had excelled in college. Although small for his age, Jim played the traditional Taylor position of guard. He was fast and tough; no one pushed him around, on the field or off. This rugged, aggressive sport seemed well-suited to his temperament, and he played the game well.

Jim had especially shown promise during his middle school years when he met *the* coach who changed his life. Jim idolized Billy Hoppers, the outgoing young coach who had guided him through his seventh-grade season at Lamar.

Coach Hoppers was tough and demanding on the field, but he taught Jim the importance of discipline and dedication and teamwork. Hoppers had a way of getting through to Jim like no one else could. Although Jim had already begun to balk at other "authority figures" in his fourteen-year-old world, he never questioned Hoppers' directives, on the field or off. He obeyed instinctively, without argument or complaint. The coach and the game brought out the best in Jim.

Coach Hoppers not only knew a great deal about football, but he also knew a lot about young boys. He encouraged his players to be positive, in both the game and in life. "Believe in yourselves," he told them. "Never settle for less." He urged them to form an attachment to something: band or choir or athletics. "Be able to say 'I belong.' Don't be just a number," he said.

Jim belonged to Coach Hoppers' football team, and he took pride in that. He worked hard every afternoon, proving himself worthy to wear the maroon-and-gold of Hoppers' Bearcats. He didn't mind the long hours or the grueling drills because Hoppers was always there on the sidelines, explaining and encouraging and spurring him on. Jim admired and respected the young coach, and would have walked through the fires of hell for him, if asked to do so. There was a special bond between them. No one could ever measure up to Coach Hoppers; he was the best. And certainly no one could ever replace him, as far as Jim was concerned.

11

Perhaps that's why Jim felt deep resentment and hostility when another coach attempted to do so. Reporting for football practice his eighth-grade year, Jim learned that Coach Hoppers had been transferred across town to Bonham Middle School, the arch-rival "with all the rich kids." He had left without saying a word to his players. Jim felt betrayed; he didn't understand how the coach could run out on him like that. He wouldn't have deserted Hoppers, no matter what. Yet Hoppers had broken the code.

Angered by Hoppers' defection, Jim made little effort to get along with the replacement coach. He resented the changes that the new coach made. The plays were "stupid" and didn't work. Coach Hoppers would have done things differently, and better, Jim thought.

After two weeks of carrying a chip on his shoulder, Jim finally balked. He was tired of the new coach telling him what to do, and he wanted no part of the game any longer. Despite his starting position in the line-up, Jim turned in his football equipment and walked off the field. If he couldn't play for Hoppers, he wouldn't play for anybody.

Arriving home earlier than usual, Jim stalked into the kitchen and told his parents he'd quit the team. Slouched in his chair at the table, he explained that he was tired of those "stupid coaches" trying to boss him. Not once during his tirade did Jim glance at his All-American father.

When Jim had finished, Von Taylor glared at his son. Clamping his jaws like an iron vise, the former pro player tried to cap the anger that welled within him. He knew, all too well, what Jim was throwing away. The memory was indelible.

Reared in the oil fields of Abilene, Texas, Von Taylor had been a roughneck kid with a singular dream: to play professional football. Like most young boys growing up in West Texas, he had learned to love the game at an early age. As a third-grader, he and his neighborhood friends had converted their front yards into sandlot stadiums, running the spectacular plays that they'd seen the high school team executing out on the practice field nearby. Von longed for the day when he, too, would wear the black-and-gold trappings of the Abilene Eagles and make big plays like his daddy had made at the University of Arkansas.

But unlike most Texas schoolboys who could only dream the dream, Von would have his shot at the brass ring. He was good. His performance earned him a position on the Texas All-State team, as well as an opportunity to play in the High School All-American game in Memphis, Tennessee. As a result of his exceptional ability, Von received scholarship offers from four major universities: Nebraska, Texas Tech, Texas A&M, and the University of Houston. His hours of hard work on the gridiron had paid off; he could write his own ticket in college football.

Although he wanted to play for a Big 8 school like Nebraska, Von couldn't go out of state. He was no longer a "free agent." He had gotten married right after graduation from Abilene High School.

Von couldn't recall the exact moment he fell in love with Carolyn Garrett, the pretty Central Texas girl who came to visit her cousin in Abilene each summer. He had probably loved her since they were thirteen, when Carolyn showed him that she could shoot a BB gun as well as any boy. She was bright and determined and outspoken. Unlike the Abilene girls who worshiped him as a "football hero," Carolyn stood up to him and kept him in line. He admired her spirit.

Carolyn had a way of bringing out the best in him, and Von couldn't risk losing her. He knew about the boys back home, including the one who wanted to marry her. Long-distance romances were difficult to sustain, especially if he were off somewhere playing football. So, he had married her in May, right after graduation. Whatever future he had in football, he wanted Carolyn to share the dream with him. Just the two of them.

But the two soon became three. With a baby on the way, Von had to consider what was best for his family financially. Despite the scholarship offers and a chance for glory at a big-name university, he decided to remain in Abilene, where he had been offered a football scholarship by McMurry College.

Von attended McMurry for one year, while Carolyn worked to put him through school. The birth of their daughter Gena, although adding to their happiness, further increased their financial problems. Von's grades dropped, and he decided to leave college. Like his father before him, Von abandoned his dream of football and went to work on a drilling rig in the oil fields near Houston.

But some dreams die hard. A year and a half later, Von returned to McMurry, where he struggled to earn the credits that would restore his football eligibility. Under the mentorship of Grant Teaff, later head coach at Baylor University, Von proved he still had the edge, winning the Little All-American award for two years in a row. Scouts from Houston and Philadelphia courted him, while Green Bay, Chicago, and New York sent letters of inquiry.

Although things were going well on the field, the sidelines still posed problems. Von became a father a second time with the birth of his son, James Edward. He delighted in his first-born son, yet Jim's arrival was ill-conceived. Once again, Von's studies were disrupted by financial hardship, not to mention the turmoil of having two small children underfoot.

Dropping out during his senior year at McMurry, Von signed a contract to play professional football for the Houston Oilers. Looking back, Von realized that he probably made a mistake in signing with Houston. The Oilers, having won the American League championship the year before, already had its stable of seasoned veterans. Only two rookies were kept; Von was not one of the "chosen."

He had played in three pre-season exhibition games with the Oilers, taking the field beside football greats such as George Blanda and Billy Cannon. Despite his promise as a young defensive lineman, Von was released from the team during the last cut. The veterans had "no cut" contracts, and Houston didn't need any new players on the line that year.

Recruited by the Jacksonville Bears of the Florida Football League, Von signed to play semipro ball. Leaving his young family behind in Texas, he traveled east, hoping to earn a second shot at his boyhood dream. Von proved himself a standout on the defensive line. He probably would have been picked up by a pro team the following season, if he'd stayed.

But the weekly phone calls from Carolyn had become more frantic. She couldn't work and take care of the children by herself. She had already sent two-year-old Jim to live with his Grandma Garrett, something that she'd vowed never to do to one of her own children. She remembered, all too well, her own unhappy childhood of being shipped from aunt to aunt. She had wanted her children to know the stability of a Christian home.

14

Tearfully, she had issued the ultimatum: Von would have to choose between football or his family.

He chose as she knew he would. The roughneck returned to the oil fields of West Texas, where he labored to support his family, which now included a second son, Glenn. He'd had trouble finding a job at first because employers were reluctant to hire him. They believed that he would eventually return to professional football. Everyone knew that Texans deified their football heroes, worshiping the helmeted idols who paraded across the gridiron arena in spandex splendor. What man could long resist the roar of the crowd or the thrill of the TV camera? they asked.

Yet when the phone call came from another football team, Von refused to go back. He had already accepted the inevitable. It was over.

"I'm not going back," Jim said, slamming his empty tea glass on the kitchen table and swallowing hard. Despite Von's strong objections, Jim's mind was made up and no amount of reasoning could make him reconsider. Hoppers had burned him, and he was through with football. Jim stormed out of the kitchen, down the hall, and into the bedroom he shared with his ten-year-old brother, Glenn. The slammed door reiterated his message. It was over.

Von sat at the kitchen table and stared out the window, struggling to keep his anger under control. He searched the overcast sky for something more that he could say to reach his headstrong son. They'd always found it hard to talk to each other, but the last few months had been especially difficult. Jim had become withdrawn and sullen.

Football had been a kind of coded language between them. Even though Von worked the night shift at a local printing company, he made time to attend Jim's games. Perhaps his scrappy young son reminded him of another young boy whom he had known, back when the dream was still alive.

"Jim had a lot of natural ability," Von recalled. "He was tough and strong. He would have made a good defensive back." The All-American saw a lot of promise in his son, and he believed the game would have been good for Jim.

"If a boy doesn't want to play football, I can't blame him for that," Von said. "But Jim had already started the season. I felt if he'd stayed and played another year, he would probably want to play some more. And that would have helped him. Football keeps many a boy out of trouble."

That's what bothered Von Taylor. He wasn't angry about Jim's quitting football so much as he was riled by what Jim would do with his spare time. He knew that his son had started hanging out with a rough crowd before school and during lunch. The principal had telephoned, advising him of Jim's association with these "bad influences." Von had forbidden Jim to run with the group, but he knew that Jim would be on the streets with them now, causing problems.

Von couldn't understand the sudden change in his oldest son. As a Christian father, Von had followed the Bible's admonition to "train up a child in the way he should go." He had struggled to set a good example for his children and to provide a godly home where they were reared with love and discipline. He had taken his children to church regularly, and he had prayed that each would someday find a personal relationship with God. Yet, despite his efforts, Jim seemed to be rebelling against every Christian principle and moral value that he had been taught.

How could a boy from a good home get into trouble in a place like Temple, Texas? Von wondered. This wasn't Dallas or Houston, where coveys of bored teenagers stalked the shopping malls in zombie-like trances. This was Temple, a conservative, God-fearing community in the middle of the Bible Belt. Kids weren't supposed to get into trouble in Smalltown, USA. Especially not his kids, not after what he'd given up for them.

Yet he was losing control of Jim, and he didn't know how to stop him. Nothing seemed to work anymore, not talking or grounding or punishing. Von had always been a strong disciplinarian, yet he knew he couldn't "take a picket out of the fence and work Jim over. He was too old for that."

Despite his great prowess on the football field, Von Taylor felt powerless to deal with his rebellious son. The former All-American had, therefore, accepted his son's impulsive decision, knowing the price that would be paid. Football had been a common ground for them, a way to reach out to each other. Now that, too, was over.

16

*   *   *   *   *

Jim had quit midseason in a town where football was king. He had walked away from a game that assured him success and acceptance and popularity. He had committed social suicide. For the first time in his life, he was small and insignificant. Feeling as though he no longer belonged to anyone or anything, Jim searched for something to fill the emptiness. He soon found it in drugs.

Jim smoked his first dope at a party with Don Folger, a friend since their third-grade year at Jefferson Elementary. Both were fun-loving and devil-may-care, often prone to take risks and get into trouble. Mischievous but not mean, they became natural allies.

Jim's decision to leave football may have been influenced, in part, by Don's similar action. Don had quit the team several days before, insisting that football wasn't worth the hassle. He'd found better things to do with his time, and he often bragged to Jim about the "real action."

Although Don came from a good home, he, too, had rebelled against his parents' values and had begun running with the rougher element at Lamar Middle School. The group congregated at the local convenience store, where they smoked cigarettes, played pinball, and acted cocky. By the end of their eighth-grade year, they had outgrown the kid-stuff routine; they were ready for some real excitement. So was Jim.

That's when he joined them in guzzling booze and smoking dope. Jim hated the taste of alcohol, but he went along with the weekly partying. He had an image to protect.

He liked dope a lot better; smoking grass was fun. By the time Jim entered the ninth grade at Temple High School, he was using several sticks a day. To finance his drug habit, Jim started pushing marijuana joints. At first he made deals in the school restroom. Later, he and Walter Frye went for the bigger bucks on the high school parking lot. Within a forty-five-minute lunch period, they once turned a $200 profit.

Jim knew Walter from football days at Lamar, although they didn't start hanging out together until that ninth-grade year of high school. Unlike Jim, Walter fit the "throwaway" image; the product of a broken home, he was always into trouble. Walter had been fighting a large seventh-grader when Jim first saw him.

17

"Walter didn't let anybody push him around, either," Jim said. He liked that.

Jim also liked the fact that Walter did whatever he wanted, whenever he wanted, without answering to anyone. Unable to get along with his mother or stepfather, Walter lived with his elderly grandfather, who permitted the boy to come and go as he pleased. That lifestyle appealed to Jim.

Similar in their temperament and in their thinking, the youths shared another bond: They were cowboys who liked to rodeo. The rodeo attracted modern-day mavericks like Jim and Walter who longed for the rough-and-tumble action of the Old West.

Together, Jim and Walter rode the Central Texas rodeo circuit and competed in the most dangerous event of all: bull riding. Weekly, they climbed onto the backs of 2,000-pound Brahman bulls, dug in their spurs, and attempted to stay aloft—and alive— for the next eight seconds.

Jim enjoyed bull riding for the danger. He had what psychologists called a "T-type" personality: a thrill-seeker who needed an element of risk. Even after he was gored in the ribs, Jim climbed on a bull the following week, looking for more action. He didn't have a death wish. On the contrary, Jim wanted to feel alive. He didn't want to miss out on anything.

That's why he began to dislike school so intensely. Jim felt he was missing out on something by going to those "boring classes" each day. He saw no point in doing homework when he could have a lot more fun getting high with his friends. He was absent much of his ninth-grade year, spent numerous days in detention, and lost all of his credits. Jim didn't care. He was having a good time and feeling no pain.

However, he had to find some way to finance his dope. He turned to burglary. The first job he pulled was strictly for fun, just to see if he could get away with it. He and a friend hit Immanuel Baptist Church, where Jim and his family had attended worship services for years. The boys hadn't planned to take anything that night; they were hungry and wanted to "borrow" a late-night snack from the kitchen, that was all. Several weeks later, however, Jim remembered what an easy target churches made.

Despite his religious upbringing, Jim had no qualms about robbing churches. He rationalized that the insurance money would pay for whatever was stolen, so there was no real harm done. He and his buddies pulled several more church jobs before his mother found out and turned him in to their minister. Reverend Guinn Williams called the Temple police, and Jim was picked up. He spent his first night behind bars at age fifteen.

When Jim was brought before the Bell County juvenile court, the judge sentenced him to six months' probation and required his parents to pay restitution. Jim's mother further insisted that he attend weekly counseling sessions with Reverend Williams. Under coercion from his parents, he went four or five times before tiring of "the religion game." He didn't need Bible verses or stories about God; he'd already outgrown that.

Jim intended to run his own life, and nobody was going to tell him what to do. Not his parents or the coaches or the police or the church. Like the rampaging Brahman bulls that he rode, Jim bucked wildly to leave the chute. He wanted his freedom, and nothing could hold him back.

Perhaps that's what had drawn me to the quiet leader of the Dozen — his rugged, independent spirit. He was an outlaw kid who did bad things, yet he wasn't bad. Impulsive and reckless, he went off half-cocked, without considering either the outcome or the consequences.

But if Jim Taylor were dangerous, he was most lethal to himself. Without help, I knew that he would self-destruct and be lost forever. That frightened me because I cared about him. I'd always had a soft spot for stray dogs and lost boys.

During the fall semester I held a tight rein on him, trying to turn him around. Jim, more than any other member of the Dozen, I had wanted to succeed. He was the one who tugged at my heart. Bonnie Neal, his math teacher that year, felt the same way. "There was something very special, almost charismatic, about Jim," she said. "You couldn't help but love him."

With missionary zeal, I searched for a way to make Jim Taylor feel good about himself and about school. I tried to place him in leadership roles, showing him that he could contribute in a positive way. I tried to take a personal interest in the things that interested him, showing him that he was important and that somebody cared. I used every educational technique that I'd

19

studied, every creative trick that I'd learned, every insight the GIs had taught me, everything and anything to reach him. And for a while, I thought I had.

Although he had been habitually truant the preceding year, Jim missed only one day that fall semester. His school file, which had previously bulged with disciplinary referral forms, remained uncluttered. Jim hadn't been sent to the principal's office or to detention a single time since school started, something of a record for him. He was polite and mannerly and cooperative, the "model" student. And we saw no sign of his using or pushing drugs at school.

But what thrilled me most as a teacher, I suppose, was Jim's academic performance. Bright and perceptive, he became an avid reader that semester. Although most of the Dozen read on a fifth-grade level and had to be tested orally, Jim was working above grade-level and his comprehension was excellent. He seemed interested and eager to learn, always reading chapters ahead of the group. For the first time in three years, he managed to pass an English class — with an A average.

My colleagues were clearly impressed by Jim's progress, and I almost broke my right arm in patting myself on the back. I had accomplished with him what I had set out to do: prove that there was a way to salvage problem kids. All it took was love and patience, and a little Army know-how.

While basking in my success as "super teacher," I forgot the proverb's warning that pride "goeth before a fall." My idealistic reverie was short-lived. I learned of Jim's decision to quit school when Donny Hill, the mouthpiece for the Dozen, made the announcement in class that Tuesday morning.

"Jim's in the office," Donny blurted out during roll check.

"Is he in trouble?" I asked.

"Naw. He's just getting some papers. He's dropping out today."

"Why would he do that?"

"He got off probation. He don't have to come no more." Donny brushed his blond hair to one side as he peered at me through wire-rimmed glasses and waited to tell me the rest.

During the Christmas holidays, Jim had quarreled with his parents and had left home. No longer on probation, he had

20

moved in with Walter Frye, and they had started partying "big-time." Walter, who had dropped out of school the previous year, convinced Jim to quit so they could run wild and free together, enjoying alcohol and dope and girls without any hassles from anyone. Jim thought it sounded good. The boys had forged a note, supposedly from Jim's mother, stating that the family was moving from Temple and requesting that Jim be withdrawn from school.

When Donny concluded his narrative, I quieted the Dozen and began reading aloud, trying to conceal my hurt and carry on as if everything were routine. I kept battling the lump in my throat, swallowing hard to steady my voice and drive back the tears. I felt devastated by Jim's defection.

Perhaps it was my professional pride; I hated being proven wrong. But it wasn't pride exactly, either. I knew that I'd lose some of the boys; the odds were against my keeping all of them, I knew that. But I hadn't counted on losing Jim. He was the one who had such promise, the one who had come so far and could have made it. Why him? Why now?

When his knock came at the door several moments later, I felt my heart pounding as I rushed to complete the paragraph I was reading. I didn't want to answer. My mind began to reel, searching for some miracle that I hadn't yet used. What could I say to him, I wondered, that would make him stay? Surely there was something I had overlooked. But even before I opened the door and stepped into the hallway, I knew the answer: there was nothing.

Jim handed me his withdrawal form and then looked away, the brim of his black cowboy hat concealing his eyes. "Where are you going?" I asked.

"Moving."

"Will you go to school when you get there?"

"Probably," he lied.

"I hope you'll finish school, Jim. You've got a good mind."

He didn't say anything. He only flashed that mischievous grin he used to mask his feelings. He had a tough image to protect; he couldn't break character.

When I reached over to hug him goodbye, I saw a look in his piercing blue eyes, a flicker of doubt about what he was doing. I suspected that part of him wanted to stay, and probably would have stayed, if Walter Frye hadn't been waiting for him in the parking lot. Peer pressure was a hell of a thing to live with.

"Adios," he called as he turned and walked away. I listened to the thudding of his cowboy boots on the stone hallway. When I could no longer hear his footsteps, I leaned against the classroom door, feeling empty inside. Once again, I'd been reminded of the teacher's occupational hazard: being hurt if you cared too deeply. I had allowed myself to become too attached to the impulsive, head-strong member of the Dozen. I knew better, yet Jim had seemed worth the risk. I had gambled, given it my best shot, and lost.

Now, like the errant prodigal son, Jim had fled into the wilderness. Restless and defiant, he was in a hurry to become a man. And about to pay such a terrible price.

CHAPTER THREE

Murder Wasn't Part of the Plan

Jim Taylor knew something bad was going to happen the night of the robbery. He could always tell beforehand, as if some sixth sense alerted him to impending danger. But he hadn't counted on the old man dying. Murder wasn't part of the plan.

If he hadn't smoked the dope earlier that evening, perhaps he might have realized that the plan was dangerous and deadly and destined to fail. But the sticks of marijuana had altered his judgment and slowed his thinking. As if trapped in some bad dream, Jim found himself standing outside Chester Brooks' general store in Coit, Texas, waiting for the robbery to go down. What happened during those next ten minutes could only occur in nightmares.

Shivering in the icy temperatures that paralyzed Central Texas on that cold winter night, Jim tried to shake the chill that ran up the back of his neck. The numbness which racked his slight body was caused by more than freezing weather, he knew that. This job terrified him; he had never attempted a robbery before.

Jim specialized in burglaries, and he had the lengthy juvenile record to prove it. During the six weeks since he'd run away from home, he and his best friend, Walter Frye, had pulled off at least one burglary a night. They had ridden around in the white Ford pickup and randomly knocked off easy targets like a grocery store or a liquor store or a school. They preferred small places in small towns because there was less risk of being caught or getting hurt. Sometimes they stole because they needed money to finance their drug deals. But mostly they stole because it was fun. Or at least it had been until that night in Coit.

23

Coit stood on the rolling plains of Central Texas, a lonesome region in the remote southwestern corner of Limestone County. Lying out "in the middle of nowhere," its countryside had changed little since the days when Comanche tribes roamed the prairies, raiding frontier settlements.

Cowboys driving longhorn cattle to northern markets saw the same panorama of mesquite grass and matted thickets, with stands of prickly pear, briars, cactus, and brush mingling among the native cedar and pecan trees.

European immigrants gazed out over the same ravines that creased the rugged blackland and sandy loam terrain, exposing limestone rock amid the thousands of acres of farm and ranch land. The land had changed little since those early Texas days; only its people were different.

The community of Coit was located twenty miles from the county seat at Groesbeck. The town had been founded in 1848 by Ben Eaton, an early pioneer who brought the first horse-powered grist mill to the region. The construction of the Houston and Texas Central Railroad through the county after the Civil War had further increased settlement, especially after the abundant ranch land was opened up for farming during the 1890s. English immigrants planted the first cotton in the area, and Coit became the center of a thriving farm community. Then the price of cotton dropped, and folks moved to the cities.

The settlement had become a near-ghost town with its four weathered buildings standing stoically beside the intersections of Farm-to-Market roads 339 and 1771. The Fairview Presbyterian Church, its small parsonage, and Chester Brooks' house and general store were all that remained of Coit's 130-year history on the Texas prairies. The howling coyotes prowling about at night far outnumbered the town's fewer than ten residents.

Coit's population swelled on weekends whenever area farmers and ranchers dropped by the old general store to "sit and visit for a spell." The men wore sweat-stained Stetsons, weathered from hours of back-breaking labor in the hot Texas sun, or they donned hunting caps with slogans such as "This Country Boy Can Survive." They toted Red Man chewing tobacco or Skoal snuff tins in their back jeans pockets, and they punctuated their conversation by spitting beyond the turned-up toes of their cowboy boots, cracked and crusted like the land. On Sunday afternoons, they drove their pickup trucks to Chester Brooks' store for a "soda water" and some old-fashioned socializing like their daddies and granddaddies before them had done.

The old store and the town had been there for as far back as folks could remember. Yet on that January night the town of Coit would die, at the hands of four young outlaws committing their first robbery.

Jim pulled his jean jacket tight and edged closer to the rear of Chester Brooks' ramshackle farmhouse sitting some forty feet off FM 339. Built near the turn of the century, the dilapidated wooden structure had been covered with tarpaper shingles, resembling slate gray stones. The small, one-story farmhouse offered Jim little protection against the numbing-cold wind that whipped against his back and legs. Digging his boot heel into the packed earth, he pivoted slightly and peered into the midnight shadows that shrouded Coit.

The full moon and a solitary streetlight enabled Jim to see the darkened outlines of two other buildings. To the west stood the Fairview Presbyterian Church, a weathered, two-story structure dating back to the 1890s. Sitting cock-eyed on its pier-and-beam foundation, the old church loomed forty yards beyond the barbed wire fence that outlined the perimeter of Chester Brooks' house and barn. Earlier that day, the sounds of "Amazing Grace" had been lifted up by the church's half-dozen members; now the building stood silent and empty, like the town itself.

Adjusting his black ski mask, Jim glanced northeastward toward the target — Chester Brooks' general store. Standing some twenty yards beyond the farmhouse, the single-story structure resembled a rectangular box, ten feet wide and twenty feet long. The store had been built in the "shotgun" style of early Texas. The name "shotgun" came from the fact that a bullet fired through the front door would exit through the back door without hitting any walls in between.

Built around 1900 by Chester Brooks' father, the store had weathered badly. Its rustic exterior resembled a primitive smokehouse, like the dark, windowless shacks used by early Texans to cure beef or pork. Strips of slate-gray tarpaper nailed to the walls concealed the rotting planks and plugged the drafty cracks. Rusty tin signs hanging haphazardly around the peeled-paint doorway advertised Camel and Chesterfield and Winston. Scarred by time and bleached by the Texas sun, the metal relics reflected the same abuse as the battered tin roof. Stacks of wooden crates, crushed boxes, discarded junk, and concrete blocks littered the hard-packed ground around the store, indicating the proprietor's reluctance to part with anything from the past. Even the rusty horseshoe nailed above the door showed an attempt to cling to the good luck of yesteryear. But the old storekeeper's luck had run out.

Pulling his leather gloves snug against his numb fingers, Jim turned and glanced at the older boy standing beside him. He'd known Wes Folger for a long time, but he'd never worked with him before. Jim often partied with Wes' younger brother, Don, so he'd visited the Folger home many times. He had talked casually with Wes, but he had never hung out with him or pulled off a job with him. As far as Jim knew, Wes Folger had never been involved in anything like this before. Aside from smoking weed, Wes seemed pretty straight. A good student and a regular church-goer, Wes was probably the most law-abiding of the lot.

Wes' younger brother was a different story, however. Jim had worked with Don Folger before. The younger Folger had been with Jim and Walter Frye the night they stole the pickup truck in their hometown of Temple and drove some forty miles to Coit, intending to case this same country store.

Jim and Walter had told Don about their wanting to rob the Brooks place because the old grocer kept large sums of money hidden in his store. The youths had tried to devise a burglary scheme for several weeks, but they couldn't solve one dilemma: Chester Brooks lived in a farmhouse near his store and would probably hear them if they attempted a break-in.

Jim didn't want a confrontation with the old grocer. Despite Chester Brooks' sixty-seven years, he was in prime physical condition. Standing five foot eight and weighing over 200 pounds, Chester was built like a Hereford bull. His broad shoulders, muscular arms, and massive hands reflected a strength that had diminished little with age. Although Jim wasn't afraid of Chester

26

Brooks, he didn't want to tangle with him either. He couldn't risk the old man, or someone else, being hurt. Nor could he chance being recognized. Chester Brooks knew Jim.

As far back as he could remember, Jim had come to this dirt-bottom country store whenever he visited his maternal grandmother on weekends or during summer vacations. Jim's Grandma Garrett lived three miles south of Chester's store, so the family knew the old grocer well. As a hot and thirsty youngster, Jim had often ridden horseback to the rustic country store for a "soda water." One of Jim's earliest memories was riding in Chester's Model-T truck and listening to the old man talk about early Texas.

But through the years, Jim's relationship with Chester had changed. The old grocer disapproved of Jim's long hair and the smart-aleck friends he brought to the store. Chester seemed gruff and indifferent toward him, so Jim had no qualms about robbing the store for drug money. However, he didn't want to do so as long as the old family friend was nearby. So until he thought of a way to keep Chester from being hurt and himself from being caught, Jim had postponed the burglary scheme.

Wes Folger eventually thought of a way. Sometime after the Coit casing job, Don Folger told his older brother about the country store, the hidden money, and the burglary that Jim and Walter were contemplating. Perhaps it seemed like easy money, and Wes needed money badly. At seventeen years old, Wes had gotten a girl pregnant, married her, and faced a large hospital bill. With a baby coming soon, he needed money — fast.

Accompanied by his younger brother, Wes drove to Jim and Walter's place that Sunday afternoon and confronted them with the idea of robbing Chester Brooks. Together, the four youths began to construct a plan. By the time the Folger brothers returned that night, Jim had smoked enough dope to make himself believe they could pull it off.

After making a couple of stops, the four outlaws had driven the forty miles to the store in Coit. Turning off the car headlights several hundred yards away, Wes coasted the yellow Cougar into the gravel parking lot on the far side of the Fairview Presbyterian Church, out of sight of the Brooks farmhouse to the east.

Sitting outside the darkened church, the boys glanced north

beyond the intersections of FM 339 and 1771, toward the property of Manuel Cordova, the nearest neighbor. His house stood dark and silent, like the one belonging to Chester Brooks.

The four young robbers felt confident as they verbally rehearsed their plan, making it up as they went along. They would divide into two-man teams. Walter and Don, the younger pair, would approach the house from the front road, FM 339, pretend to be out of gas, and call the old grocer outside. While Chester walked the twenty yards from his farmhouse up to the gas pump beside his store, Jim and Wes, wearing black ski masks, would dart inside the old man's darkened bedroom, hide, and wait. When Chester returned to his house, the two older youths would jump him, tie him up, and leave him inside the bedroom while they joined Walter and Don up front at the store. There, they would break in, get the money, and be on their way. Even Jim thought the scheme sounded good. Chester wouldn't get hurt and Jim wouldn't get caught.

Although Jim would have preferred working with Walter Frye, he had to be one of the guys in the ski masks; otherwise, Chester would have recognized him. Wes Folger, probably the strongest of the youths, insisted that he be the other member of that team.

So everything was settled, except for the gut feeling that gnawed at Jim as he stood outside Chester Brooks' house. He knew, even then. Something bad was going to happen and they had to call it off. Jim turned to his older companion and whispered, "Let's go. This doesn't feel right."

"We can't," Wes said. "Don and Walter are already up front."

About that time, two voices began calling the old man. The job was going down. Chester's mongrel heard the voices and sounded the alarm. Charging from out of the shadows, the black dog raced to the house, where it stood barking directly at Jim and Wes.

If the dog had continued barking, it probably would have drawn attention to the boys and foiled the robbery attempt. But, for some unexplained reason, it suddenly ran away without Jim or Wes having said or done anything to it.

Within seconds, the old wooden door of Chester's back

room creaked open. Jim watched a massive, shadowy form emerge through the threshold, carrying a .410 shotgun in one hand. Jim and Wes glanced at each other, their dark ski masks unable to conceal the terror in their eyes. They hadn't counted on the old man being armed. And certainly not with a shotgun.

"Who is it?" called Chester Brooks, walking the moonlit path toward his store like a wary hunter stalking his prey. "What is it that you boys want?" he asked as he saw two small forms silhouetted in the moonlight near the gas pump.

"We're out of gas up the road," said one of the young voices. "We need to get some gas. We'll pay for it."

Chester clicked back the hammer on the old .410 and approached Walter and Don. The boys continued with their contrived story about the gas, keeping their eyes on the old grocer. They'd heard stories that he would shoot on sight, and they didn't want to arouse the old man's suspicion.

Chester lowered his gun, told the boys where to find the gas cans, and began walking back to his darkened house. Walter and Don called out to the old man again, pretending not to understand what he said. They were stalling for time, trying to give Jim and Wes a chance to get into the back bedroom and hide. The ploy proved unnecessary. As soon as Chester's large, shadowy hulk had disappeared from view, Jim and Wes had darted inside.

Wes stood close to the part-opened door and breathed heavily. "We've got to get that gun away from him," he whispered.

Jim stood silently, allowing his eyes to adjust in the darkness. The small back room felt hot and stifling, and a rank, musty odor added to the smothering feeling. The glow of the blue flames in the gas heater illumined a corner of the room, and Jim thought he could see Chester's bed and an old dresser. It occurred to Jim that, in all those years, he had never been inside Chester's room. Not once.

Jim didn't want to be there now, either. He knew that this was wrong. Something bad was going to happen, and he wanted no part of it. For a moment, he considered lunging past Wes and running out the door before the old man returned. He wanted to run, but he couldn't.

Jim remembered Walter Frye. His best friend was standing out front. A man didn't run out on his partner, no matter what.

He'd read enough Louis L'Amour novels to know about the "code of the West" that couldn't be broken. He'd have to ride it out and see what happened. So he stood there, waiting against his will.

Two or three minutes passed before Jim heard the old man's heavy footsteps on the frozen ground outside. Jim braced his back against the wall, clenched his fists, and glanced at Wes Folger. The older boy stood in the half-open doorway, primed for the strike. Although the darkness and the mask concealed Wes' face, Jim could feel the tenseness in his companion. Wes was scared. He'd never done anything like this before; neither had Jim. Both were unknowns, about to face a brutal rite of passage. They held their breath.

Even before the old grocer stepped inside the bedroom door, Jim had made the decision. He couldn't go through with this. But Wes Folger could.

As soon as Chester Brooks entered the darkened doorway, Wes lunged into him, slamming the old man against the west wall. Grabbing a firm hold on the .410 in Chester's hands, Wes tried to wrestle the weapon from the grocer's grip. Chester's massive fingers tightened on the gun, and he mustered every ounce of strength in his 200-pound body to protect himself.

The two figures struggled and fought just inside the bedroom doorway. Jim saw one darkened form pounding the other, again and again and again. He heard Chester's voice cry out in pain. Then, the black shadows disappeared through the open doorway, and Jim had his chance. He ran outside.

No sooner had he cleared the door than a hand grabbed him and pulled him down into the fight. Suddenly, he was lying on the frozen ground with Wes and Chester wrestling on top of him and then all around him. He struggled to get away, but a five-foot metal gate leaning against Chester's house crashed on top of him and pinned him to the ground.

As he lifted the metal gate and maneuvered to free himself, Jim saw the struggling bodies tumble toward him a second time. Instinctively and with all of his might, he shoved the gate like a battering-ram against the two, sending them sprawling into the darkness. He heard voices cry out. Later, Wes would tell him, "You almost killed me with that gate."

Having freed himself, Jim hurled the gate away from him.

He glanced toward the store in time to see Walter and Don running toward Wes, who still wrestled with the old man on the ground. Walter carried something in his left hand: a large concrete block.

Fearing that the neighbor across FM 339 might have heard a noise or Chester's cry, Jim ran around the opposite corner of the farmhouse to watch for signs of trouble. "Lookout" was a role that he had often played in recent burglaries; he did it almost instinctively, without thinking.

From where he stood on the southwest side of the farmhouse, Jim saw nothing of what happened during the next sixty seconds. But through the crisp country air of that chilling January night, he heard everything.

The old man's voice came in hoarse, raspy gasps, almost choking on the words. "Please, don't hit me anymore. Please."

The voice sounded unfamiliar to Jim, like some stranger's. All the fight had gone out of it. He had never heard Chester Brooks crawl, not in all those years he'd visited the country store. Chester Brooks was old Texas, too proud to know when he was licked. He wouldn't back down from anything, not unless he was . . .

Jim shut his eyes, like a terrified child watching some horror movie and knowing what's about to happen on the wide-angle screen, in living Technicolor, frame after frame after bloody frame. He tried to block the thought from his mind, tried to shut down the projector before the horrible image took form. But it was too late.

"I have a little money," said the voice. "You can have it. Please, don't hit me anymore."

A moment of silence followed. And then, *thump, thump, thump.* The pounding of the concrete block.

The muscles in Jim's throat tightened like a tourniquet, and he struggled to breathe. He had known something bad was going to happen that night. From the beginning, he had known. But he never expected this.

CHAPTER FOUR

Nobody Goin' to Heaven

*L*ater, when we talked about the events of that evening, I asked Jim why he hadn't gone to help Wes, instead of running around the corner of the house.

"I didn't want to," he said.

"If you didn't want to help Wes, then why didn't you try to stop him?"

Jim fell silent, as if he had considered that same question a thousand times before. "How?" he asked. "You can't stop something like that, not once it's started. It was going to happen, and there was no way to stop it."

"Are you saying that you couldn't have taken Wes?"

Answers bounced around in his head like pinballs ricocheting off the sides of the game machines he played. "Somebody else would have gotten hurt," he said finally. And then, as an afterthought, he added, "Bad."

So he had stood there in the darkness, feeling powerless to control anything that happened.

Jim stood guard at the southwest corner of Chester Brooks' farmhouse, listening to the thumping of the stone block. With each hammering blow, his heart pounded, and he wanted to run around the side of the building and see what was happening. He could hear the terrible sounds of struggling and thrashing and smashing, not more than twenty feet from where he stood. Filled with an anxious dread, he had turned and moved in that direction once, but he caught himself in midflight and forced his legs to stay put. He couldn't leave his lookout post; someone might come. Besides, he told himself, there was no need to go back. Not really. He had already guessed what was happening there in the shadows. It was bad.

Feeling the muscles in his neck flinch with each blow, Jim tried to control his fear by focusing on the Cordova place, some 200 yards northwest of where he stood. Watching his frozen breath rise in a vapory mist, Jim searched for signs of movement at the neighboring farmhouse. He looked past the shadowy stand of oak trees near the house, their twisted trunks touching the crystalline sky like gnarled, bony fingers.

Nothing stirred. No light appeared at the window; no voice called through the night; no dog howled in alarm. The farm family slept on, unaware of their neighbor's nightmare.

For the endless seconds that he watched from his lookout post, Jim stood like a statue, stone-still and icy-cold. He didn't move, except perhaps to distance himself from what was happening. He tried to mentally run away, to pretend he was somewhere else. He told himself he wasn't supposed to be in Coit and this was all a mistake.

He had made a date with Connie Aiken, and they had planned to do some heavy-duty partying that evening. Connie was a fast-moving, pseudo-hippie type that he'd started dating after he left home. He hadn't canceled their date because he didn't take the Folgers seriously when they talked about pulling a job that night. He thought they were just talking big, like guys sometimes did when they wanted to impress people. Big talk—like he himself had done several times when he mentioned robbing the old man's store. It was just talk, only talk.

Jim had been waiting for Connie to pick him up when the Folgers came by to get him and Walter around 9:00 that Sunday night. Had Connie arrived first, he would have left with her. Instead, he had no choice but to go with Wes and Don. He couldn't back down. Not then, not ever. He'd have to ride it out and see what happened.

He became conscious of a shadowy shape near the southeast corner of Chester's house, and the sudden movement jarred him from his mental stupor. He realized that the pounding had stopped, and an eerie silence enshrouded the night. With a sense of anxious dread, he forced himself to go back.

33

He approached Walter and Don, who stood several feet away from the house with their backs toward him. They were watching Wes, still hunkered on his knees astraddle the old man's body. Several moments passed before Wes staggered to his feet, arched his back as if in pain, and lumbered toward them. His frozen breath came in great gusts through the hole in his ski mask, now splattered with the old man's blood. He appeared tired and out of breath.

"I thought I'd never get that old man knocked out," Wes said. "He wouldn't stay down."

Jim glanced sideways toward Chester's house. He saw the old grocer thrashing about, moving his feet as though he were trying to get up. Jim couldn't see the upper part of Chester's body because the shadows of the house concealed it. But he could hear Chester's breathing—deep, raspy, life-wrenching. Jim tried to block out the sound, but the old man's anguish amplified in his ears. Chester was hurt bad.

"Come on," Wes said as he nudged Jim's arm, forcing him to turn his back on the spectral figure lying in the shadows. "I've knocked him out. Let's go ahead and rob the store, like we planned."

Mechanically, Jim walked back toward Chester's exterior bedroom door and picked up the pair of bolt cutters that he had dropped there earlier. He clutched the cold steel tightly, as though he were grateful to hold something familiar, something that gave him a grip on his sanity.

Jim had used those bolt cutters often during the six weeks that he and Walter Frye had burglarized Central Texas. They were the tools of his trade. That's why Jim had insisted that Wes stop by Ricky Dominick's place before driving over to Coit. Jim wanted to pick up his bolt cutters and a shotgun.

Ricky Dominick, the twenty-two-year-old son of a prominent Central Texas family, had been Jim and Walter's employer since the boys left home. He hired the two runaways to do "custom farm work," although neither of the young outlaws did anything while they were under Dominick's employment. Harboring the runaways by providing them with a hideout, Dominick allowed his employees to have free run of his two-bedroom frame house on Wall Street in Belton.

Located six miles from Jim's hometown of Temple, Belton was a small place of distinction. In addition to being the county seat and the home of a small Baptist college, Belton was also a haven for the two-fisted, hard-drinking cowboy element that cruised around after dark in shiny pickup trucks, looking for some action. Jim and Walter felt right at home.

They moved into Dominick's place around mid-December, just a few days before Christmas. Although Dominick still had some clothes and personal belongings in one of the bedrooms, he seldom stayed at the house on Wall Street. Recently divorced after a brief marriage, Dominick preferred to live, instead, at his mother's mobile home near Lake Belton, a recreation area some five miles west of town.

Dominick hadn't acted surprised when the youths appeared at his trailer that Sunday night, asking to borrow the bolt cutters and the shotgun. Dominick had walked with them to his brown-and-white pickup, where he searched for the bolt cutters while Jim explained that they needed them "to rob an old friend near Marlin."

"Who's that in the car with you?" Dominick asked, nodding his head toward the yellow Cougar that waited in the driveway, motor running.

"Wes Folger and his brother," Jim said matter of factly. Dominick nodded, handed Jim the bolt cutters, and began walking toward his trailer. When Jim repeated his request for the double-barrel shotgun, Dominick refused.

Walking back to the Folger car, Jim wondered why he had asked to borrow the shotgun. He and Walter never used a weapon when they were "taking care of business." They were burglars, not armed robbers. Besides, they had several guns back at the house on Wall Street. He could have brought any of them along if he'd wanted to. Perhaps he was just showing off that night, trying to impress Wes with his outlaw image.

Placing the long-handled bolt cutters in the floorboard of Wes' car, Jim climbed in and began the forty-minute drive to Coit. Before the night was over, he would have gone too far.

*   *   *   *   *

35

Carrying the bolt cutters in his left hand, Jim led his three partners along the hard-packed dirt trail to the back of Chester Brooks' store, some seventy feet beyond where the old grocer lay. The back door, hanging scarred and splintered from rusty metal hinges, posed no obstacle for the young intruders. Breaking-and-entering was their specialty. Jim maneuvered the bolt cutters into place around the metal hasp and squeezed hard. The hasp snapped in two, the lock fell to the ground, and the weathered wooden door creaked open several inches.

Jim reached inside the darkened doorway and fumbled along the wall until his leather glove found the overhead light switch. The naked bulb, suspended by a cord from the cracked and cobwebbed ceiling, cast an eerie glow over the cold, cluttered store.

The place was just as Jim remembered it. To the left stood the red-and-white Coke machine, elevated on a wooden platform that made it tower above him. Jim had opened its narrow glass door many times, pulling a bottled soft drink through the metal slot that encased it. He liked to watch the next bottle snap sharply into place, like a gun being loaded with shells. He always got a soda water when he went to Chester's store. Except that night.

To the right of the door stood an old wooden counter some six feet long and containing a glass-topped, domed case on the far end. Jim had often reached inside that glass compartment, for it housed the candy bars and chewing gum and cigarettes that he usually bought. He could smell the aroma of the candy and cigarettes above the musty odor of the store. But he hadn't come for candy or cigarettes.

Along the east and west walls were row after row of wooden shelves, bowed long ago by the weight of Folger's coffee tins, Del Monte canned vegetables, Kerr's canning jars, things that his Grandma Garrett usually bought. Interspersed with the grocery items were stacks of old magazines, boxes of tarnished coins, and cardboard containers with old letters and yellowed papers. Jim never understood why Chester kept such junk around, cluttering the limited shelf space.

Jim stepped down twelve inches onto the hard-packed, dirt-bottom floor inside the store and walked behind the counter, toward the front door. He didn't worry about the overhead light being seen because the primitive store had no windows, only two

36

wooden doors that were propped open with stone blocks during regular business hours. The back door, now standing ajar, couldn't be seen from the side road.

Jim walked past the white meat scales sitting on the counter-top, careful not to disturb the cans of Planters peanuts or Hershey's cocoa or Campbell soup collecting dust nearby. When he reached the glass display case, Jim ignored the bread loaves stacked on top, as well as the warped boxes of Snickers and Juicy Fruit and Camels inside the domed compartment. His mind was on something else.

Instead, he bent down on his knees, scanned the half-dozen shelves beneath the counter, and began rummaging through the empty King Edward cigar boxes. He knew that Chester didn't have a cash register or a safe. The old grocer usually stashed his money inside boxes throughout the store. Or, he buried it in fruit jars beneath the dirt floor—a fact unknown to the boys that night.

As he searched for money, Jim felt in control of himself once again. He was doing something that he'd done often during the last six weeks. In his mind he was simply burglarizing a store—not Chester's store, just a store like all the rest. His natural instincts took over as his hands moved mechanically and methodically through the old cigar boxes. He found a wad of money right away and stuffed the crumpled bills inside his right boot top. He'd split the take with Walter later; they were partners and looked out for each other.

While Jim worked behind the counter, Don and Walter ransacked the shelves on the opposite wall near the Coke machine. Don pulled boxes off and handed them to Walter, who rummaged through the contents before stacking the boxes on the dirt floor. Several minutes passed, and the boys became frustrated. They weren't finding the hundreds of dollars that the old man supposedly kept in his store.

As his three accomplices looted the shelves, Wes stood in the doorway, glancing from the store to the shadowy darkness outside. He gripped the door with his bloody gloves, leaving red smears along the edges of the white frame. Suddenly and without warning, Wes' eyes widened in terror. "Jim!" he yelled. "Somebody is out there!"

"You sure?" Jim asked as he raised up from behind the counter.

"I saw something move. Out by the barn. Let's go."

Obeying Wes' order, Jim grabbed several unopened cigar boxes as he made his way to the back door. Don and Walter filled their arms with as many boxes as they could carry, including the useless ones they'd opened. They couldn't leave anything behind; they hadn't worn gloves.

Frantically, the four outlaws fled the store, not bothering to turn off the overhead light. Jim led his friends down the dirt trail and past the darkened house without glancing toward the battered body lying in the shadows. Had he thought about it, Jim might have remembered that Chester always kept money in his front shirt pocket. Jim could have taken it easily, but he didn't go near Chester Brooks. He didn't know whether the old man was dead or alive; he didn't have time to think about it. He was on the run, and he was scared.

Rushing helter-skelter into the night, the boys ran behind Chester's farmhouse, climbed over the two barbed-wire fences around the pasture, and darted through the church yard. During their flight, one of them dropped a box of old coins. The tarnished tokens lay splattered on the ground—like the old man who had collected them.

When the boys reached the west side of the Fairview Presbyterian Church, they raced across the crushed-stone parking lot and ran toward the car. Wes removed his bloody gloves, fumbled for the keys in his front Levis pockets, and opened the trunk of the yellow Cougar. The boys threw their robbery loot inside, and Wes slammed the lid shut.

Jim glanced beyond the farm-to-market intersection and toward the house of Manuel Cordova. Still no light shone from that direction. Apparently, no one had heard anything. Wes had probably seen one of Chester's cows, milling around in the pasture back of the store. Somewhat reassured, Jim tried to steady his hands as he flung open the passenger door.

Walter and Don scrambled into the back seat, and Jim took the shotgun position beside Wes. Once inside, the youths noticed something unusual: None of the car's interior lights worked. The lights had worked on the drive up, and they would work fine on the following day, but they didn't work that night. Frantically, Wes inserted the key into the ignition, pumped the gas pedal, and sighed with relief when the Cougar's engine turned over. For an agonizing moment, he had feared that the car wouldn't start.

Wes edged the Cougar across the church parking lot and onto FM 1771. Turning right at the intersection of FM 339, some seventy feet beyond, he drove along the narrow blacktop road that ran in front of Chester Brooks' store. No one looked as they passed.

Not wishing to attract attention, Wes waited until the car was hundreds of yards beyond the Brooks place before he turned on the headlights. Farther down FM 339, when he judged that he had gone a safe distance, Wes pulled over to the side of the road, stopped the car, and motioned for Jim to get out. Together, the boys frenziedly tore off the duct tape they had placed over the tail lights earlier that evening. For some reason, that was the only detail of their plan they had thought out in advance. Wes had borrowed the idea from some TV show.

Climbing back inside, Wes gunned the motor and accelerated to over 70 mph along that narrow back road toward Kosse, the nearest community, with some 500 residents. Wes fumbled to turn on his tape player, hoping the rock music would replace the loud silence that throbbed inside their heads. But the tape player didn't work. There had been no problem earlier that evening, and there would be no problem the following day. But on that night, it didn't work. Nothing worked that night.

The boys sat in silence, each lost in his own nightmare. Finally, Wes spoke. "Well," he said, gripping the steering wheel with white knuckles, "I guess I'm not going to heaven now."

A somber laugh came from the back seat. "I guess none of us are."

The others nodded in silent assent. They had broken the commandment carved in stone and there was no turning back for any of them. They knew that.

As the yellow Cougar sped through the night, Jim peered out the icy windshield, staring at the dark void that engulfed them. The familiar fields of his childhood had changed somehow to a cold and bleak expanse that stretched on and on forever, consuming him with its emptiness.

He didn't know about his chances of going to heaven, but he knew about hell. He was already there.

CHAPTER FIVE

Live by the Gun; Die by the Gun

He Who Lives by the Gun, Dies by the Gun.

I wrote the words on the chalkboard in bold letters, hoping the Dozen would read and heed the clichéd axiom of the Old West. At the time, I had no way of knowing that Jim Taylor would learn the same lesson that week, standing there in the shadows of Chester Brooks' farmhouse.

I had ridden roughshod over the Dozen after Jim left, prodding them to finish the Western Lit unit before final exams. We pushed to complete the novel *Shane,* the story of a mysterious gunfighter unable to escape his past. I read aloud to the boys, instructing them to use their fingers in underlining the words in the book. I wanted them to learn to see groups of words; it was a reading improvement skill we practiced often.

Despite their reluctance to read, the Dozen had enjoyed *Shane,* especially the part where Shane sided with the homesteaders and stood up against Fletcher, the powerful cattleman. Most of them thought Shane was a "bad dude" after the saloon shootout with Fletcher and his hired guns, although some still considered the gunfighter a fool for unstrapping his six-shooter in the first place. All agreed that they wouldn't have faced the enemy unarmed. The four-inch switchblades they carried inside their jeans pockets proved their point.

As I listened to the Dozen's comments, I wished Jim Taylor had stayed to hear the he-who-lives-by-the-gun discussion. I had chosen to teach the novel because of him and the other boys in class with juvenile records. It was part of my behavior modification strategy, a subtle way of using literature to focus on acceptable or unacceptable behavior. I selected classic novels that focused on ethical principles and fostered moral behavior.

Rather than "preaching" traditional values to the Dozen, I used positive role models in literature to demonstrate responsible actions. I let the books "show" rather than me "tell." Schaefer's story about the notorious gunfighter provided a classic example of behavior modification. Shane tried to teach Bob Starrett alternate methods of dealing with anger and hostility. A man could be a man without resorting to aggression. It was okay to turn the other cheek.

Jim would have enjoyed reading about the gunfighter. I felt he belonged to that wild, ruthless era of six-guns and shootouts. As if he were a wayward time traveler, Jim had been trapped in the wrong century. He belonged to the days of Pat Garrett, Billy the Kid, and Jesse James.

Jim agreed. "If I had lived a hundred years ago," he said, "I would have been a bank robber. Of course," he laughed, "I'd probably got hung."

As far back as the third grade, Jim had daydreamed about an adventurous outlaw career. His hero was Jesse James, the legendary bank robber who terrorized much of Missouri during the 1870s. In schoolboy fashion, Jim had envisioned himself raiding railroads, robbing banks, and eluding the Pinkertons. He saw nothing wrong with his hero's actions because Jesse James had been "driven to it" by the aftermath of the bloody Civil War. As an impressionable youngster, Jim believed the romanticized legends about the daring outlaw, America's version of Robin Hood.

Mrs. Fikes, Jim's third-grade teacher at Jefferson Elementary, hadn't shared those views about a misguided Missouri marauder. Like many historians, she considered Jesse James a ruthless, paranoid killer. Clearly, Jesse was no role model for impressionable young children to emulate. When a student brought a record of American folk ballads to class, Mrs. Fikes played all of the songs except the one about Jesse James.

Jim seldom contradicted his teachers, but he angrily spoke out in defense of his outlaw hero. He demanded to know what was wrong with Jesse. Mrs. Fikes attempted to explain her objection to the badman's ballad, yet Jim remained unconvinced. His loyalty to the Missouri bandit never wavered, even during the years that followed. Subconsciously, Jim may have patterned his own lawlessness after Jesse's exciting exploits.

He and the outlaw held much in common, especially in appearance and temperament. Each had blue eyes, sandy-colored hair, and rugged good looks. They stood approximately five-foot-eight, had slight frames, and handled a gun with their left hands. Reared in strict Baptist homes, they knew about the Bible and rarely drank anything stronger than beer. They held Victorian beliefs about women and seldom swore in the presence of ladies. During their criminal careers, both used the alias of "J. T." and stole from friends as well as enemies. Despite frequent bouts with insomnia, they maintained light-hearted, reckless, devil-may-care dispositions.

An even stranger similarity was their gift for premonitions. Once Jesse and his wife, Zee, hastily fled to Tennessee after the outlaw had a premonition about impending danger in Missouri. Several days later, Pinkerton detectives raided the home of Jesse's mother and threw a railroad potflare through the farmhouse window. A freak explosion followed, and shrapnel tore open the stomach of Jesse's nine-year-old half-brother. The boy died soon thereafter. Jesse's mother, also injured during the explosion, suffered such a mangling of her right hand that surgeons later had to saw it off above the wrist. Jesse, forewarned about the danger, hadn't been in the house at the time of the Pinkerton raid.

Jim, too, had escaped similar close calls with law enforcement officers because some "bad feeling" alerted him to danger. During three different burglary attempts, as Jim and Walter Frye were about to enter a darkened store, Jim's sixth sense held him back. Within moments, a police car or sheriff's car drove past the targeted store. Experience had taught him to listen to those gut feelings; they usually kept him out of trouble.

Jim shared still another link with the famous desperado: a miracle. Both had defied death by surviving near-fatal injuries. In 1865, after raiding and looting with Bloody Bill Anderson's guerrillas, the eighteen-year-old Jesse rode under a white flag into Lexington, Missouri, attempting to surrender to Union troops. He was shot through the right lung and, according to the doctor who later tended him, should have died from the injury. But Jesse fled into the woods and survived the night by dragging himself to a creek, where he constantly bathed the wound in his chest. In the morning, Jesse crawled to a nearby field where a farmer was plowing, and collapsed. The farmer took the young marauder home with him, tended the near-fatal wound, then summoned Jesse's family. Although the lung injury plagued him for the rest of his life, the Missouri bandit was lucky to be alive.

Jim shared the same fortune as his boyhood hero, miraculously surviving an accident that should have killed him. On a December afternoon, eleven-year-old Jim disobeyed his mother by not going straight home after school. Instead, he and a friend sneaked off to their favorite neighborhood hideout, the drainage culvert by the small creek in their housing area. The tree-shaded, brush-covered gully provided an idyllic retreat for young boys, a place where they could talk or smoke or crawdad fish without fear of detection.

With only an hour of freedom before Jim's mother came home from work, the boys took a shortcut to the creek that Monday afternoon, cutting through the New Hope Cemetery. New Hope was a plot of ground set aside for the black community of Temple, a deserted area where large patches of Johnson grass overran the many untended, pre-World War II gravesites. Located beside the Missouri, Kansas, and Texas (KATY) railroad tracks, the cemetery's ground vibrated as northbound or southbound trains rambled past each day, filling the air with stale diesel stench and interrupting the solitude with nerve-grating sounds of clicking, clacking, squealing, and screeching.

The boys' flight through New Hope was slowed that December afternoon, for heavy rains had turned the cemetery ground into a quagmire, bogging them down as they ran past the water-filled, half-sunken graves. With his friend in the lead, Jim sludged through the tombstoned mounds as fast as he could, for he hated being around graveyards and dead people.

As he neared the east entrance, suddenly and without warning, a four-foot section of the massive tombstone ahead broke away from its one-and-a-half-foot base and toppled toward Jim. Unable to stop in time, he reacted by putting both hands in front of his chest, hoping to shove the falling tombstone away from

43

him. The weight of the mammoth white slab slammed against him, forced him backward, and pinned him to the marshy ground beside a grave.

Dazed and in pain, Jim cried out from beneath the rock that buried most of his small body. After what seemed like an endless wait, Jim saw his schoolmate's face, hovering above him and mouthing something, but he didn't understand what. Then the face disappeared, leaving Jim trapped and unable to move, unable to feel his arms or his legs. He lay stone-still, like the occupant in the grave beside him.

Some five minutes later, the frantic schoolmate returned with an older, bigger boy who had been riding a bicycle on a nearby street. The two rescuers, working to free the ashen-faced Jim, struggled to move the 44x20x10-inch stone block. While the older boy somehow hoisted the 330-pound tombstone, the schoolmate pulled Jim from beneath. Then they loaded Jim onto the back of the bicycle, carried him to the nearest house, and telephoned his mother.

When Carolyn Taylor arrived fifteen minutes later, she saw her son sitting beside the neighbor's curb, crying. Jim's mouth was bloodied, his arms were scraped, his chest was bruised, and he complained of a sharp pain when he breathed. With her training in medical records, Carolyn suspected that Jim had injured his lungs or had other internal injuries.

Carolyn cried while driving the five miles to the hospital, afraid that her eleven-year-old son might die. Jim also continued to cry, but not solely from the pain. He cried because he feared what his mom would do to him for disobeying her. Carolyn Taylor could be tough.

When Jim arrived at the emergency room, the doctors were amazed that he had survived the accident. "It's a miracle your boy is alive," a physician told Carolyn as she stood nearby, watching the doctor read the X-rays. She had been to the emergency room often with Jim; he was always taking risks and getting hurt. But his injuries had never been this bad before.

The tombstone had lacerated Jim's scalp, crushed his right arm, and bruised his chest and abdomen. His lungs had not been punctured (that would come later in a bull-riding accident). Jim had, however, sustained another injury: the third finger on his left hand. The coincidence seemed almost contrived, for according to historians of the Old West, the injured middle finger on the left hand marked another young outlaw who had roamed the Texas frontier. Every lawman in the territory knew about the bandit with the missing nub on his left hand. The Missouri badman, Jesse James.

When Jim was released from the hospital four days later, he put the bizarre tombstone incident behind him. How could he explain why a 330-pound stone suddenly toppled over on him, without anyone having touched it? It was creepy, like something out of *The Twilight Zone*. He vowed not to take any more short-cuts through New Hope Cemetery.

Had he returned to the scene of his near-fatal accident, he might have noticed the names on the surrounding tombstones. The stone that crushed him belonged to Aggie Harrison, a seventy-four-year-old laundress who had died in 1945. Her five-foot monument was unique in its design. Lying horizontally across the top of the marker was a two-foot section of log, resembling those found on Woodsmen of the World tombstones. Except Aggie Harrison wasn't a member of that insurance company, for the elderly black woman would have been excluded from the Woodsmen's all-white policyholders. Perhaps the stone symbolized something else, though its significance had long since been forgotten. But Aggie Harrison's grave couldn't be forgotten, towering above the Johnson grass in New Hope Cemetery and clearly visible from the Missouri, Kansas, and Texas railroad nearby.

Immediately north of the Harrison gravesite rested Joel Folger, a World War I veteran. Folger had served with the Negro 813 CO Transportation Corps in Italy, loading dead bodies into Allied ambulances. He told stories about the horrors of war up until his death on July 7, 1938. The Christian cross etched on his tombstone was reminiscent of those found in the Argonne Forest or Flanders Field.

East of Folger's marker was the grave of Edward L. Wilson, a veteran of World War II. The black technical sergeant bore the Star of David on his tombstone, in contrast with Folger's cross. Jew and Christian buried side by side, two old soldiers resting beneath government-issued headstones in New Hope Cemetery.

45

A fourth marker completed the circle of graves surrounding the spot where Jim Taylor fell that December afternoon. The gray marble monument appeared modern in comparison to the others. It bore a single surname chiseled across its face: Garrett. Garrett was the name of Jim's maternal grandmother, who lived three miles from Chester Brooks' store.

Had he returned to the scene of his near-fatal accident, Jim Taylor probably wouldn't have made a connection with the names on the four tombstones. Yet, Garrett, Wilson, Folger, and Harrison formed a cast of characters he was destined to meet again. For Jim, the Twilight Zone had only begun.

The old cemetery beside the MK&T tracks began a series of coincidences that connected Jim Taylor with a time and place far removed. Students of history might well have recognized the name of the graveyard: New Hope.

More than one hundred years before Jim's accident, a Baptist minister stood before a small congregation in Clay County, Missouri, preaching the gospel. Seated there on the pew of his father's rural church was a blue-eyed schoolboy who would grow up to break most of the commandments he had been taught.

The boy was called Jesse James, and his father's Baptist church was called New Hope.

New Hope Cemetery provided still another link with the Missouri outlaw. When I visited the graveyard years later, I was intrigued by the tombstone of Joel Folger, the World War I vet who had loaded bodies into ambulances. Perhaps my curiosity stemmed from the coincidence in surnames. Folger, I remembered, was the name of the boy who had wielded the stone block against Chester Brooks.

Searching for more information about the old black man, I rummaged through a 1938 issue of the *Temple Daily Telegram,* looking for Folger's obituary. I found no record of his death. In the rural South of the thirties, blacks seldom made the news unless they were arrested for crimes against whites.

But on the obituary page where Folger's name would have appeared had he been white, I found an article of interest. The headline read:

In an Associated Press news release, a Dallas resident named Robert F. Cole related an incident from his boyhood days. Cole reported that an old black man once told him about helping an outlaw gang bury its last haul in Texas:

> A Negro told the youngster (Cole) he dug the hole when the treasure was buried.
> "It was betwixt the smokehouse and the plumb thicket," the old darky was quoted as saying.
> Cole pointed to an old excavation now thickly overgrown with weeds and underbrush . . .

Ordinarily, I would have filed that information under the heading of Texas tall-tales and forgotten it. But a gnawing suspicion made me read on. The site of the old excavation was a place near Dallas called White Rock. And the notorious outlaw leader whom the old man had helped was Jesse James.

White Rock. Black man. Jesse James. I made the connection with New Hope Cemetery and the "old darky" beneath the white headstone where Jim Taylor fell. The "darky" whose missing obituary had led me, instead, to a little-known story about the Missouri bandit. Of all the outlaws who robbed and looted on the Texas frontier, why had I been led back to this one?

Had I followed Jesse's exploits more carefully, I might have read about a train robbery near Muncie, Kansas, in December of 1874. Five armed men forced the train crew to uncouple the express and baggage cars from the rest of the Kansas Pacific train before ordering the engineer to pull ahead. The robbers removed approximately $30,000 from the express car safe, then rode away.

The Muncie holdup outside of Kansas City was routine and uneventful, and skipped over by most historians who like to dwell on the James–Younger bloodbath at Northfield, Minnesota, some two years later. Yet the train robbery may have had a significance for an outlaw kid taking a shortcut through New Hope Cemetery.

Jesse James had used one of his favorite tricks to stop the locomotive at Muncie: piling stones and logs across the tracks.

Stones and logs like the ones carved on Aggie Harrison's tombstone, lying there in the shadows of the MK&T railroad tracks. Train tracks like the ones running north to Missouri and the New Hope Baptist Church, where a blue-eyed boy listened to his father's dictums about thou-shalt-not-steal.

A blue-eyed boy like Jim Taylor, who lay with a stone log piled across him on that near-fatal December day.

The exact same day in December that, ninety-seven years before, Jesse James had piled the stones and logs across the railroad tracks in Muncie, Kansas.

All trails led back to Jesse James. But why?

Perhaps my English-teacher training made me find "foreshadowing" at every turn, as if I were cursed by some sort of professional paranoia about persistent patterns and recurring motifs. Jim's connection to Jesse James was purely circumstantial, I told myself, not to mention far-fetched. Even if Jesse James believed in psychic perceptions and out-of-body experiences, as some historians alleged, I certainly did not.

Still, I felt uneasy about Jim Taylor, for I remembered all too well the fate of the Missouri outlaw who had refused to hang up his six-guns. As a child growing up during the *Gunsmoke* and *Bonanza* era, I had sung the ballad that Mrs. Fikes refused to play for Jim's third-grade class: "It was a dirty little coward that shot Mr. Howard and laid poor Jesse in his grave."

Although I, too, had once reveled in the myths of the daring Jesse James, I wanted the Dozen to realize that the day of the badman had ended long ago. That's why I had wanted them to hear the message of *Shane:* He who lives by the gun, dies by the gun.

I wanted them to find other ways to settle their differences with people and school and society. If they were to survive, their lawlessness had to stop and their attitudes had to change.

I had hoped Jim would be in class to learn that lesson. But like the mysterious gunfighter Shane, he had already ridden off into the sunset, and there was no calling him back.

CHAPTER SIX

Battered and Broken and Bent

As the yellow Cougar and its stony-eyed passengers sped away, Chester Brooks lay in the shadows of his rural farmhouse, dying. He rested face-down with his head perpendicular to the car shed wall, inches away from the blood-splattered siding. Nearby, the old .410 shotgun lay in three pieces: the barrel, bowed; the stock, broken; and the receiver, dislodged.

The front of Chester's face bore evidence of the brutal shotgun beating he had endured moments earlier. A large, T-shaped laceration had been gouged deeply into his forehead; the tissue from the left eye to the bridge of the nose had been badly bruised; the skin at the right temple had been lacerated; a thick, bloody discharge oozed from his mouth and nose. In addition, his left shoulder and right wrist had been broken during the terrible struggle for the gun.

Against the side of his head rested a twenty-five-pound concrete block, smeared with matted gray hair and bloody tissue. The back of the old man's head lay cracked open from the base of the skull upward. Through the bloody six-inch crevice of fractured skull bone, brain tissue lay exposed in the freezing January air. The car shed wall resembled a blood-splattered slaughter pen, as if the head of a hog or a cow had recently been bashed open by a sledgehammer's blows.

The massive hemorrhage of underlying brain tissue ended the life of the sixty-seven-year-old grocer. He died violently and brutally and needlessly following a hold-up in which he was not supposed to be hurt.

On the day of his death, Chester Brooks had done two things

49

that he rarely did: He dressed in clean khaki clothing, and he swept the dirt floor of his store. He appeared to be getting ready for something and wanted to have his affairs in order. Perhaps he, like Jim Taylor, had been forewarned of what was to happen on that gruesome January night.

One customer noticed that the old grocer seemed noticeably edgy on the afternoon prior to the robbery, which wasn't characteristic of the old man at all. Chester Brooks had been the most loving, forgiving, trusting soul in all of southern Limestone County. His kindness and generosity, as well as his eccentricity, had made him a living legend.

Dressed in his faded khakis, baseball cap, and high-topped shoes, Chester had presented a colorful picture of rural Americana, like the subject of a Norman Rockwell painting. At a time when modern technology propelled people forward at an accelerated pace, the genial old grocer had clung to the ways of the past, when life was slower and simpler and, perhaps, better. He had been a nostalgic reminder of a time when people talked to one another, called each other "neighbor," and didn't lock their doors at night.

His rustic general store had served as a favorite gathering place for locals. It was a rural mecca that drew folks together for miles around. Country people sat in ladder-back chairs outside the weathered, one-room structure, drinking sodas and exchanging news about the price of crops or who had married whom. City slickers who happened by gawked at the rusty tin signs tacked to the sun-bleached walls, or gaped at the towering glass-topped, hand-cranked gasoline pump that stood out front like a solitary sentinel.

Chester's store — with its dirt floor, cobwebbed ceiling, grist mill, and meat scales — had remained a welcome relic of an age past. Small children on a Sunday outing to Grandma's house had immediately clamored to "go see Chester." They knew that the old man would not only give them candy or gum or silver dollars, but that he would also spend time talking to them and making them feel important. Young people, especially girls, had delighted in the fact that the old grocer always remembered their birthdays, and that he would have a card or an Avon brush waiting for them on their next visit to his store.

Chester's generosity had extended to adults, as well. If a neighbor were out of work and couldn't afford the price of groceries, Chester had supplied the needed items, saying, "Pay me when you can." Or, if an impoverished family couldn't afford to pay, Chester had simply given them the food; after all, he reasoned, that's what neighbors were for.

He also had gone out of his way to provide conveniences for his regular customers. He stocked hard-to-find items that his shut-in neighbors had requested. He opened up his store late at night to accommodate customers who had run out of bread or cigarettes and didn't want to drive into town for the items. He also cashed sizable checks when folks ran out of money and couldn't get to their banks on weekends or at night.

"Chester Brooks was everybody's granddad," said Dennis Wilson, a Limestone County deputy who had often stopped at the store while patrolling the area late at night. Drinking a soda and talking about the ballgame, Dennis had enjoyed the old man's company. "With Chester, there wasn't a 'generation gap.' He loved people," the deputy recalled.

While the old grocer had delighted in providing for the needs of others, he had thought very little about his own comfort. With the exception of electricity, he enjoyed few of the modern conveniences. The old man lived without air conditioning or running water or indoor plumbing. For many years, he had used a wood-burning cookstove to heat his meals, which he usually ate from the cans. He had preferred to sleep outside on the front porch, under a tarpaulin, year round. Only during recent months had he enclosed the back porch of his house and begun sleeping in that room.

Chester had, undoubtedly, inherited his eccentricity from his mother, Carrie Steele Brooks. As a young woman, she had suffered a severe mental breakdown that impaired her ability to care for her two preschool sons. Following the tragic death of her youngest boy, Woodrow, she had grown progressively worse. Whenever her behavior became too bizarre, neighbors saw Chester's father load the young boy into the buggy and take him to his grandmother's house until Mrs. Brooks had "calmed down."

Except for a brief stint in the U.S. Army during World War

II, Chester had remained in the rural community of Coit, caring for his feeble-minded mother and running his father's general store. After his father's death, Chester assumed sole responsibility in caring for his mentally-infirm mother, as well as for his eccentric Aunt Annie, who had taken refuge with them after a family quarrel had left her homeless.

By the time his mother died, Chester's house had been overrun by ceiling-high columns of newspapers that Aunt Annie had saved, leaving only small trails between the stacks for her and Chester to walk through. After his aunt's death, Chester had refused to discard the musty, yellowed collection of old newspapers. And, he never again slept inside the house; perhaps, some speculate, it was because his old, eccentric aunt had died in there.

The most bizarre behavior that Chester had inherited from his mother was his tendency to hide money in out-of-the-way places. Mrs. Brooks had often stashed paper money inside the pages of old magazines and books that she read. Chester had chosen to conceal his money inside inconspicuous jars, such as Carter's Little Liver Pill bottles, on his store shelves. In addition, he had also buried over 300 pounds of coins in the dirt floor of his store, carefully concealed in cigar boxes or fruit jars.

Neighbors, concerned for his safety, had warned him about the danger of keeping so much cash inside his store. Yet, although he maintained a sizable checking account at the Kosse State Bank for store business, the old grocer had still enjoyed keeping a private collection of money on hand. Late at night, he had been seen inside his store, counting his money over and over again. Because his habits were well known, Chester Brooks made a prime target for a robbery.

Well-meaning friends who were fearful for his safety suggested that he think about retirement. And, for a time, Chester had talked about "kicking over a stone" on the door of the store and shutting up shop for good. But he had continued to postpone the closing date; he couldn't disappoint his customers.

When friends realized that the old grocer wasn't going to close his store, they urged him to buy a modern gun for his protection. His old .410-gauge Stevens shotgun was an antiquated piece of artillery, they insisted. But Chester, wielding the worn-out weapon in his massive hands, had ignored their urgings and gone about his business. After all, he lived in the country, far away from big-city crime and violence. He had nothing to fear, he assured them. "This ain't Houston," he said.

And yet, he had seemed jumpy on that last Sunday of his life, as if he had half expected trouble. Perhaps his edginess stemmed from the fact that a red sports car with three long-haired, suspicious-looking occupants had stopped at his store the day before. Or maybe he felt tense because he had heard, off and on for several nights, the sound of small stones striking the walled-in back porch where he slept.

Then again, perhaps he felt apprehensive because of the confrontation that had taken place in his store earlier that afternoon. Luis Torres, a neighbor from down the road, had entered the store with two illegal aliens and asked to borrow money. Because Chester had already given the man a $100 loan that hadn't been repaid, the old grocer refused to advance any additional money. Annoyed, Torres had then suggested that Chester make a loan to one of the aliens. Again the old man refused, saying, "What guarantee do I have that he won't skip over the border into Mexico without paying me?"

Angered by the old grocer's refusal to cooperate, Torres had become verbally abusive. Following a heated exchange of words, Chester had yelled, "Get out of my store, all three of you. And don't come back!"

Although he was kind-hearted and generous, the five-foot-eight, 210-pound grocer could be tough when he was riled. He wasn't the type to start a quarrel, but he wouldn't back down from one either. In the frontier tradition of early Texas, the old man would fight to protect what was his.

And that's what worried his neighbors — the fact that he would fight back. On several occasions, friends had told him, "If someone tries to rob you, let 'em have the money." But they knew that their words were wasted. Chester Brooks and his .410 shotgun would fight to the death.

And so, that's what they had done on that bitter cold January night. Now, as the yellow Cougar sped away, Chester and his shotgun lay in the shadows of the rural Texas farmhouse. Battered and broken and bent.

CHAPTER SEVEN

Dumping the Evidence

On the day Chester Brooks died, national attention focused on another violent death many miles from the blood-splattered Texas farmhouse where the old man lay. Shortly after sunrise on the same morning, convicted killer Gary Mark Gilmore faced a firing squad at the Utah State Prison south of Salt Lake City. The execution marked a media melee.

Gilmore, a thirty-six-year-old high school dropout, had gained national headlines by demanding his civil liberty: the right to die for what he had done. Gilmore had walked into a Utah service station and gunned down David Jenson, the twenty-five-year-old attendant. The next night he confronted Bennie Bushnell, the night manager of a Provo motel, and shot the twenty-five-year-old Brigham Young University student twice in the head. Each robbery victim left a widow and a young child.

Gilmore had been convicted for the motel murder and sentenced to death. The Utah Supreme Court granted a stay of execution only days before Gilmore's sentence was to be carried out. That routine gesture of mercy touched off a unique legal crisis and a national sensation. Gary Gilmore refused to accept the court's clemency and demanded that his execution take place as scheduled. He became known to the media as the man with a "death wish."

Two days after the court stayed his execution, a handcuffed and shackled Gilmore went before the Utah Supreme Court judges to plead his case personally. "I am ready to accept my execution," he said to the jurists. "I believe I was given a fair trial. The sentence is proper, and I'm willing to accept it with dignity, like a man. I hope it will be carried out without any delay," he concluded.

The court reversed itself and gave the go-ahead for Gilmore's execution. Civil libertarians picked up on the death penalty controversy and contacted Gilmore, demanding that he change his mind. No one had been executed in the United States since 1967, and the anti-death penalty advocates wanted to continue the ten-year moratorium. Despite pressure from the American Civil Liberties Union, the NAACP Legal Defense Fund, the National Coalition Against the Death Penalty, and the National Council of Churches, Gilmore remained steadfast in his decision. He wanted to die.

As the sun rose behind the rugged peaks of the Wasatch Range, inmate No. 13871 got his wish. Gary Gilmore was loaded into a prison van, driven to a cinderblock shed, and strapped into a wooden chair with nylon strips loosely binding his neck, elbows, wrists, and ankles. A black hood was placed over his head, and a priest administered last rites to the calm inmate clad in a black T-shirt, white pants, and red-white-and-blue tennis shoes.

A black target with a white circle was pinned to Gilmore's T-shirt, and the convicted murderer was asked for his final words. "Let's do it," Gilmore said.

Utah State Prison warden Samuel Smith motioned to the five anonymous men with .30-caliber rifles standing ten yards away behind a burlap screen. Seconds later, a volley of rifle fire sent four steel-jacketed bullets into the white circle pinned to Gilmore's shirt. One weapon held blank ammunition so that none of the marksmen could be sure that he actually killed the condemned murderer.

There was a slight movement of Gilmore's hands as the red blood slowly oozed from under the black T-shirt and onto the white pants. The body continued to move for twenty or thirty seconds, then sat stone-still. The prison doctor moved forward, examined the body, and pronounced Gilmore dead.

When prison officials led 150 newsmen into the cinderblock shed moments after the corpse had been removed, blood still dripped from the green chair and unpainted plywood execution stage.

* * * * *

In class that Monday morning, the Dozen had been fasci-
nated as we discussed Gilmore's execution. I had brought up the
current event as a grand finale to our he-who-lives-by-the-gun discussion from the previous week. I liked to tie the "real world" to
our literature study whenever possible, and to reinforce object
lessons.

Unlike the gunfighter Shane, Gary Gilmore had not tried to
modify his behavior or abandon his lawlessness. In and out of
reform schools since he was fourteen, the high school dropout
seemed bent on getting into trouble. The Utah robberies had
been the climax to a lifetime of crime, I told the Dozen, hoping
they'd make the connection with their own misdeeds. Then I
quoted an observation made by Democritus: "Hope of ill gain is
the beginning of loss."

They hadn't bought the idea and were quick to react. "Crime
does pay, unless you're stupid," one of them insisted. "Gilmore's
only mistake was getting caught."

"Yeah, he was dumb; he deserved to die," another voice
chimed in.

Despite my attempt to introduce moral ethics, I soon realized the discussion wasn't headed where I had intended, and I
steered the Dozen toward another activity. So much for current
events and object lessons, I thought. This behavior modification
trick was going to be tough. I hoped the nation had greater success than I had.

Local newspapers carried follow-up articles on the Gilmore
execution, soliciting reaction to the first use of capital punishment in ten years. Texas law enforcement officers applauded the
return of the death penalty, reflecting the brand of justice left
over from frontier days. Local juries were tough on crime and
criminals. Central Texans preferred to lynch their murderers and
be done with it.

Bell County Sheriff Lester Gunn reflected the views of many
folks when he commented on the Gilmore execution by saying,
"That's the finest thing that's happened since 1964 [the date of
the last execution in Texas]. Now people are going to think before they pull some of these crimes," the sheriff stated.

Sheriff Gunn's tough words were welcomed by the citizens

of Bell County who wanted law and order restored to Central Texas. Fear of capital punishment was the only way to deter would-be criminals, they insisted.

Yet, four young robbers knew nothing of Gary Gilmore as they sped along the darkened back roads of Bell County during the pre-dawn hours of that Monday morning. Despite the hourly newscasts and the special bulletins interrupting network television, they had paid no attention to the execution of the convicted Utah murderer. They were too busy with their own wrongdoing to heed society's message.

At about the same hour blood oozed from beneath Gary Gilmore's shirt, Jim had opened his eyes, focused on the bedroom wall, and seemed surprised that he had been asleep.

He remembered lying awake for a long time after they got back to the house, staring into the darkness, and trying to force his mind to turn off the terrible picture-making machine. But the images kept flashing: the old man, the shotgun, the stone block.

The drive back from Coit had seemed like an endless odyssey through time. The yellow Cougar raced through the darkness at break-neck speeds, straddling the yellow lines as it wound along the narrow roadways that twisted and turned like coiled copperheads.

Jim had stared out the front windshield, focusing on the white highway signs illumined by the thin headlight beams piercing the night. The numbers on the road signs blurred together in repetitious configurations of seven: FM 1771, Highway 7, Junction 77. Everything was sevens, even the date — the seventeenth of January. He remembered reading something about the number seven in the Bible, but he had forgotten the significance long ago. He had blocked out everything he'd learned about God or religion; that was sissy stuff and he had no use for it.

As if he had been consumed by some black hole and propelled into an abyss of nothingness, Jim rode on through the void of the night. He scarcely noticed when the Cougar braked to a stop in front of the north Temple home of Don Folger's parents, dropped off the youngest of the four conspirators, and sped away.

Some ten minutes later, Wes wheeled the car to a stop in front of a small frame house on the corner of Wall Street in

Belton, the place where Jim and Walter had been hiding while they did "custom farm work" for Ricky Dominick. Jim smelled the odor of stale marijuana as he opened the front door and walked inside. He wished he had a joint right then, but he had smoked the last of his stash before the robbery and would have to wait until morning to buy more. For the moment, he concentrated on getting the stolen loot out of Wes' car trunk and into the house without being seen.

Jim carried an armful of stolen boxes through the living room, navigating his way around the couch, two chairs, and old player piano. Except for the dozen bullet holes in the wall, the room appeared well-kept. The boys had enjoyed a game of target practice several nights before, using their pistols to shoot bugs crawling across the sheetrock walls. The gaping holes attested to their poor marksmanship, but they had been high at the time.

Jim and his two companions carried the loot into the front bedroom, where it would be out of sight from unexpected visitors. They sorted through the pyramid of old cigar boxes and wooden crates, laying the cash on a card table and throwing everything else to one side.

Chester Brooks had been a pack rat, all right. The boxes contained outdated coupons, yellowed papers, sets of U.S. collector's coins, assorted Canadian coins, and old keys. Jim tossed the coins and old keys into a King Edward cigar box for safekeeping; he'd decide what to do with that stuff later on.

The rummaging ended minutes later, and Jim counted the take, almost $280 in crumpled bills. Plus, there was a stack of old two-dollar bills and several sets of silver coins. Not much, Jim thought, as he cut the cash four ways, handed Wes a $70 share, and put the remainder on the card table. They'd settle up with Don Folger later.

Wes was anxious to get rid of the evidence and go home to his trailer house nearby. He wanted to wash the old man's blood from his face and hands and get out of his stained clothes before his pregnant wife, Jill, woke up. Stuffing handfuls of papers into a metal trash can, Wes took a cigarette lighter from his jeans pocket and lit the fire.

When the small bedroom filled with smoke, the boys realized it was too risky to dispose of the papers right then. Stowing the trash inside a black garbage bag, they decided to drive to Cedar Ridge Park later that afternoon, where they could start a campfire and dispose of the evidence without arousing suspicion. Having agreed on a plan, Wes walked outside to his yellow Cougar, climbed inside, and drove away. He didn't look back.

Within ten minutes, Jim and Walter had washed up and climbed into bed. Their heads throbbed, their insides ached, and their muscles felt twisted and torn. They wanted to sleep and block out the memory of the Coit nightmare.

But sleep didn't come. Jim heard Walter tossing on the twin bed beside him, rearranging his pillow and tugging at the bed sheet. Jim tried to lie still, but he was just as fidgety. He couldn't turn off the picture machine inside his head. He kept seeing the old man's feet, struggling to get up.

"Jim?" Walter whispered as he raised up on one elbow.

"Yeah."

"Can you sleep?"

"Naw."

"I'm gonna turn on the light."

Walter's feet thumped across the hardwood floor toward the light switch. The overhead fixture blinked on, chasing the darkness from the small bedroom. The ceiling light burned all night, long after there was anyone awake to see it.

Just like the light inside Chester Brooks' store.

When the yellow Cougar pulled up in front of the house that afternoon, Jim crushed the butt of his joint in the living room ashtray and met Wes at the door. The oldest Folger stepped inside and explained that Don wouldn't be coming with them to Cedar Ridge Park, as planned. Instead, Wes would take Don's cut of the money to him, preferring not to involve his kid brother any further.

Wes stood beside the space heater in the living room, warming his hands and looking edgy while Walter introduced him to Dominick and some girl who had dropped by the house earlier that afternoon. Wes seemed anxious to escape Dominick's gaze, so he followed Jim and Walter into the bedroom to retrieve the black bag with the tell-tale papers.

When the three black-hatted cowboys emerged from the

front bedroom with the garbage sack in tow, the girl began bantering, "What's in the bag? What's in the bag?" as she tried to steal a glimpse. Dominick ran interference, playing keep-away with the girl while the trio of robbers made their way outside to the car. Wes popped the trunk, moved his blood-stained clothes to one side, and tossed the sack on top of the two gas cans taken from the old man's store.

Jim returned to check the house, making sure that they had left no trace of their crime. He saw the two King Edward cigar boxes from Chester's store, but decided not to take them. There were just Canadian coins and old keys inside. What harm could they do?

Dominick stood in the doorway, watching as the yellow car and its incriminating cargo disappeared down the street. He had been curious about Wes Folger and his brother after the two had remained in the darkened car while Jim and Walter borrowed the bolt cutters the night before. Now that Dominick had met the older Folger brother, he wondered how Wes had become involved in Jim and Walter's criminal activity. He didn't seem the type.

Dominick's curiosity about the sleepy-eyed Wes would intensify later that evening after the girl told him what she had heard on the six o'clock news. Amid the hype about Gary Gilmore, she had heard something about an old man being beaten to death during a robbery near Marlin. She couldn't recall the victim's name or the specific details, but she didn't need to. Ricky Dominick made the connection right away.

Dominick saw the older Folger brother only one other time. A couple of days after the Coit robbery, the twenty-two-year-old Dominick stood outside a Belton convenience store with Jim and Walter, buying gas. As he finished filling his brown-and-white truck at the self-serve pump, Dominick saw Wes approaching with a brisk step and a sense of urgency.

Wes looked visibly shaken, for he had heard the newscasts about Chester Brooks' murder and was trying to come to terms with his involvement in the crime. As Dominick stepped inside the store to pay for his gas, the three conspirators began to talk about that night. Dominick heard only one line of their conversation, but it was enough.

"If the old man is dead," Wes said, "I guess I killed him."

The yellow Cougar stopped beside a concrete picnic table at Cedar Ridge Park. The park lay at the eastern edge of Belton Reservoir, a $13 million dam and lake project on the Leon River that had been built in 1954 by the U.S. Army Corps of Engineers as part of the Flood Control Act. The lake itself stretched twenty-six miles in length, ran three miles across at its widest point, and had 136 miles of shoreline. Its thirteen parks and recreation areas drew thousands of Central Texans to the federal property for boating, swimming, fishing, picnicking, and camping.

Cedar Ridge was one of the more scenic camping areas on Lake Belton, with its rocky cliffs jutting out over placid Cedar Creek. The acres of twisted and gnarled cedar trees stood out in rustic beauty along the brush-covered ridge, creating a secluded hideaway for campers. The spot was also a favorite hangout for area teenagers. Jim had come here often to smoke dope, chug a six-pack, or fool around with some girl in the bushes.

The area was deserted that afternoon as the three boys made their way toward the top of the ridge, pushing aside the low-hanging tree branches with their hands and dodging the recoil of the barren limbs. The only sound they heard as they carried the black bag toward the campsite-clearing was the scrunching and crunching of their own boots as they trudged up the winding, stone-covered trail.

When they reached a secluded clearing, the boys ripped open the garbage bag and dumped handfuls of yellowed paper atop the powdery ashes of a recent campfire. Wes took out his cigarette lighter, and the three conspirators watched the refuse from the old man's store crackle and cringe in charred protest against the flames. The boys continued to feed the fire, making sure every piece of tell-tale evidence was consumed in the fiery holocaust.

Sparks spewed upward like a volcanic upheaval when Wes added his bloody shirt and jeans and the two black masks to the pyre. The boys stood somberly, as if they were attending some pagan ritual of purification, some purging of body and mind and soul.

When the flames died down, Wes stirred from his vigil and took two other items from the trunk of his car: the gas cans

Walter and Don had touched while setting up the old man. Walter watched as Wes and Jim filled the five-gallon cans with small rocks, walked over to the rocky ledge, and flung the containers into Lake Belton.

The stone-laden gas cans refused to sink beneath the twenty-foot water, but instead floated farther and farther away from the ledge where the boys stood. The three youths picked up handfuls of small stones and began chunking at the cans, firing again and again and again. The cans, battered by the relentless fusillade of pounding and pelting, retreated beneath the murky waters of Lake Belton and sank.

Returning to the smoldering fire, Jim scattered the embers with the scuffed toe of his boot and examined the scraps of charred cloth, the remnants of his black ski mask. He, unlike the black-hooded train robber from Missouri, would never again pull an armed robbery. One time was enough for Jim, more than enough. He was through with black hoods.

And so was Gary Gilmore. Had Jim listened to the radio that Monday, he might have heard about the other armed robber with a black hood over his head. A robber who, hours before, sat slumped in a bullet-riddled chair with a white target pinned to a bloody T-shirt. Another modern-day Jesse James who had lived by the gun and scoffed at Democritus' warning about ill-gotten gain, just as the Dozen had done in my classroom that morning.

To a nation bent on restoring law and order, Gary Gilmore's execution symbolized society's solution for deterring crime and criminals. To the sixteen-year-old outlaw stirring the embers of a campfire, the Utah killer's death would come to mean something more: an object lesson not taught in books or discussed in classrooms. The price of ill-gotten gain. The beginning of loss.

CHAPTER EIGHT

Rusted Plates . . . Like Tombstones

The metal gate was a bad omen. The five-panel Lifetime enclosure stood open at the west end of Chester Brooks' store; that's how Frank Mitchell knew something was wrong when he pulled into the crushed-stone driveway out front. Chester wouldn't have left the gate open for his cows to get out.

The rural mail carrier raced the Dodge's motor as he sat outside the Brooks store, waiting for Chester to open up. The old grocer always came outside when he heard Frank's car pull up to the pump; he usually carried a Snickers in his leathery fist because Frank liked to munch a candy bar while they talked. Frank, in turn, always handed Chester his mail, mostly newspapers and such. It was a ritual the two old friends had had for more than twenty years, ever since Frank moved back to the area.

Frank's friendship with Chester, however, began long before then. As a Depression-aged youngster growing up near Coit, Frank had walked the gravel road to Brooks' store many a time to fetch "store-bought" light bread, a real luxury in those days. Even though Chester was eight years older than Frank, the grocer took an interest in the younger boy and made him feel welcome. Chester had a knack for making people feel good about themselves.

Frank still reminisced about a time, long ago, when Chester took him for his first pickup ride to the Brooks farm over in neighboring Falls County. It was a Fourth of July that Frank would long remember, for the day marked not only his eleventh birthday but also his first taste of chewing tobacco. That "rite of passage" had made him sick, and Frank remembered the way Chester had tried to console him on the bumpy, dusty ride back

63

home. Chester cared about people — even little green-gilled, mischievous boys without a lick of sense. That genuine caring became the basis of a camaraderie that would last a lifetime.

Frank thought it strange when his old friend didn't open the door to welcome him that morning. Turning off the car's motor, Frank got out and walked the five or six paces to the store's front door, and pushed against it. When the door didn't budge, Frank began pounding and calling, "Chester? Chester, are you in there?"

The only sound he heard was the whistling of the north wind as it nipped at the back of his neck. Frank turned up the collar of his coat and walked to the west end of the store, where the five-foot gate stood unfastened. He called toward the barn, thinking perhaps Chester was out back with a sick animal and hadn't had time to open up yet.

But the open gate and the terrible dread he felt inside told Frank that something more than a sick cow had changed the old grocer's routine. Putting the mail under his right arm, Frank placed his hands inside his front coat pockets and nudged the gate aside. He was careful not to touch anything with his hands because he had already guessed what he was about to find out back. Something bad.

Walking across the frozen ground toward the barn, he called the old grocer's name as loudly as he could, beating back the sound of the wind that roared in his reddening ears. When he stood parallel with the house, he saw something lying in the grass at the edge of the car shed. Frank altered his course and moved in that direction for several yards, never once taking his eyes off the gray-khaki mound that loomed before him. Then he saw the bare foot.

Frank stopped abruptly. His eyes focused on the stiff foot turned heel-up, with its white sole exposed to the numbing cold of that January morning. Then his eyes took in both of Chester's feet, crossed at the ankles and resting atop a five-foot metal gate lying on the ground beneath the body.

Frank stood staring at the feet, noticing that the top one wore a high-top work shoe, loosely laced as if the old man had hurriedly slipped it on. The other foot lay bare with a lifeless big toe wrapped around the rung of the gate.

Poor Chester, the mailman thought as he stared at the frozen foot. Chester had always worried about his feet getting frost-bitten, like they had during the war. He must be awful cold lying there like that, Frank said to himself.

But Frank Mitchell had already guessed the terrible truth about his boyhood friend, and so he returned through the open gate beside the store. His breath came in icy gusts as he hurried back to his car, climbed in, and drove 200 yards to the neighboring Cordova house just beyond the intersection of FM 339 and 1771.

Mrs. Cordova met him at the door, explaining that her husband, Manuel, was in the shower when Frank asked to speak to him. As the mail carrier explained why he needed to use her phone, the woman's eyes widened and her hands shook. She led Frank inside the former parsonage and listened without interruption as he called Earl Wilson, the local constable, and then Neville White, the nearest undertaker. Mrs. Cordova offered to telephone Travis Arney, Chester's nearest next-of-kin, while Frank told Manuel what had happened.

Frank waited for Manuel to dress before returning across the road to wait for the constable. He wanted someone with him this time. He couldn't face Chester alone.

Constable Wilson drove up in front of the store as Frank and Manuel crossed the intersection. Together, the trio of somber-faced men passed through the open gate and moved toward the southeast corner of the car shed, where they stood staring at the blood-splattered wall above the old man's head. Within minutes, Justice of the Peace Bob Angle and two units from the Limestone County sheriff's office arrived on the scene, responding to Constable Wilson's radio dispatch for assistance. The deputies moved quickly to secure the area and make sure evidence was not disturbed by the crowd of farmers and ranchers who had heard the news via the telephone party-line and had begun to gather outside the store.

Within twenty minutes, Chief Deputy Bill Fletcher drove out from the sheriff's office at Groesbeck to take charge of the investigation. Tall and lean, the middle-aged Fletcher liked to boast about the time he had cleaned up one Central Texas town single-handedly. Fletcher had walked into the raunchy bars with nothing more than a blackjack, as he told the story, and the villains cowered in fear. In the Dirty Harry tradition, Fletcher enjoyed intimidating his prey with his massive size and his wild-eyed stare. He was a tough hombre.

Fletcher took charge of the investigation, instructing a young deputy to take Frank Mitchell's statement before the elderly mail carrier left to complete his run. When Frank emerged from the crowd of curious onlookers, Fletcher ordered the neighbors to move back and stay out of the way. The chief investigator then stalked the area around the old car shed, trying to piece together what had happened. He focused his attention on the broken shotgun and the blood-smeared concrete block near the victim's body.

Frank Mitchell recited his story to the young sheriff's deputy. His words seemed cold and numb and mechanical. He stood staring at the gray-khaki mound lying in the grass before him, disbelieving what his eyes told him to be true. When he had finished, Frank climbed into his Dodge, cranked the sluggish motor, and sat gripping the steering wheel with reddened knuckles.

He stared at the locked front door of the old store, half expecting his childhood friend to emerge through its weathered threshold carrying a Snickers in his hand and smiling that toothless grin. But Chester Brooks was dead, and with him, those boyhood days of growing up in Coit.

Chester had been the heart and soul of the rural Texas community, the last storekeeper in a town that had almost disappeared after more than a hundred years on the Texas prairies. He had been the antiquated relic that had linked folks with the simple traditions of a time gone by, a time when men honored God's commandment and loved their neighbors as they did themselves. Now there was nothing left. The man and the town were gone.

Frank Mitchell pulled out onto FM 339, glanced through his rearview mirror, and fought back the tears. Things like this didn't happen in Limestone County, he told himself. And certainly not to a man like Chester Brooks. The old grocer had gone out of his way to help people; he would have given the shirt off his back to anyone who needed it. There was no reason to kill him. No reason at all.

Who could have done such a thing?

* * * * *

66

The same question reeled through Sheriff Dennis Walker's mind as he sped along the icy back road toward Chester Brooks' store. Tall, handsome, and powerfully built, the thirty-seven-year-old sheriff resembled the hero in a Hollywood film, racing toward a crime scene and trying to make up for lost time.

Walker had been investigating a complaint about a stolen trailer house when the dispatcher received Constable Wilson's call about possible "foul play" at the Brooks place. The sheriff had sent Chief Deputy Fletcher on ahead to investigate while he concluded his meeting and dropped off a prisoner at the Limestone County jail across the street.

Sheriff Walker had just picked up the crime lab photo equipment when he received a radio message from Fletcher, advising him that he was needed in Coit "right away." The urgency in Fletcher's voice reminded Walker of the hectic life he had known before becoming the sheriff of Limestone County.

Although Walker had grown up in Groesbeck as the barefooted son of a row-crop farmer, he was no small-town peace officer. What he knew about law enforcement he had learned on the big-city streets of Houston.

Deciding at the age of seventeen that he wanted more from life than cotton farming, Walker had dropped out of high school during his senior year, hopped into a '41 Ford with five dollars in his pocket and two pairs of jeans and shirts in a paper bag, and headed for Houston. He grew up the hard way in the big city, pumping gas for a dollar an hour while he finished night school at San Jacinto High School. Too proud to go back home and live, he returned only briefly to marry his high school sweetheart. He was eighteen and she was seventeen, and they had dreams of a better life.

Walker knew from the age of fourteen that he wanted a career in law enforcement, so he applied for the Houston Police Academy. He was the youngest cadet ever accepted to the academy, and he distinguished himself prior to his graduation.

Walker was smart and honest and committed to a code of ethics that didn't allow compromise. He believed in doing what was right, come hell or high water. He was a throwback to that rugged individualism of John Wayne and Gary Cooper, and God help the man who got in the way of him doing his job.

But the job in Houston took its toll on the idealistic young officer. He could handle the shootouts and the high-speed chases on city streets, but the twelve-year-old kid got to him. Staring at the tiny corpse lying in its own vomit after a drug overdose, Walker decided there had to be a better place to raise his three sons. So he packed up his family and returned to his father's farm in Central Texas.

His law enforcement dream was finally fulfilled when he was appointed sheriff of Limestone County after the elected sheriff died of a heart attack while breaking up a street fight. Friendly and easygoing, Walker found favor with the voters who trusted him as a man of honor and integrity. He commanded the people's respect without wearing a gun strapped to his hip, like some law enforcement officials did. Folks in Limestone County honored him by calling him "Dennis." He had come home, at last.

But as Walker began to transform the sheriff's department into a modern-day operation, he made waves in a town where rocking the status quo wasn't permitted. He offended people in high places, refusing to bend or bow in the power struggle. As a result, he became controversial, being hauled before the grand jury eleven times during a twelve-year period.

His most publicized scandal would come later when three black youths, who had been arrested by Walker's deputies following a Juneteenth free-for-all, drowned while being transported by boat across Lake Mexia. As a result of the tragedy on Black Independence Day in Texas, Walker would be targeted by the NAACP, crucified by a Dallas television station, and profiled by *Time* magazine.

But on that January morning, Dennis Walker was still a little-known sheriff on his way to investigate the death of an old man.

Why Chester Brooks? he wondered as the car sped along the winding roadways in rural Limestone County. This wasn't Houston.

Sheriff Walker glanced at his watch as he pulled up in front of the old Coit store at 9:20 A.M. He knew he'd have to file a report later on, and years of training had taught him a precision for details. What his training hadn't taught him, however, was how to numb his feelings whenever he examined the mangled bodies of violent crime victims. Even after working in Houston, he never got used to seeing man's inhumanity to man. Walker's compassion for the innocent was still an occupational hazard that gnawed at his insides, like that morning when he leaned over the corpse of Chester Brooks and saw the bashed-in skull and the blood-splattered wall.

Walker rose from his kneeling position beside the old man's body and instructed a deputy to take pictures of the victim lying in the position in which Frank Mitchell had found him. When the deputy had finished, Walker authorized the justice of the peace to pull Chester's body away from the car shed wall and conduct a coroner's examination there at the scene. The small crowd of onlookers, including Chester's relative Travis Arney, scarcely recognized the old grocer's face, caked with frozen blood and swollen from bruising. The iron-stomached men, long accustomed to the hardships of life, felt sickened and disgusted as they watched the deputy take the final pictures.

After the justice of the peace completed his examination and pronounced Chester Brooks dead, he instructed Neville White to take the victim's body by hearse to a nearby funeral home in Mexia. There an autopsy would be conducted to determine the official cause of death.

Someone on the funeral home's staff, however, embalmed Brooks' corpse before the autopsy could be held at 10:00 the following morning. As a result, the doctor conducting the autopsy could not determine the exact time of death, but estimated that the victim died somewhere around 2:00 A.M. on the morning of the robbery.

The funeral home employee had made an honest mistake, and those conducting the investigation overlooked the blunder. But one person, who reached a different conclusion about what actually happened that night, remembered the error. The exact time of death had not been established — beyond a reasonable doubt.

As soon as Chester Brooks' body had been hauled past his dirt-bottom store, Sheriff Walker ordered his deputies to spread out and search the surrounding area for evidence. Chief Deputy Fletcher made his way to the back of the store, where he found the cut hasp and the open door. Fletcher examined the bloody hand prints smeared along the splintered edge of the old wooden door, then summoned the sheriff.

When the two officers entered the store, they found a few papers and boxes scattered on the floor, but very little evidence that the store had been burglarized. They theorized that someone had been looting the store when the old grocer heard a noise and came to investigate. Brooks had probably recognized the perpetrator and may have been killed to keep him from identifying the burglar, Walker reasoned.

Another deputy reported that he had found a trail of spilled coins leading from the back of the store toward a barbed wire fence at the west end of Chester's property. When the sheriff went to investigate, he found two blood stains on the fence, as if someone had put two hands on the wire while climbing over it. Walker ordered the section of bloody wire to be sent to the Department of Public Safety crime lab in Waco for analysis.

As the investigation continued, Sheriff Walker received a radio message that he was wanted back at his office in Groesbeck. A deputy from neighboring McLennan County needed to speak with him right away concerning an urgent matter. Walker left Fletcher at Brooks' store to wrap things up while the sheriff hurried back to Groesbeck.

What next? Walker wondered.

Fletcher and two deputies, along with Justice of the Peace Bob Angle, remained at the murder scene until after 5:00 P.M. The officers collected evidence, made sketches, interviewed neighbors, and inventoried the victim's property. The crowd outside Brooks' store continued to grow as word spread of the grocer's brutal death. Folks from miles around dropped by to help, but the increasing number of people only added to the confusion.

The deputies placed the broken shotgun pieces and the bloody concrete block inside a patrol car's trunk for transfer to the sheriff's property room at the Groesbeck courthouse. From there, these alleged murder weapons would be taken to the DPS lab in Waco for examination. In the surrounding confusion of that afternoon, the sheriff's deputies forgot to tag the stone block, violating the "chain of custody" procedure. It was a legal blunder that would be pointed out later in a court of law.

The deputies also confiscated the five-foot metal gate that had lain beneath the victim's body when Frank Mitchell found him. They wanted to dust it for possible fingerprints, hoping it would give them a clue to the murderer's identity.

The deputies then took statements from two people gathered outside the store. Charles Stone of nearby Otto stated that Brooks had told him about three long-haired males in a sports car who had come to the store the preceding Friday, asking if the grocer sold soda water. As Brooks handed them the soft drinks, he asked where the boys were from and was told Bremond, a small town several miles east. Brooks had related the incident to Stone, commenting that the boys acted "very strange."

The deputies also spoke with Travis Arney, the victim's next of kin. Arney stated that a neighbor, Aubrey Stevens, had told him about two long-haired, thug-looking men who came by the Stevens' residence, looking for the "dirt-bottom store." Travis remembered being concerned for Chester's safety when Stevens told him the news, because Travis had been trying to get the old grocer to either buy a better gun or close his store. But Chester hadn't listened to him.

The inventory of Brooks' store revealed an odd assortment of items, listed by a deputy on a piece of yellow legal paper. In addition to the many boxes and cans of food items, the deputy listed five old guns: a Spanish Mauser, two Winchester rifles, a Springfield rifle, and a Marlin shotgun. Other items of value included a silver Westclock watch, a billfold with cash and currency totaling $89, and four checks from customers.

The deputy paid little attention to the names on the checks as he listed them on the makeshift inventory sheet. He had no reason to do so. Yet one of the checks would have given him a clue to the person he sought. As part of her regular Sunday afternoon ritual, Carolyn Taylor had driven to Coit, visited the old grocer, and written him a check for $25. She was there just hours before her son stood outside the store, wearing a black ski mask.

Neighbors watched as the old man's personal effects and valuables were loaded up and carried off in the trunk of the justice of the peace's car. Darkness came to Coit, and one by one, the somber crowd began to disperse from the old store and head home to supper. They'd be back tomorrow and the next day, trying to come to terms with what had happened at Chester's place. But for now, they were numbed and needed time.

The deputies secured the back door of the old store and closed the open gate to the west, so the old man's cows wouldn't get out. Somebody else would have to dispose of the animals in the barn and the two old cars up at the house.

Nobody paid much attention to the cars that day, sitting discarded like locust husks within feet of where the old man died. Chester had loved those old relics, refusing to part with them when he was offered top money from Model-A antique dealers. He kept the old pickup truck out front beneath the overhang that had once been part of the front porch. More than likely, it was like the truck that eleven-year-old Frank Mitchell had ridden in on the day he learned about the evils of chewing tobacco.

The old panel truck stood beneath the car shed roof that Chester had had built in recent months, when he closed in the back porch and took residence in the small room. It was similar to the panel truck that Jim Taylor and his mother had ridden in when they visited Chester on another Sunday afternoon, long ago, and listened to the old man talk about the "good ole days" in Coit, when times were prosperous and folks hung horseshoes over their doors for good luck.

In the excitement of the day, nobody paid any attention to the rusty old trucks, or to the battered license plates they bore. Bleached and faded by the Texas sun, the numbers were barely legible on that chilling January day. If folks had tried, they might have made out the digits 280 on the pickup's tag or the numbers 665 on the old panel truck. But no one thought to read them, and certainly not to combine the digits into any particular sequence.

Yet 280665 became a number that Jim Taylor was fated to see again, years after he stood outside the Coit farmhouse wielding a metal gate against the two dark figures that tumbled toward him. The license plates on Chester Brooks' trucks foretold the tragic fate of the young outlaw in the black mask, for those numbers would become part of Jim's destiny.

Perhaps the rusted plates, like the tombstones in New Hope Cemetery, had tried in vain to warn him.

CHAPTER NINE

Tottering on the Edge

I didn't recall hearing about the old grocer's death on the evening news, probably because I was preoccupied with media coverage of the Gilmore execution and its aftermath. Like much of the nation, I became caught up in the legal debate about the virtues of restoring capital punishment. The volatile controversy over the death penalty obscured any local news coverage about a small-town robbery/murder, or a bludgeoned victim found lying atop a metal gate.

It wasn't until weeks later that I learned of Jim's connection with the murdered man, yet my mind often associated him with the image of a gate. I remembered seeing him straddle a wooden one almost a month before the murder occurred. The image was indelibly etched in my mind, for it had marked a turning point for Jim: the end of a beginning.

Jim had invited me to watch him ride Brahman bulls in the Junior Rodeo competition at the Sheriff's Posse Arena in Temple, and, although the event unnerved me, I had promised to come. Whenever a student asked me to attend an out-of-school activity, I made every effort to do so. If one hour could make a difference in a child's life, I considered the time well spent.

And so, I had bundled up my two-year-old son and braved the elements of that bitter-cold December evening. As I drove to the arena, the thought occurred to me that the trip might be in vain; I might be jeopardizing our health and risking pneumonia for nothing. Jim hadn't been in class that Friday morning, and his absence concerned me. He hadn't missed school since it started in September, which was something of a record for him. Perhaps he was ill and wouldn't ride in the rodeo, I thought.

I hadn't wanted to consider the other possibility — that he had reverted to his old tricks and cut my class. I had worked hard to make Jim feel good about himself and school, believing he would change for the better if he found love and acceptance and a sense of belonging.

He, like the rest of the Dozen, had seemed to respond to my maternal nurturing. I sensed an enigmatic force pulling us together and creating a bond. Jim seemed willing, despite his disappointment in a coach, to take a chance and trust a teacher again. The recent car-bash incident had proved that I was making some headway with him, and I felt encouraged.

The Auto Mechanics Club had tried to raise money for a school project by sponsoring a car-bash fundraiser at lunch. For a twenty-five-cent contribution, a student could pound a sledgehammer against a wrecked jalopy on the Temple High School parking lot. As an added incentive to attract customers, the club had painted teachers' names on the body of the car, thereby enticing students to take out their frustrations against faculty members. The avenging arms of the student body pommeled the vehicle relentlessly, according to the Dozen's version of the event, given spontaneously in class the following morning.

"But nobody hit your name, Mrs. Post," said Donny Hill, his blue eyes flashing through the wire-rimmed glasses.

"Oh, I find that hard to believe. After all the homework I assign?"

"Nobody touched it," Donny insisted.

"Well, that's strange."

"Jim wouldn't let 'em."

"What do you mean?"

"He stood guard. There'd been a fight if anybody tried."

Surprised by Jim's protectiveness, I glanced at him, but he merely flashed that notorious grin and said nothing. He seldom spoke in class; he didn't have to, for his eyes said everything. Deep blue and strikingly intense, they seemed to reflect what the Indians called the "tunnel to the soul." In time, I learned to read them well.

When we later talked about the car-bash event, I thanked Jim

74

for defending my honor, and asked why he'd done something like that in front of the entire school.

"Respect," he said. And then as an afterthought he added, "You're the only teacher I've ever respected. Right from the first day, you seemed to care. I only come to school because you're here."

I had wanted to light Roman candles in celebration of this small victory, but I knew my rejoicing was premature. Jim was caught in the middle of a power play; I tugged to keep him in school while Walter Frye pulled to get him out on the streets. When the pressure was on, I feared who would win.

I had hoped that the rodeo might show Jim that I genuinely cared about him, as a person as well as a student. And so my son and I had gone to watch him ride bulls. As soon as I made eye contact with him inside the Sheriff's Posse Arena, I knew he'd cut my English class. Walter had wanted him to go partying, so Jim had taken the day off from school.

I waved to him as he stood beside Walter at the chute gate, but he pretended not to see me. All that evening, he avoided looking at the stands where I sat, trying to corral my squirming two-year-old, who behaved as frisky as the baby calves in the roping event. I sensed that Jim didn't want to face me. He'd let me down, and that bothered him. It was a matter of respect.

When the bull-riding competition began, Jim climbed atop a gray Brahman bull and gave the signal for the chute gate to open. Almost immediately, over 1,800 pounds of bucking beef came charging out, with the black-hatted young outlaw spurring its flanks and goading it forward. As the bull careened down the length of the dirt-bottom arena, I clutched tightly to the twisting toddler in my lap and forced myself to keep my eyes open.

I watched as Jim's lithe body flailed in the saddle, up and down, back and forth. With each hammering blow of the bull's hooves, Jim's neck jerked, his head snapped, his body pounded. Four seconds . . . five seconds . . . six seconds. Then, on the count of seven, he came flying off the Brahman's back as if he'd been ejected.

Like a rag doll tossed through the air by a careless child, Jim landed on his knees in the dirt. Slowly, he got to his feet and limped toward his black hat lying several yards away, careful to watch the bull's movements from the corners of his eyes. As expected, the angry brute turned and charged in Brahman-fashion. Jim ran to the nearest fence and climbed atop a gate, narrowly escaping the bull's twelve-inch horns. Once astride the fence, Jim smiled the mischievous grin.

That's how I remembered him, straddling a gate. Inches away from danger and tottering on the edge, he could go either way.

I knew that he had a good heart and that he felt guilty for disappointing me. But I also knew that when it came to choosing between what was right and what was wrong, Jim would do whatever came easiest. And that's what bothered me.

Jim was like the nursery rhyme character perched atop the stone wall, headed for a great fall. Once he had touched the metal gate at Chester Brooks' store, the Humpty Dumpty prophecy had been fulfilled. Now nothing could put him together again.

CHAPTER TEN

Incriminating Evidence

It didn't fit, Sheriff Dennis Walker told himself. He pushed away from his cluttered desk, leaned back in the wooden armchair, and stared at the crooked black-and-white picture hanging on the wall of his cramped first-floor office in the Limestone County courthouse at Groesbeck. Within two weeks of the Brooks murder, his deputies had arrested a suspect and collected enough circumstantial evidence to convince most Central Texas juries, yet something was wrong with the case and he knew it.

Walker took a sip of black coffee as he reached for the inch-thick folder on his desk and thumbed through his deputies' reports, searching for some fact they had overlooked during the two-week investigation, some clue that would ease his gnawing suspicion that they had arrested the wrong man. Yet all the evidence pointed to Luis Torres, a forty-two-year-old Mexican who had quarreled with the victim on the day of Brooks' death. Walker had enough to hang him.

The Limestone County Sheriff's Office had first questioned Torres three days after the Coit robbery/murder in response to an informant's tip. According to the source, Torres and two "wetbacks" had gone to Brooks' store on Sunday morning, while everyone else was in church, and demanded money. A heated argument had broken out when Brooks refused Torres' demands, and the old grocer had ordered the three angry Mexicans from his store. The incident had riled Brooks, and he related the details of the altercation to several customers that afternoon, including the informant.

Sheriff Walker had asked Chief Deputy Fletcher to question

Torres about a possible motive for murder, suggesting that the deputy first contact Texas Ranger Jim Ray at Company F headquarters in Waco and ask for his assistance with the Brooks investigation. Walker's department frequently worked on felony cases with the barrel-chested, cigar-chewing Ranger. Jim Ray, a seventeen-year-veteran of the Texas Rangers with jurisdiction over four Central Texas counties, was a top-notch investigator and an old friend of Sheriff Walker. Relying on Ray in felony investigations was a matter of necessity as well as courtesy. With only four deputies to cover a county of 1,000 square miles, Walker's department was understaffed, overworked, and in need of all the manpower it could muster. In Ranger tradition, Jim Ray was happy to oblige.

Despite his modest and easygoing manner, Jim Ray was considered "tall in the saddle" by most folks who knew him. He belonged to Texas' elite unit of law enforcement, with a proud tradition dating back to the wild-and-woolly days on the frontier. The Texas Rangers were the stuff of which legends were made, blazing a trail in western folklore with their colorful exploits and daring deeds. Tall, quiet, and ramrod-straight, they were the valiant force of men who had tamed the Southwest.

Historically, the Rangers comprised a rare breed of law enforcement because their authority differed from the local peace officer or the state militia officer. Unlike local law enforcement, the Texas Ranger's commission authorized him to operate throughout the state, and, unlike the militia officer, the Ranger was not subject to military rules or regulations. He was not even required to wear a prescribed uniform, although most Rangers opted to wear the wide-brimmed, white Stetson as a unifying symbol. This top-of-the-line hat set them apart as the anointed white knights of the Texas frontier, riding forth to do battle with the forces of evil, or so the legend went.

With its present-day force headquartered in Austin and affiliated with the Texas Department of Public Safety, the Ranger organization operated six active companies, selecting its men from distinguished DPS officers throughout the state. The Waco unit comprised Company F, and consisted of a Ranger captain, a sergeant, and two "working Rangers."

Jim Ray fell into the latter category. He had worked with law enforcement officers in McLennan, Falls, Milam, and Limestone counties since 1969, when he left behind an outstanding twelve-year career with the DPS to become one of Texas' finest.

While Ray took pride in his Ranger affiliation, he didn't buy the western myth about his unit. He didn't walk on water, and he didn't take over from local law enforcement when things got tough. Instead, Ray offered his expertise whenever police or sheriff's departments asked him to assist with felony investigations. Hard-working, dedicated, and committed to law enforcement, Ray responded to Walker's request for assistance with the Brooks investigation.

On January 20, three days after the murder, Ray met Walker and Fletcher at the Limestone County Sheriff's Office, where the two officers briefed him on the Brooks case before taking him out to the Coit community for a firsthand look. Standing beside the blood-splattered car shed, the Ranger made sketches of the murder scene while Walker reconstructed the crime for him.

The sheriff moved mechanically through the scenario of the broken shotgun, the blood-smeared stone block, the metal gate, and the blood-crusted fence out back. This was Walker's third trip to the murder scene in as many days, so the details of the crime were familiar to him. Too familiar, perhaps. He had a gnawing suspicion that he had overlooked something important.

Like he had almost done on the day of the murder when he missed the pile of fresh dirt behind the counter of the old man's store. Neither Walker nor his deputies had paid much attention to the dirt-bottom floor that first day, except to note in their reports that paper and boxes had been scattered about during the apparent robbery. No mention was made of the small mound near the meat scales area.

It wasn't until the next day that Walker got the notion to search the store again. He recalled neighbors' rumors about the old hermit: Chester Brooks had buried a lot of money beneath the dirt floor of his store. Walker decided to check out the stories.

The neighbors had been right. Beginning at the freshly dug mound, Walker and his deputy spent several hours digging twelve inches down into the packed ground. There they found dozens of dusty coffee cans and rust-crusted fruit jars filled with the old man's money, mostly collector's coins. Over 300 pounds, in all.

Walker radioed for the justice of the peace, Bob Angle, to come to the store and assist with an inventory of the victim's property, just as he had done the day before. The JP was met by seven or eight neighbors who had seen the sheriff's car outside the store and dropped by to supervise the digging.

Walker asked the JP to take custody of the money and turn it over to Jimmy Bradley, the Groesbeck lawyer serving as temporary executor of the Chester Brooks estate. The sheriff preferred not to be bogged down with the responsibility or the paperwork. Walker's office had received several tips in the Brooks investigation, and he wanted to check them out while the trail was still fresh.

The first tip led him to Luis Torres.

On January 21, Walker sent Fletcher out to question Torres about his alleged argument with the old grocer on the day of the murder. When the suspect agreed to submit to a voluntary polygraph exam, Fletcher telephoned Texas Ranger Jim Ray, asking him to meet them at the DPS office in Waco.

There the two veteran lawmen led the solemn-faced Torres into the interrogation room, where polygraph operator Cockran strapped the detector sensors to the suspect's arm and began monitoring the machine. Fletcher and Ray took turns in questioning the middle-aged farm worker, zeroing in on the Mexican's quarrel with the victim and his demands for money.

Torres' muscles tightened and his voice tensed as he responded to their questions, wiping his damp palm on his pants leg as he shifted his weight in the chair, crossed his legs, then recrossed them. Each time he answered, the suspect repeated the same story. He hadn't gone back to the store that night. He didn't know anything about the murder of Chester Brooks. They had the wrong man. He was innocent.

Sheriff Walker was sitting at his desk, reviewing the autopsy report, when the first break in the Brooks case came. Fletcher telephoned from the DPS office. Torres had failed the polygraph test. Badly.

Fletcher and Ray brought the jittery suspect back to the

Limestone County Sheriff's Office, where Walker continued the interrogation for over an hour. As he listened to Torres' story, Walker could tell that the suspect was hiding something. He didn't need a polygraph test to tell him that; years of law enforcement experience had given him a sixth sense about people. Torres had been at the Brooks store on the night of the murder. Walker could feel it.

Protesting that he was innocent, Torres had voluntarily allowed the sheriff's deputies to search his blue pickup. When they found nothing in the truck to incriminate the rattled Mexican, Walker thanked Torres for his cooperation and released him.

The sheriff watched from the window as the suspect climbed into his truck and drove away. Give a man enough rope, and he'll hang himself. It was an old cliché in law enforcement, Walker knew that. But he also knew it worked.

Already, the noose was tightening around Luis Torres' throat.

The second break came two weeks later, when a "reliable source" contacted the sheriff's office and urged Walker to search Torres' pickup for possible evidence in the Chester Brooks murder case. The informant, an employee at the funeral home that embalmed Brooks' body, reported that he had recently peeked through the truck's window and had seen a substance on the gas pedal that appeared to be blood. Although deputies had previously searched Torres' vehicle and found nothing, Walker followed up on the tip.

Obtaining a search warrant from the justice of the peace at 2:25 A.M. on February 1, sheriff's deputies contacted Luis Torres and asked him to drive his vehicle to the courthouse and park it. Torres complied.

At 10:30 A.M., deputies drove the blue 1969 Chevy pickup to McGilvry's Gulf Station in Groesbeck, where it was again searched. Using a large spotlight and a vacuum cleaner to collect evidence, the deputies found a small quantity of grayish-white hair and blood matted together on the bottom half of the gas pedal. Removing a sample of the hair and blood, they bagged the evidence and labeled it before Deputy Dennis Wilson took it to the DPS lab in Waco. In addition, Wilson also took the gas and brake pedals, as well as a dirt sample from the floorboard of the Chevy.

When Deputy Wilson received the chemist's lab report later that afternoon, he rushed into Sheriff Walker's office with a sense of urgency. The blood and hair samples taken from Torres' pickup were human. And, they were similar in type to those of the murder victim, Chester Brooks.

Walker reached for the phone and called the justice of the peace, requesting that an arrest warrant be issued for Luis Torres. He then alerted his four deputies and placed them on stakeouts along the two highways entering the town. Torres had reportedly been seen leaving the neighboring town of Mexia and was en route to Groesbeck.

At 6:15 P.M., Deputies Lewis and Pike spotted the murder suspect in a white Ford sedan. Following Torres through town, they pulled him over as he turned right onto Highway 164. Deputy Lewis approached the white car, asked Torres to step outside, and advised him that he was under arrest. When Torres demanded to know for what, the deputy told him that he had been charged with the murder of Chester Brooks.

The Mexican looked stunned as the deputy searched him, cuffed him, and placed him in the back seat of the squad car. As Lewis drove to the sheriff's office at the courthouse, Deputy Pike read Torres his Miranda rights from a card, asking the suspect if he understood. Torres nodded, muttered a barely audible "yes," and then stared out the window in silence.

Torres said little as he was brought before Justice of the Peace Marvin Pruitt and charged with capital murder. Pruitt set bond at $150,000 before Torres was booked and taken to the Limestone County Jail two blocks away.

The final piece of incriminating evidence came the day after Torres' arrest. That's when the money talked.

At 10:00 A.M. on February 2, Walker received a phone call from Gary Vogel at the Farmer's State Bank in Groesbeck. Vogel had heard of Torres' arrest and thought the sheriff might be interested in a recent deposit that the murder suspect had made. Walker was.

Within minutes, the sheriff was sitting inside Vogel's office, staring at the three-pound Folger's coffee can with the particles of dirt clearly visible on the outside. The can reminded Walker of the ones he had seen when he dug up the floor of the old man's store two weeks earlier.

According to Vogel, Torres had brought the canful of pennies to the bank and requested to cash them in. The teller who assisted Torres remembered the transaction, for she had to count and roll more than $25 worth of coins.

Walker took the dirt-covered coffee can as evidence, requesting that the bank keep the rolled coins in a safe spot until further notified. Walker wanted to send the can, along with dirt samples from the store floor, to the DPS crime lab in Waco. The sheriff remembered the mound of fresh dirt he had discovered near the meat scales, and he had a hunch about the source of Torres' newfound coin collection.

The lab proved him right.

The second phone call came from Vogel later that morning, about an hour after the sheriff had left the banker's office. A bank employee had just brought a $20 bill to Vogel's attention because she was suspicious of the dark stains on the front and back. They appeared to be blood stains.

Walker returned to the Farmer's State Bank, where Vogel assisted him in tracking down the origin of the $20 bill. The money had been brought to the bank by an employee of Rand's Food Store in Groesbeck.

Walker drove to the local food store and spoke with each employee, trying to determine who had cashed the stained currency. It was a long shot, but it paid off. A cashier remembered the grimy bill all too well, for she had closed her checkout stand and gone to wash her hands after touching it. She didn't like the feel of it, and she didn't like the feeling she had as she stared into the eyes of the customer who handed it to her.

She told Walker about that Sunday morning of January 30, some two weeks after the murder, when the man came into the store to purchase soft drinks, cigarettes, and several other small items. He acted "nervous and ready to get out of the store" as he handed her the stained bill and waited for change. The cashier turned the bill upside-down as she placed it inside her register drawer because there was something funny about it. She wanted to look at it again after the customer left. She didn't want to arouse the man's suspicions because he lived near her.

The man was Luis Torres.

It was all there, Sheriff Walker told himself as he closed the Torres file and shoved the folder across his desk. The motive, the opportunity, the evidence linking the suspect to the murder scene — all there. Torres was a dead man now that Gary Gilmore's execution had restored capital punishment throughout the land.

The God-fearing, law-abiding folks of Limestone County had loved Chester Brooks, and they would, no doubt, string up the Mexican. Like their Old Testament counterparts, they believed in the biblical teaching of "an eye for an eye." Retribution would be hard and swift, and carried out for all to see. Just like in the picture.

Walker leaned back in his chair, flexed his neck muscles as he rolled his head from shoulder to shoulder, and glanced at the black-and-white print hanging crooked against his office wall. The scratched and faded photo offered a graphic reminder of frontier justice — the last public execution in Limestone County.

The camera lens of some forgotten citizen had captured the carnival atmosphere of April 12, 1895, when men and women and children drove from miles around to sit in their buggies, eat their picnic lunches, and watch the black man hang for allegedly raping a white woman. The spectators saw the "nigger" climb the scaffold steps, lower his eyes when the noose dropped around his neck, and gasp for breath as his body plummeted through the hole beneath the scaffold floor. Law and order had been restored; justice didn't take long in those days.

The old picture was titled "The Last Hanging in Groesbeck," but that was a misnomer. There'd soon be another legal lynching, and Walker knew it. And yet, despite the mound of circumstantial evidence weighing against the Mexican, the sheriff still suspected he had the wrong man. Like a piece of chain with several links missing, it just didn't fit. But why not?

If the sheriff had glanced at the two nostalgic reward posters hanging on the opposite wall in his office, he might have caught a glimpse of the truth that alluded him. There the pair of yellowed flyers hung side by side, reminiscent of the posters tacked up in sheriffs' offices across the Old West almost a hundred years before. The bold, black print advertised the dollar value of two notorious outlaws wanted for robbery and murder.

The poster hanging on the left would have been of little consequence in the Brooks case, for it told about the exploits of an Easterner named Harry Longbaugh, who had come west and carved out a name for himself as a member of Butch Cassidy's "Hole in the Wall" gang. Longbaugh had a $6,500 price on his head before he fled south to Bolivia, where he and Cassidy reportedly died in a bloody shootout with federal troops. Thus ended the outlaw career of the prince of the Wild Bunch: the Sundance Kid.

It was the poster hanging on the right that would have given Walker a clue about the young desperado whom he sought. The flyer advertised a $25,000 reward for the legendary bandit that Mrs. Fikes had fought so hard against there in her third-grade classroom, when she confronted the little blue-eyed boy and tried to keep him from following in the badman's bootsteps.

"WANTED: DEAD OR ALIVE," the poster read. Payment in full, for the prodigal son of a Baptist preacher, the outlaw Jesse James.

CHAPTER ELEVEN

"Chester's grave is my grave"

"I wonder if Jim Taylor did it."

"Alice! How can you say such a thing?"

"I don't think he liked Chester very much. I wonder if he had anything to do with it."

Carol Fairbairn stared in horror at her fourteen-year-old daughter, wondering what had possessed Alice to think such a thought. They had been friends with the Taylor family for years. Alice's grandmother and Jim's grandmother were neighbors in Coit, so the children had grown up playing together. Carolyn Taylor was one of Carol Fairbairn's dearest friends.

"Alice, don't ever breathe that to anybody, do you hear me? What an awful thing to say!"

Carol watched her red-eyed daughter run from the room, and she winced seconds later as she heard the bedroom door slam. Tears welled in her eyes, and she hated herself for lashing out at Alice. She knew her daughter was having a hard time coping with Chester's death, but then so was she.

Carol hadn't even had the chance to say goodbye. No one had thought to call her home in Houston and tell her about the funeral. It would have meant a four-hour drive on icy roads, but she would have been there for Chester. He had always been there for her.

Carol had first met Chester seventeen years earlier, when she married into the Fairbairn family, an old and highly respected Central Texas clan who owned a hilltop farm one mile south of the Brooks store. The "Fairbairn place," with its fertile fields and one-story, white-frame farmhouse, dated back to the days of early Texas. For more than a hundred years, generation after generation of Fairbairns had worked the land with the same love and tenacity and fierce determination that had characterized their forbears.

Since 1930, the Fairbairn place had been largely run by "Miss Ruth," the bright-eyed, quick-witted matriarch who worked the fields by day and tended her family by night. Warm and generous, yet strong-willed and hearty, she was a throwback to that rugged breed of pioneer woman who carved her mark on the land.

Miss Ruth raised a bundle of young 'uns, sent them off to get a good education, and understood when they wanted to seek their fortunes elsewhere instead of returning to the farm. Her eldest son, Jim, had gone off to the big city and married Carol, a dark-eyed beauty from New York, whom Miss Ruth had adored right away.

Bright and personable and artistic, Carol was enthralled by the rustic beauty of the Central Texas countryside. An accomplished art teacher, Carol often brought her sketch pad with her whenever she and Jim came to visit Miss Ruth. That's how Carol got to know Coit's living legend, Chester Brooks.

Recognizing the Brooks store as an irretrievable part of the past, Carol had set out to capture it on canvas. She spent hours sitting outside the dirt-bottom store, sketching its rustic exterior with the cigarette signs, the old glass-topped gas pump out front, the Model-T panel truck sitting in a weed patch, the Rhode Island Red chickens wandering about at random, and the mange-ridden old dog panting in the shadow of a nearby oak tree. She later transferred her sketches into original watercolor works that she hung throughout her Houston home, making Chester's world a part of her own.

As she continued to visit the store, year after year, she felt a bond with the genial old grocer, as if she'd known him for a very long time. She spent hours talking with him while she worked on her sketches, probing his mind and delving into his thoughts. Unlike so many of the people who came to Chester's store, Carol wasn't content merely to "shoot the breeze." She found the old man to be brilliant; he was like a living encyclopedia or a high-speed computer. Carol wanted to tap into his mind, and so she pressed him to tell her things — about the war, about the land, about life.

Sometimes she brought her camera to the store and, despite Chester's protests, took pictures of the shy old grocer standing behind his beloved counter, with the twenty-five-year-old cobwebs hanging in the background. Chester was such a gentle soul; he couldn't bring himself to destroy anything of Nature's, not even a dust-covered spider web.

Carol found it impossible to believe that anyone could harm such a kind and caring man. And yet, half an hour before, Miss Ruth had telephoned with news about the funeral, followed by the details of the old grocer's brutal murder. His brains splattered against the car shed wall, his body frozen stiff — images that Carol tried to block from her mind as she stifled the silent scream inside her head: *No! Please, God, no.*

That wasn't how she wanted to remember Chester; he deserved better than that. And so, Carol retreated into the darkness of her photo lab, where she found negatives for the pictures she'd taken at Christmas, during her last visit to Chester Brooks' store.

Filled with grief and anguish and anger, Carol worked on for endless hours, enlarging the pictures of the wrinkled old man in the lop-sided baseball cap, smiling that shy, toothless grin as he said, "Oh, Carol, don't take my picture. Save your film." That was Chester. Her Chester. That's how she would remember him.

A few days later, Carol wrote the poem. An English-teacher friend helped her arrange the stanzas, but the words were her own. They were the words she would have said to him at the Thornton Cemetery if she'd been given the chance to say goodbye.

DEAR CHESTER

Someone took you from us,
You are gone from your store.
We'll pass, remembering you, but we'll be on our way
Because there's no need to stop anymore.
Time will pass; seasons come and go,
And I'll always feel the absence
Of the friend I grew to know.

Who didn't welcome the nice things you did,
Your smile, comfort, and thoughtfulness, too.

88

Everyone loved you, it's easy to see,
Everyone will miss you, especially me.

An hour of talk or laughter
Gives a memory which will linger forever after.
Just words of kindness made a difference in your day
And the hours were a little brighter,
And dark times seemed less gray.

The hands that took you away
Belong to the real loser because
They never felt your gentle touch
Or enjoyed the warmth of your friendship.
Those hands and the conscience of stone have stolen
    your life,
But your spirit cannot be destroyed,
For it will last despite your absence
And you will live in our hearts eternally.

How can anyone forget you?
When I was with you, life was good,
Time stood still while you reminisced
Pictures from the past, loved ones all remembered.
To sit and pass a minute here, an hour there with you
Gave you your greatest thrill.
For time was all you had.

When Miss Ruth's husband died of a stroke within a month
of Chester's death, Carol and her two daughters accompanied
Jim Fairbairn back to his family farm in Coit for his father's funeral. As she packed her husband's clothes, Carol remembered
to include several copies of her poem, along with the prints of
Chester's smiling face, captured on film as well as in memory.
With so much grief to bear in such a short time, perhaps her trib-
ute to the old grocer would help to heal the broken hearts of others.
    Mr. Fairbairn's funeral proved an ordeal for his grieving
family, but the service was especially hard for Carol. As she
watched the pallbearers carry her father-in-law's casket down the
front steps of the Fairview Presbyterian Church and slide it into
the waiting hearse, Carol glanced eastward toward the old gen-

eral store, now empty and deserted. For the first time since she had come to Coit more than seventeen years before, she saw no trace of the gentle old grocer who had touched her life so deeply. Even Chester's old cars were gone, hastily sold off like most of his possessions. There was nothing left; everything had been sold or trashed once the will had been probated.

Carol felt robbed. She had wanted to make a shrine of the store, to buy the land and keep the place exactly as Chester had it, a sacred museum with dusty spider webs and all. How dare someone touch his things, she thought. She felt as if the old grocer had been defiled, as if his memory had been raped, as if she had failed him somehow by not stopping the desecration. If only she had known about his death in time.

Chester had left his property to a young girl who had, as a child, visited his store and brought him plate lunches on holidays. Folks reasoned that the lonely old grocer had merely repaid the girl's kindness by naming her his heir.

Some were surprised that Chester had failed to remember Carolyn Garrett Taylor in his will. Everyone in those parts knew that the old grocer loved Carolyn as if she were his own. And Carolyn's affection for the old family friend was as equally deep and abiding. She had proven that, time and again.

From the moment the fiesty little Garrett girl first toddled through his store during Depression days, Chester Brooks melted whenever Carolyn dropped by to visit for a spell. Her childhood laughter warmed the musty old store as she sat there by the icebox, whiling away the hours and telling him about her latest tomboy adventure or some good-natured prank. He gave her bubble gum, candy, and soft drinks, opening up for her a magical world of rare childhood delights. She gave him a sense of feeling needed, as if the little girl depended on him for love and warmth and acceptance that she didn't find at home. They were friends, two lonely souls bound together, and nothing could change that.

Even after Carolyn grew up, married, and moved to Houston, she always went to see Chester whenever she and Von and the children visited her mother up the road at the "Garrett place." When the Taylor family relocated to Temple, after Von had given up the dream of returning to professional football, her visits to the store became more frequent.

It was Carolyn Taylor who made the weekly runs to the Temple discount stores, buying Cokes and bread and staples to restock the shelves of the old Coit general store. After years of doing business, the wholesale trucks had finally taken Chester's store off their regular routes because the old grocer didn't buy enough merchandise to make the trip worth their while. So, Carolyn had assumed that job by picking up whatever Chester needed and bringing it to him on Sunday afternoons. She had a full-time job and four children to rear, but she always made time for Chester. He had always taken time for her.

That's why Carolyn had been at the store just hours before the old man's death. She was, perhaps, the only person who loved and understood Chester Brooks better than Carol Fairbairn did. That's why Carol wasn't surprised when Miss Ruth told her about how hard Carolyn had taken the old grocer's murder.

"Chester's grave is my grave," Carolyn had said on the day they buried him in the Thornton Cemetery. And folks who knew her agreed; she was never the same after that. Something had died within her, as if the best part of her had somehow perished with her old childhood friend. At the age of forty, she looked old and tired and spent.

Miss Ruth had also told Carol about Carolyn's violent rage once the shock of Chester's death had abated and anger had replaced her grief. "If I could get my hands on whoever did this," Carolyn had said through clenched teeth, "I'd kill him."

Maybe that's why Carol Fairbairn had lashed out when Alice suggested that Carolyn's son might have had something to do with the robbery. It was impossible, Carol told herself, and she resented her daughter for having thought it.

And yet, the fourteen-year-old Houston girl had known in her heart what Sheriff Dennis Walker already suspected: the real murderer of Chester Brooks was still out there.

CHAPTER TWELVE

The Wrong Man

When the phone rang at the Limestone County Sheriff's Office at dusk on February 18, Dennis Walker reached for the receiver matter of factly. He'd stayed late to finish some paperwork after a hectic week of investigating routine burglaries and suspected drug deals. He looked forward to the weekend and to the hunting trip that would get him out-of-doors and away for a much-needed breather. He didn't know that the phone call would alter his plans and send him off on a different kind of hunting expedition.

The Jesse James saga was about to be replayed, complete with its bushwhacking gang member and its betrayed leader. Only this time, the traitor wasn't motivated by money, like the $25,000 that was advertised on the reward poster in Walker's office. And this time, the "dirty little coward" wasn't a trigger-happy kid named Bob Ford, but a nineteen-year-old ex-con named Hank Worley.

As Walker lifted the receiver to his ear and continued to sign papers with his other hand, he heard the familiar drawl of the cigar-chewing Jim Ray. "Dennis, hang on to your socks," the Ranger told him. "This is gonna blow your mind."

Walker straightened in his chair as he heard the Texas Ranger confirm what he had suspected all along. "You've got the wrong man."

Walker listened while Ray related the bizarre set of circumstances that had ripped the Brooks case wide open. The sheriff sat mute, sorting through the maze of information.

Ray broke the silence. "I think you'd better saddle up and

ride on over. We've got somebody here at the Bell County Jail you need to talk to."

Walker picked up Chief Deputy Bill Fletcher at his home in Groesbeck and briefed the deputy during the fifty-five-minute drive along the darkened Interstate 35 that ran southwest toward the Bell County Jail in Belton. The Belton Police Department had picked up a kid named Hank Worley earlier that afternoon in connection with a theft charge. Worley, an ex-con on parole for a motor vehicle burglary conviction, had no desire to return to the Texas Department of Corrections. He had, therefore, asked to speak with Lieutenant Cosper of the Belton PD, offering to make a deal in exchange for information about a murder case where the wrong man had been arrested.

Lieutenant Cosper had contacted Ed Gooding, the Texas Ranger assigned to the Bell County area. Cosper asked the Ranger to speak with Worley and decide whether his information merited a "deal." In addition, Cosper called Al Shoore, an assistant district attorney in Belton, and asked him to join them at the jail to arrange a deal if Gooding gave the go-ahead.

When the Ranger and the assistant DA arrived, Worley laid his cards on the table. He said he knew who had killed the old man up near Marlin, and he would give a statement implicating the murderers if all charges against him were dropped.

Making deals with law enforcement was to become a specialty for Worley. In 1992, he would gain national attention for turning in his partner, Kenneth Allen McDuff, a convicted mass murderer and the subject of a nationwide manhunt. Worley would admit to helping McDuff kidnap, rape, and torture a young Austin woman named Colleen Reed before McDuff "used her up" and stashed her body at an unknown location. In exchange for his testimony against McDuff, Worley would not be charged for the woman's murder.

But in 1977, the assistant DA balked at Worley's demands; theft charges against the ex-con would stand. However, the DA did agree to let Worley serve "jail time" in Belton rather than send him back for a second hitch at the Texas Department of Corrections. In exchange, Worley would have to make a written statement and testify against the alleged murderers in court. That was the only deal they could offer him. Take it or leave it.

Worley dropped his head and nodded in assent; he would take it. Anything was better than going back to the TDC. Despite the efforts of U.S. District Judge William Wayne Justice to open the state prison system to sweeping reforms, as mandated in his *Ruiz vs. the State of Texas* ruling, little had changed. Texas prisons were still hell-holes, and Worley wasn't going back, no matter what.

And so, Hank Worley began the tale that would nail Jim Taylor just as surely as Bob Ford's bullet had pierced the unarmed Jesse as he turned his back to straighten a picture on the wall of his St. Joseph, Missouri, home some ninety-five years before.

Ranger Gooding listened to the ex-con's story, then telephoned Jim Ray at the Company F headquarters in Waco. Ray arrived within an hour, and together the two Rangers listened while Worley repeated his statement for the DA's stenographer. When the ex-con had signed the voluntary statement naming three murder suspects, Ray placed the call to Walker. He sounded like a chicken snake with a half-grown pullet in its mouth, about to choke on his good fortune.

Sheriff Walker and Deputy Fletcher arrived at the Bell County Jail around 8:00 that Friday night with Limestone County Assistant DA Dick White, who had followed them over in his private car. Walker had telephoned White earlier, asking him to sit in while they questioned Worley about the Brooks case. The sheriff wanted to make sure that they followed correct procedure, avoiding any slip-ups that might overturn a possible conviction. His years in law enforcement had taught Walker to be cautious about legal loopholes.

Walker, his deputy, and the assistant DA met Ranger Ray inside the booking area of the jail, where they were briefed on the content of Worley's statement. Afterward, the three Limestone County officials followed the cigar-chewing Ranger down the hall and into one of the jail's interrogation rooms, where the long-haired ex-con waited.

Walker introduced himself and the others, then explained that he wanted to question Worley about the statement he'd given to the Texas Rangers earlier that evening. Worley sat with his elbows propped against the table, fingering a cup of black coffee as Walker reexamined every detail of his story.

"How long have you known these other two boys, Taylor and Frye?" the sheriff asked.

"For about a month. They've been staying in Belton with Ricky Dominick. Dominick is a friend of mine."

"And when did these boys tell you about the murder?"

"I rode around with Jim and Walter, and they told me several times about robbing and killing the old man in Marlin. Jim told me the old man's name was Chester, but I can't remember the last name."

"All right, son," Walker said. "Tell me again what Taylor said about robbing the store."

"Jim said they went with Wes Folger in his car to Marlin. They were going to break into the old man's store and get some money and cigarettes. Jim said he knew the old man, and he knew he kept money in the store. They said they took a fourth man with them, but I don't know his name."

"According to Taylor and Frye, what happened after the four boys got to the store?"

"They said they went out back and jumped on the old man and took a shotgun away from him and beat him with it. They told me they bent the barrel of the gun on him. They said the old man wouldn't pass out, so they got a hydite block and beat the old man over the head with the block."

"And you're sure that's what they said happened?" Walker asked, peering across the table at the long-haired ex-con and sizing him up.

Worley nodded, took a sip of his lukewarm coffee, and continued. "Jim and Walter have told me about that night several times."

"Now, why do you suppose they'd do that?"

"It first came up one day when I went to Dominick's house, and I saw several cigar boxes full of change. I asked them where they got the money, and that was when they told me about trying to rob the store and beating the old man."

"And you believed them?" the sheriff asked.

"At first I didn't, but a day or two later I heard about the murder, and the radio said the man's name was 'Chester,' but I can't remember the last name."

When Walker paused for a moment, Worley continued his narrative without waiting for the sheriff's questions. "Jim has talked more about this than Walter, but what Walter told me is the same as what Jim said. Walter told me he was the one who hit the old man on the head with the hydite block, and Jim told me he had picked up the iron gate leaning against something, and lifted it up and threw it on the old man."

Worley concluded by adding that he had later helped Jim hide the cigar boxes full of Canadian coins. Worley related how they had climbed up into the attic through a hole in the kitchen closet. There, they had stashed the robbery loot between two rafters so it would be out of sight. Jim had acted nervous, Worley recalled.

Satisfied with Worley's information, Walker turned the ex-con over to the Bell County Sheriff's Department. Worley was booked on the theft charges and spent the night in the Bell County Jail in Belton.

Walker, Fletcher, and White, meanwhile, returned to Groesbeck and arrived at the sheriff's office around 10:30 P.M. Walker roused Justice of the Peace Marvin Pruitt out of bed, telephoning him to come to the courthouse on urgent business. When the elderly JP arrived moments later, Walker signed formal complaints against the three suspects implicated in Worley's statement. Pruitt, in turn, issued capital murder warrants for Jim Taylor, Walter Frye, and Wes Folger. He also gave Walker a search warrant for Ricky Dominick's house on Wall Street in Belton.

The sheriff asked Fletcher and White to meet him at the Bell County Jail around 9:00 the following morning. At that time, they would join Ranger Ray and the Bell County Sheriff's Office in executing the warrants.

As he watched his deputy and the assistant DA drive away through the moonlit shadows of the courthouse square, Walker glanced toward the three-story, red brick building looming in the darkness two blocks away. There, in a second-floor cell, slept Luis Torres, unaware that the scaffolding had just been torn down and the lynch rope loosened.

96

Walker breathed deeply. Now it all fit.

The manhunt began early that Saturday morning, February 19, as scheduled. At 9:35 A.M. two cars approached Wes Folger's mobile home on South Pearl Street in Belton. The lead car, with the Bell County Sheriff's Office insignia on its side, braked to a stop, and Texas Ranger Jim Ray and Bell County Deputy E. L. Wilson stepped out onto the gravel driveway. They were joined moments later by Sheriff Walker, Deputy Fletcher, and Assistant DA White, occupants in the Limestone County vehicle.

The five somber-faced men approached the run-down mobile home, and Ray knocked twice. The officers took a step backward as the door opened six inches and a face appeared. Jill Folger, the pregnant wife of the principal murder suspect, peered out through the open doorway as the Ranger stated their business. She seemed startled as she listened, explaining that her husband was not at home. He had gone to see a doctor, but she expected him to return within a few minutes.

Walker and Ray agreed to stake-out the Folger home and wait. In the meantime, Fletcher, White, and Wilson were to conduct a simultaneous raid on the home of Taylor and Frye. Once the suspects were in custody, they were to be brought to Sheriff Lester Gunn's office at the Bell County Jail.

Wes Folger drove up a half-hour later, and he made no attempt to run when Walker showed him the murder warrant and placed him under arrest. The seventeen-year-old suspect sat stoically in the back seat of the squad car as he rode to the Bell County Jail, where Ranger Ray read him his Miranda rights before questioning him about the Brooks case.

Ranger Ray and Sheriff Lester Gunn questioned Folger for thirty minutes, but the youth denied any knowledge of the crime. Meanwhile, a tearful Jill Folger had arrived at the jail, having first telephoned Wes' parents in Temple and advising them of his arrest.

Walker stood out in the hallway with the girl, trying to calm her. He'd always had a soft spot for kids, especially for those who were in trouble. In a soft-spoken, sympathetic voice, Walker explained the situation to Jill Folger. She then asked to speak with her husband, alone, and Walker agreed. Perhaps she could persuade him to do what was right.

The couple sat in the room, talking quietly. Fifteen minutes later, Wes Folger agreed to give a voluntary statement. "I've been lying to you," he said. "I was there, but I didn't do the beating."

Ranger Ray and Sheriff Gunn continued to question Folger, using the "good guy" interrogation strategy. Sheriff Gunn pretended to be on Wes' side, urging the boy to "come clean" while the villain Ray was out of the room, and things would go easier for him.

Wes gave an oral statement to Gunn, admitting that he had participated in the robbery, but insisting that Taylor and Frye had planned the entire thing. At no time did he admit having killed Chester Brooks; he accused the other boys of the murder.

But, unknowingly, Wes Folger did provide the officers with a piece of information they hadn't known before: the name of the fourth accomplice. Wes incriminated his own brother.

When Wes' parents arrived at the jail with a lawyer, the youth was advised to make no further statement. The first of the conspirators was taken before the Bell County justice of the peace, Joe Harrison, where he was arraigned and bond was set at $300,000.

Walker made arrangements to transport the murder suspect back to Limestone County later that afternoon while he waited for Fletcher's group to return with Taylor and Frye.

When his showdown with the law finally came, Jim Taylor was caught off-guard. Although he had expected to bite the dust with six-guns blazing, he hadn't gotten off a shot. Like Jesse James, his sixth sense had failed him at a crucial moment. Probably because he had blitzed his brain with dope until 5:00 that Saturday morning.

While the lawmen closed in, Jim and Walter slept on in the south bedroom of Walter's grandfather's house on Water's Dairy Road in Temple. The old one-story frame house sat right across the road from two churches that Jim had burglarized the year before, back when his outlaw days had first begun.

For some reason, Jim and Walter hadn't spent the night at Ricky Dominick's house in Belton. Instead, Dominick's younger brother had dropped them off at Walter's grandfather's place, and they'd climbed into bed without awakening Mr. Mahler. The old man was hard-of-hearing, anyway.

At the time, Jim didn't think much about the change in hideouts. He and Walter were too stoned to pay much attention to details. Later, however, he wondered how the deputies knew to come to the address in Temple. He and Walter hadn't stayed there in weeks.

Drowsy from drugs and weary from partying, Jim finally stirred around 11:00 as the sun beamed through the dingy window pane and onto his back. He yawned, stretched, and turned over to glance out the bedroom window. When his groggy eyes focused on the sheriff's car out front, he bolted upright. "Walter, wake up! The cops are here."

Still in his underwear, Jim ran toward the bedroom door as two deputies stormed into the room with their .38-caliber weapons drawn. Jim stopped abruptly in midflight, staring down the barrel of the revolver.

"You boys get dressed," Fletcher barked, towering over them with his knees slightly crouched and his gun gripped with both hands. "Right now."

"What for?" Jim asked.

"You're both under arrest for murder. Let's go."

The two deputies and the assistant DA watched while Jim and Walter dressed in their wrinkled flannel shirts and faded Wrangler jeans. Once the boys had slipped on their scuffed cowboy boots, the deputies snapped the handcuffs on their wrists and led them outside.

Mr. Mahler stood on the front porch, his weathered face wrinkled in anguish as the deputies led his sixteen-year-old grandson toward the light-colored squad car. He had suspected that Walter and Jim had been up to no good. They were, after all, high-spirited boys. But this was more than their usual mischief — he knew that.

The old man gripped the porch railing and tried to steady himself as he watched the sheriff's car pull away. He saw Walter and Jim's bowed heads through the rear window, and he realized that he hadn't spoken a word to either boy. What could he have possibly said?

*   *   *   *   *

Neither Jim nor Walter spoke during the ten-minute ride to the sheriff's office in Belton. Both sat in stony silence, staring out the windows and trying to get a grip on what was going down. Their minds fielded the same question over and over: How had the cops found out? They had heard that a suspect had been arrested, a Mexican man who had quarreled with Chester on the day of his death. What, or who, had led the cops to them?

Jim tried to clear his mind, but his thoughts seemed fragmented and blurred. That was how his life had been during the month since Chester's death: fuzzy and disoriented and out-of-focus, like a bad picture show. Reel after reel after reel.

He looked at the handcuffs shackled to his wrists and wondered why he hadn't run. There had been plenty of chances, and he'd thought about it often. Like on the afternoon he and Walter had gone out to Cedar Ridge Park with Wes Folger to burn the bloody clothes and the useless papers from Chester's store. As he stared at the flames, Jim had felt seared by fear and guilt, and he burned to run away. Later, when he watched the gravel-filled gas cans disappear beneath the murky waters of Lake Belton, he had considered doing his own vanishing act and just dropping out of sight, permanently. He could have thumbed his way to who-knows-where.

But for some reason, he had ignored his instincts and remained in Belton. Probably he was reluctant to leave because of Walter Frye. If his best friend had been willing to run, then Jim would have cut out and hit the outlaw trail. But Walter had met a girl named Leslie Golding, and she had him lassoed and hog-tied. Walter wasn't going anywhere, and Jim wasn't going any place without him. Just like that night at the store. A man didn't desert his partner, no matter what. That was the code.

So, while Walter fooled around with this new girlfriend every night, Jim started carousing with some of Ricky Dominick's friends in Belton. One of them was an ex-con named Hank Worley.

Although Jim liked Dominick, he didn't have the same regard for some of his friends like Hank Worley. Something about the ex-con made Jim leery. While Jim had no qualms about cruising around in Worley's van or smoking dope with him, Jim didn't

100

trust the former inmate. Worley was slow-thinking, and he made stupid mistakes. That bothered Jim.

Recognizing Worley's liabilities, Jim didn't know why he had agreed to pull off a burglary with him. Although he had once enjoyed a life of lawlessness, Jim hadn't hit another place since that night at Chester's store. He feared what might happen and wouldn't take the risk. Yet, on impulse, he had agreed to join Worley and another one of Ricky Dominick's friends when they pulled their next job in Belton. He had gone along for the ride, trying to kill time until Walter came home from Leslie's place. Doing something was better than doing nothing.

Worley had driven around for several minutes that night before he and his buddy selected the target: a small grocery store somewhere on the edge of town. Jim hadn't paid attention to the location. He was "busy" with a girl in the back of Worley's van. She was one of the many who hung around the house that month, offering him a sample of her wares. With his rugged good-looks, Jim rarely lacked for female companionship. He willingly took what they freely gave, playing a meaningless game without feeling or involvement. Time after time, he had merely gone through the motions. He used girls like he used weed.

Still, the girls hadn't seemed to mind his sport; they always came back for more. He was dangerous and exciting to be with. They enjoyed the challenge of trying to tame an outlaw, although none of them ever did. Like the wild, free-spirited Brahmans that he rode, Jim Taylor couldn't be broken or penned. Not by anyone or anything.

When Worley's van stopped, Jim concluded his business with the girl in the back seat and surveyed the set-up. Their target was a small country store, much like the one in Limestone County. Jim felt uneasy, but he had smoked enough dope that night to steady his nerves. He followed Worley and his accomplice around to the back door, with his bolt cutters and the young girl in tow.

As soon as Jim snapped the lock and shoved the door open, he knew that something was wrong. An alarm, shrill yet inaudible, sounded inside his head as his eyes focused on two objects in the half-shadows of the back room: a bed and an old dresser. His mind transported him to another room, similarly furnished.

101

There he had stood in terror as he waited for the old man to come inside. Not again, he thought.

His heart pounded as the muscles in his throat tightened. He swallowed hard. What if someone lived in this back room and were inside the store? Jim's instincts told him to back away from this job, but his three companions had already darted through the doorway. Reluctantly, he followed them inside.

The job that night went off without incident, although Jim had grown impatient with Worley's antics. The ex-con and the young girl, a runaway from somewhere, had raced up and down the store aisles with their shopping carts, throwing items into the baskets as if they were on some idiotic shopping spree. Worley behaved wildly and recklessly, and he took too long inside the store. That's how he had been caught before, taking chances and being careless. Worley's foolhardiness made Jim edgy; he didn't trust the ex-con.

Still, Jim had continued to run around with Worley. He even told him about the murder up in Limestone County after the dope had addled his brain and loosened his tongue one night. He had gone so far as to ask Worley's help in hiding the cigar boxes with the Canadian coins and the old keys. That was a stupid thing to do; yet, contrary to form, Jim had done a lot of stupid things that month.

He behaved as if he wanted to get caught, as if he wanted to be stopped before he went too far again and somebody else got hurt. And so, when the showdown finally came, Jim allowed himself to be taken without a fight. Neither he nor Walter offered any resistance as Fletcher and Deputy Wilson led them inside the Bell County Jail for interrogation.

They entered the building through the visitors' waiting area, a route not usually taken by prisoners. They should have gone through the side door with the electronic lock, then passed through a barred gate before arriving at the holding cells by the booking area. That was the way handcuffed prisoners were usually routed, not past the vending machines in the visitors' waiting room.

For whatever reason the deputies led them that way, Jim and Walter saw someone sitting in the waiting room that they weren't supposed to see. Hank Worley.

102

The ex-con sat on a bench beside his mother, and turned ashen when he saw Jim and Walter pass within inches of him. If looks could kill, Hank Worley would have been a dead man.

Deputy Wilson led the two boys down a hallway to the left and toward the office of Lester Gunn, the Bell County sheriff who had applauded the return of the death penalty some three weeks earlier when a black-hooded Gary Gilmore had bought the bullet. Wilson opened the door to Gunn's office and motioned the boys inside.

The balding, bespectacled sheriff rose from behind his desk when the manacled suspects entered the room and stood somberly before him. "Come on in, boys," he said. "Have a seat."

"What's this all about?" asked Jim as he slumped into a chair, adjusted the handcuffs on his wrists, and tried to act casual.

"Capital murder, boy. The sheriff of Limestone County has come to take you back for the murder of a man named Chester Brooks."

"I didn't kill anybody," Jim railed. "You're crazy!"

"For your sake, son," Sheriff Gunn said, glaring over the rims of his glasses and choosing his words carefully, "I hope I am crazy."

With that, Jim glanced at Walter, who sat stone-faced and silent. When asked if they wished to make a statement, both boys insisted that they had nothing to say. Deputy Wilson then led them to the booking area, where he placed each boy in a separate holding cell. They'd give them time to think it over while Sheriff Walker finished questioning Folger in the next room.

Jim stalked inside the 4x6-foot holding cell and pivoted on his boot heel as he heard the deputy slam the iron door shut behind him. He glanced about the dismal, windowless enclosure; it resembled a tomb.

A stark light bulb dangled from the eight-foot ceiling, which had been crudely blackened with peace symbols and rock group logo and meaningless initials, scrawled by prisoners with the carbon from their cigarette lighters or matches.

The drab beige walls, dingy and grimy from the smudges of human hands, were constructed of concrete blocks. The same kind of hydite blocks that Wes Folger had used at Chester Brooks' place four weeks earlier.

The oppressive metal door, four inches thick, contained a scratched plexiglass window with a metal flap hinged on top. If a prisoner behaved himself, the deputies left the flap up so the suspect could glimpse at the people in the booking area outside. If the prisoner proved uncooperative, the flap slammed shut, isolating the suspect from the rest of the outside world. That day, the metal flap remained closed.

Jim pushed against the door, pressing his palms against the cold metal above the speaker-box attachment and the food-drop slot. He leaned his entire weight against the door, but it did not budge; he was trapped.

Minutes later, when a deputy shoved a tray of food through the door slot, Jim shoved it back at him. He heard the dishes clattering on the concrete floor outside, and the scalded deputy railed in a volley of curse words. Jim chuckled, but his laughter sounded hollow and forced.

The odious smell of stale urine permeated the air inside the ventless cell; it came from the unflushed toilet next to the door. Jim reached for the cold chrome handle and flushed it, staring into the stained toilet bowl and watching the water swirl down, down, down into oblivion. He longed to go with it.

He stretched out on the slotted-wood bench against the wall, lying on his back and staring at the naked light fixture on the ceiling. The bulb reminded him of the one he had left burning that night in Chester's store, when he and his terrified companions had fled into the darkness.

He closed his eyes and tried to sleep. He wanted to block out the terrible reality of where he was and what was happening. If he didn't allow himself to think about these things, then they wouldn't be real. The fear and dread would go away, like the bad dreams he had when he was a kid.

He wished he were a kid again, when life was simple and good. Back when he wore the football jersey and listened to the roar of the crowd. Back when his dad came to watch him play, and he felt like he was somebody. Back, back . . .

Jim sat upright on the wooden bench, shuddering as he heard the ear-piercing scream fill the cell and ricochet off the walls. He glanced about him, trying to locate the origin of the frightful wail, only to discover that it came from his own throat, tightened and tortured.

Something weird had happened inside his head during the few minutes he slept. Perhaps it was the drugs or the depression or the guilt, but something in his psyche snapped, like a ball propelled with missile-like force.

As if he were on some forgotten football field, Jim rammed his right shoulder against the locked door, using it like a battering-ram, the way Coach Hoppers had taught him to do so many seasons before. Unable to move it, he clenched his fists and pounded scarred knuckles against the scratched metal door. *Thump, thump, thump.*

"Let me out, let me out," he screamed as tears flooded his reddened eyes. He thrashed and bashed against the door, like a crazed Brahman inside a chute, fighting to be free.

"I'll tell, I'll tell! Just let me out. Let me out!"

When the heavy metal door swung open several minutes later, Deputy Wilson stood outside, staring at the young prisoner. The boy seemed contrite and broken. The holding cell had done its job.

"Are you ready to make a statement, son?" Wilson asked.

"Yes, sir."

"All right. Let's go down to that desk there at the end of the hall."

Jim brushed his flannel shirt sleeve across his eyes and nose as he walked to the desk with Deputy Wilson. He blinked back the tears as he stood before Justice of the Peace Joe Harrison, who had set bond on Wes Folger just moments before. Jim bowed his head as Harrison read endlessly from a piece of paper, something called a juvenile warning. He didn't understand Harrison's words; he wasn't even listening. Drugged and dazed and drained, he just wanted to get it over with and be left alone. He just wanted the nightmare to end.

And so, without a parent or a lawyer present to counsel him otherwise, Jim told Harrison and Wilson everything they wanted to know about the robbery at Chester Brooks' store.

The dramatic climax should have come as no surprise to Jim, for his fate had been as carefully orchestrated as a classic Shakespearean tragedy. Long ago, as an eleven-year-old boy run-

105

ning through a black cemetery, he had met the same cast of characters.

The tombstone that had crushed him to the ground that day bore the surname of HARRISON, the same as the Bell County justice of the peace who read him his juvenile warning. The adjacent marker had read FOLGER, the name of his co-conspirator who sat in an interrogation room nearby. To the east of those two graves stood the marker of WILSON, the name of the arresting deputy who listened to Jim's oral confession in the hallway. And completing the circle of cemetery markers was the tombstone chiseled GARRETT, the name of Jim's maternal grandmother who lived three miles south of Chester Brooks' store.

Harrison, Folger, Wilson, Garrett — names carved in stone at New Hope Cemetery, each one bearing witness of the young desperado crushed beneath the slab of white rock.

Harrison, Folger, Wilson — names of men assembled in the Bell County Jail, listening as Mrs. Garrett's sixteen-year-old grandson spoke the words that would crush him with their weight.

Perhaps the four tombstones in the New Hope Cemetery had tried to warn Jim Taylor of his tragic destiny. Somehow, they must have known.

CHAPTER THIRTEEN

Notoriety in a Quiet Little Town

The folks inside Josie's Restaurant paid no attention to the boy silhouetted in the back seat of the sheriff's car as it pulled into the northwest driveway of the Groesbeck courthouse across the street. The Saturday afternoon patrons swallowed bites of chicken-fried steak, sipped black coffee, and made small talk with the waitress, who busied herself with wiping off tables and refilling coffee cups.

The denim-clad diners talked about the weather and about the toll the recent cold spell had taken on their livestock. More than a month had passed since the news of Chester Brooks' murder had shocked the sleepy-eyed town in central Limestone County, and most of the angry, vindictive talk had died down days ago, after the Mexican had been arrested and thrown in jail. Groesbeck had returned to a lifestyle reminiscent of simpler times, and the customers inside Josie's Restaurant liked it that way.

A pair of cowboy patrons finished off their last forkfuls of homemade apple pie and slapped at their stuffed bellies, bulging over shiny belt buckles etched with western logos. As they paid their checks, exited the restaurant, and climbed into the two-tone pickup out front, they paid little attention to the scenario across the street, where Deputy Bill Fletcher and Ranger Jim Ray were leading a young prisoner up the north courthouse steps and toward Sheriff Dennis Walker's office on the first floor of the three-story, red brick building.

The Groesbeck courthouse, which housed the Limestone County Sheriff's Office as well as a half-dozen county offices and two district courts, encompassed an entire city block. Its massive

1924 Greek Revival architecture, with fluted white pillars rising two stories high to support ornate cornices carved with cornucopias and garlands, seemed strangely out of place in this small town of 3,000 residents. Considered one of the most beautiful government buildings in Central Texas, the gilded courthouse stood out in stark contrast to the faded Norman Rockwell storefronts, the run-down lumber yard, and the rustic livestock barns nearby.

The provincial town of Groesbeck had been founded in 1870 by the Houston and Texas Central Railroad. Named for Abram Groesbeeck, a director of the company, the town became incorporated in 1871 and experienced a brief boom as a railroad terminus. Serving as a marketing and shipping point for farm and ranch products, Groesbeck became the Limestone County seat in 1874.

The railroad town had been a violent one during its early years, back when the outlaws Sam Bass and Jesse James first rode across the Central Texas prairies. Reconstruction had been hard, and Groesbeck was placed under martial law as a result of race riots in 1871. Resentment ran high long after the ordeal of Reconstruction had ended. In 1889, some twenty-four years after the surrender of Gen. Robert E. Lee, veterans of the Confederacy in Limestone County and neighboring Freestone County assembled as an encampment and formed the Joe Johnston Camp No. 94 — United Confederate Veterans.

For the next fifty-seven years, these CSA veterans and their families met in late July or early August for a three-day gathering at the Confederate Reunion Grounds on the Navasota River in Limestone County. Their purpose was "to perpetuate the memories of fallen comrades, to aid disabled survivors and indigent widows and orphans of deceased Confederate soldiers, and to preserve the fraternity that grew out of the war." In the hearts of Limestone County folk, the South lived on.

It was this link to the past that gave Groesbeck its greatest notoriety, for the town was steeped in colorful legends and Texas tall tales. Perhaps the most famous of these was the saga of Cynthia Ann Parker, a nine-year-old white girl captured by renegade Indians during the massacre at nearby Fort Parker. Most Limestone County citizens knew the story by heart, and they delighted in telling the tale to wide-eyed tourists who traveled to Fort Parker, hoping to gain a glimpse of the Old West by standing inside the twelve-foot-high stockade walls of the rustic frontier fort, recently restored as a state historic site.

Cynthia Ann's life among the Indians became the stuff of legends. At first, she witnessed the savagery and brutality that her captors inflicted on other prisoners. Perhaps the most gruesome spectacle was that involving Cynthia's cousin, Rachel Plummer.

Six months after their capture, Rachel had given birth to a baby boy. One day while she was nursing the infant, several Indians came to her and demanded the child. When she refused, a Comanche wrestled the child from her arms and strangled him. The Indian threw the baby's body into the air, watched it strike the ground, and then tossed the lifeless form at Rachel's feet.

Rachel gazed on the bruised cheeks of her infant son and discovered he was still alive. She washed the blood from the baby's face and comforted him, hoping the Comanches would allow her to keep him. But when the Indians saw that the child was still alive, they tore him from Rachel's arms and knocked her down.

The young mother watched in horror as a Comanche tied a plaited rope around the baby's neck and threw him into a bunch of prickly pears, pulling him backward and forward until his tender flesh was literally torn from his body. Another Indian, on horseback, tied the end of the rope to his saddle and galloped in a circle until the baby was not only dead, but torn to pieces. The Comanches untied the rope and threw the baby's remains into Rachel's lap. She dug a hole in the earth and buried them.

Cynthia Ann would witness other such atrocities before her captivity ended in 1860, when Capt. Sul Ross and a group of Texas Rangers recaptured her and her infant daughter during the Battle of Pease River. By that time, however, Cynthia Ann was thirty-four years old and, except for her blue eyes, resembled the Indians with whom she had lived. During her years of captivity, she had married Peta Nocona, a Comanche chief, and had borne him two sons, Pecos and Quanah Parker, in addition to their infant daughter, Prairie Flower.

After learning of her identity, Captain Ross returned Cynthia Ann to her relatives in East Texas; however, she could not readjust to Anglo-American society. Her life among the Indians had been a happy one. She grieved for her dead husband and her warrior sons. Cynthia Ann died four years later, shortly after the death of Prairie Flower. Legend maintains that she died of a broken heart, longing to return to the free life of the Comanches.

The Indian abduction of Cynthia Ann Parker found its way into Texas folklore because of her unwillingness to return to the ways of her childhood. In addition, she is remembered as the mother of the last great Comanche chief to raid the Texas prairies.

Cynthia Ann's legend lived on through the exploits of her half-breed son, Chief Quanah Parker, who led a band of 700 Indians in the Battle of Adobe Walls. Finally surrounded and captured in 1874, Quanah and his braves were sent to the Indian Territory, where they lived out their final days in peace.

Groesbeck's final claim to fame was having a favorite son who headed west and "made good" in Hollywood. The actor Joe Don Baker, star of the *Walking Tall* films about a small-town sheriff, hailed from Groesbeck. Folks still recalled watching Joe Don play football for the Groesbeck Goats, pointing to the hometown boy with pride. Sheriff Dennis Walker had played on that same team with Baker, never realizing that the actor would someday rise to fame playing the part of a controversial sheriff, a part that Walker played every day without a script.

Not many towns could boast a Confederate campsite or an Indian massacre or a genuine movie star. The folks inside Josie's Restaurant took pride in their town. Groesbeck was a good place to grow up and to raise a family. People taught their children to honor God and country; they respected the American work ethic of self-reliance; they voted Democratic like their daddies and granddaddies had done since Reconstruction. Groesbeck was, to their way of thinking, just about perfect.

But the boy entering the sheriff's office was about to change that. And they, like Cynthia Ann Parker, would be caught off-guard.

The hollow thud of boot heels echoed through the gray granite corridor as Deputy Bill Fletcher and Texas Ranger Jim Ray led Jim Taylor toward the sheriff's office on the northeast side of the building. Passing through the courthouse foyer, Jim glanced toward the double staircases that led upstairs to the district courtrooms on the second floor and the juvenile detention center on the third floor. Making a sharp left turn at the base of the polished gray steps, he found himself outside Sheriff Walker's office, where he heard muffled, muted voices.

Jim paused, allowing Fletcher to precede him through the opened, glass-paneled doorway with the words "SHERIFF'S OFFICE" stenciled in gold letters across the transom. Glancing quickly to his right, Jim saw a man standing beyond the drinking fountain and framing the doorway of the next office labeled "COUNTY ATTORNEY." The well-dressed, obese onlooker nodded to Ranger Ray, then leered at the young prisoner as Jim stepped across the threshold. Jim recognized the look. He had seen it on the faces of referees after they'd thrown the flag and stepped off ten yards. The smug satisfaction of catching the infraction and extracting a penalty.

Jim followed Fletcher past the receptionist's desk just outside Sheriff Walker's private office and on through the empty waiting room, with its rows of scarred wooden chairs lining the somber sheetrock walls. As they passed between a glass display case housing drug paraphernalia and an old oak bar with a brass footrail, the sound of voices became more distinct. Jim found himself in a small hallway leading to two closet-sized offices and a darkroom lab, all cubbyholed along the north rear wall.

The first office belonged to Chief Deputy Fletcher, while the second office was shared by several deputies in the Limestone County Sheriff's Department. The room at the end of the hall served both as a darkroom crime lab and as a coffee break area for the deputies. Fletcher ushered Jim down the narrow hallway, past his own office, and beyond the office where two young deputies stood talking with Sheriff Walker. Fletcher nodded to the sheriff, who halted his officers in mid-conversation until Fletcher and the young prisoner had passed.

Fletcher stopped outside the last door and, jerking his head to one side, motioned for Jim to go in. Seated around a small table were Walter Frye and Wes Folger. They had been brought over from the Bell County Jail several hours earlier by Sheriff Walker and a deputy. The two young prisoners stared at Jim nervously as he entered the room and slouched down in the hard-back chair next to Walter. No one spoke. The less said, the better.

As soon as Fletcher's massive hulk had disappeared down the hallway to join the sheriff, Walter leaned over and asked Jim where he'd been.

"Cedar Ridge," came the barely audible reply.

Fear shot through the eyes of Walter and Wes as they stared at Jim for a startled second, then dropped their heads and glared at the table. Cedar Ridge conjured up images of a smoldering, gray campfire with its last bloody remnants of a black ski mask and a red-stained shirt shriveling into nothingness. It brought back images of two dented gas cans being pelted by hastily thrown stones until they sank beneath the murky waters of Lake Belton, concealing the tell-tale fingerprints and the nightmarish deed of four young outlaws. Cedar Ridge — where Jim could have provided the deputies with enough evidence to hang them all.

Jim sensed the betrayal that his partners suspected, and the blood pounded feverishly inside his head. He felt like some animal snared in a hunter's steel trap, knowing that the only way to save itself was to gnaw off its own foot. And that, he had just done.

An hour before, he had stood on the rocky ledges of Cedar Ridge and reconstructed everything for Deputy Fletcher and Ranger Ray. Slowly and mechanically, without feeling or fear, he had pieced together the jagged memories of that January afternoon.

He had stood somberly and watched as the two officers scraped up fibers and snaps and nails from the ashes of the pyre where he had tried to purge himself of Chester Brooks' memory. He had then stood staring into the icy waters of Lake Belton, raising his right arm like a mechanical mannequin to gesture toward the spot where the old man's gas cans had been swallowed whole by the glistening depths. He had stood motioning toward a nebulous spot which, despite divers' efforts several days later, refused to yield up its metallic refuse as evidence of his wrongdoing.

Jim winced slightly. A deputy's voice intruded on his thoughts, forcing him to return to the cramped room where he and his two companions sat in stony silence. The young deputy leaned inside the doorway and, shoving a wad of chewing tobacco against the side of his cheek, instructed the boys to come along with him.

The sounds of chair legs scraping the hardwood floor and the shuffle of boot heels broke the silence as the boys rose to follow the deputy down the hall and into the booking room. There each one, in turn, added his blackened smears of loops, whorls, and arches to the sheriff's file, marking him with a stain as indelible as the ink on his fingertips.

Jim watched the deputy's methodical movement as, one by one, his own small, square fingers were pressed into the dark fluid, then mashed onto the stiff, white paper. The ebony imprints looked strange, especially the one for his left, middle finger — the one injured during the tombstone accident so long ago. He had been conspicuously marked by that finger, much like the legendary badman on the reward poster inside Sheriff Walker's office. The outlaw legacy lived on.

Back inside the small room, the boys sat waiting for what seemed like hours. None of them wore a watch, but Jim's stomach signaled that evening had come. He hadn't had anything to eat all day, and he longed for something to ease the gnawing inside his gut.

As if reading Jim's thoughts, the obese onlooker from the district attorney's office stuck his head inside the room and announced suppertime. "We ain't gonna starve you boys," Dick White said, leering at the three long-haired prisoners.

With that, the assistant DA stepped aside and motioned to a member of his staff, who had gone across the street to Josie's Restaurant and returned with several hamburgers. As the boys tore open the greasy wrappers and ate with overstuffed mouths, Dick White turned to the tobacco-chewing deputy standing just outside the doorway. "A hamburger is a small price to pay for a confession," the assistant DA said quietly, grinning at the officer and then glancing at Jim.

Moments later, the visitors came. Jill Folger and a girlfriend had driven over from Temple, hoping to see Wes. Sheriff Walker led the boys out into the waiting room, where Jill rushed forward to hug her husband and cry quietly in his arms.

While Wes attempted to console his sixteen-year-old wife, Jill's girlfriend walked over to Jim and Walter, hugging each of them in turn. She had gone to school with the boys and had partied with them often, so she tried to make small talk and offer reassurance. Sheriff Walker allowed the young people to step out into the empty courthouse hallway where they could talk more privately. No handcuffs. No armed guard.

Walker felt sorry for the three long-haired boys; he saw through their hardened, street-tough act and knew that they were frightened by what was happening. He also ached for the teary-eyed, pregnant girl who clung to Wes Folger. In his own youth, the sheriff had done some things that he regretted. He had been wild and reckless and impulsive, and he'd gotten into trouble from time to time. But Walker had been luckier than these boys. He hadn't been caught. And, unlike them, he'd been given the time to straighten out.

A few moments later, while the girls said their goodbyes, Dick White approached Jim and asked him to step down to the district attorney's office at the northeast corner of the building. White explained that Brenda Copeland, the legal secretary for Limestone County District Attorney Don Caldwell, had arrived to take Jim's written statement. Justice of the Peace Marvin Pruitt was also there, waiting to read Jim his juvenile warning.

Jim asked to speak with his parents. The day's events had seemed like a whirlwind, and he needed someone to help him think things through. Everything was happening so fast. He was scared.

"We haven't been able to get ahold of your folks," White explained. "They're not home right now. But don't you worry, son, we'll keep trying. In the meantime, why don't you just go ahead and get it over with? It'll be easier on you."

Jim stared blankly at White and said nothing. Reluctantly, he followed the assistant DA down the hall, past the drinking fountain, and into the corner office of the courthouse. Seated at a small desk next to the window was Mrs. Copeland, holding a small steno pad and waiting to take Jim's written statement in shorthand. A few feet away from her stood Pruitt, an elderly, gray-haired gentleman with a warm smile and a gentle manner reminiscent of Jim's grandfather.

The genial old JP greeted Jim with the first sign of real kindness that the boy had seen all day. Soft-spoken and reassuring,

Judge Pruitt exuded a quiet confidence that made Jim feel as if nothing bad was going to happen.

The white-haired magistrate instructed Jim to sit in the chair next to Mrs. Copeland's desk and to listen carefully to what he was about to say. With the assistant DA standing nearby as a witness, Judge Pruitt glanced at the official-looking paper he held in his hand and began reading.

The judge advised Jim that he was being charged with capital murder, that he had the right to have a parent present when he made a statement, and that he had the right to hire a lawyer and have him present to offer advice during questioning. Furthermore, Jim wasn't required to make a statement, but if he did . . .

As the kindly old judge droned on and on, Jim sat with his head bowed, listening to the sounds of the words without really hearing them. He tried to block out everything, just like he'd done that night outside Chester Brooks' store when he first heard the horrible thumping of the concrete block. If he didn't acknowledge what was happening, then nothing would be real. The game would be over, and he'd go home.

"Do you understand everything, son?" the kindly old JP asked, waiting for the boy's eyes to signal some sign of comprehension. Jim glanced from the judge to the assistant district attorney, and then back to the judge. Jim nodded, but insisted he didn't want to make a statement until his parents arrived. Once again, Dick White explained that they had been unable to locate Von and Carolyn Taylor. Jim half-turned in his chair and glanced out the window beside him, staring blankly through the slats in the blinds. He was stalling for time, trying to decide what to do.

Sensing the boy's reluctance, Judge Pruitt encouraged Jim to go ahead and cooperate with them. By doing the "right thing," Jim would make it easier on himself in the long run, the judge insisted. Dick White agreed, adding that they already knew what had happened that night at Chester Brooks' store. White reminded Jim of his confession in the Bell County Jail hours earlier. Why not tell the story again and help them to help him?

Jim agreed to cooperate with the two authority figures. After the assistant DA left the room, Jim recited a jumbled confession to Judge Pruitt. The sequence of events was out of order, and the facts were confused — evidence of the boy's disoriented mental

115

state — but the necessary information was there. Jim had implicated himself and his three companions in the murder of Chester Brooks.

After the DA's secretary had transcribed her notes into a typed confession, Judge Pruitt took the draft and read it back to Jim, attempting to verify its accuracy. Jim made one correction, initialed the change, and then signed his name at the bottom. He handed the paper back to Judge Pruitt without reading the confession for himself. Why bother? He had done "the right thing."

As the kindly old judge carried the sworn confession into the hallway and handed the paper to Dick White, Jim stood staring out the window at the railroad tracks a few yards to the east of the courthouse. He saw a freight train rattle by, bound for some unknown destination up north. Jim thought about bolting through the office door, shoving the two men aside, and hopping on the train. He wasn't handcuffed and there were no deputies around. He could certainly outrun the elderly JP and the large assistant DA. It would be easy to get away, and this might be his last chance.

Jim turned around to survey his prospects of escape, but he abandoned the idea immediately. Standing in the doorway were the two people whom he had longed to see: his dad and his mom.

Von and Carolyn Taylor stood staring at their scroungy, long-haired, sixteen-year-old son. They were holding hands, and crying.

Carolyn Taylor had known something bad was going to happen that Saturday. Call it mother's intuition, but she had known Jim was in trouble from the moment she sat down at the breakfast table and felt an icy chill run through her.

She hadn't seen her renegade son for almost a month. They had quarreled before the Christmas holidays, Jim had stormed out of the house, and she had made the decision: no more. No more would she tolerate Jim's lies and thievery and drug abuse. No more would she see her family torn apart by a rebellious, headstrong son who didn't care about anyone but himself. If Jim wouldn't respect her values and abide by her rules, then he couldn't live in her house. Fighting back the tears, she had packed his belongings, stuffed them into paper sacks, and stacked them outside on the covered porch with a note that read:

> Here are your things.
> Please don't come inside.

And he hadn't. The prodigal son had moved in with Ricky Dominick and Walter Frye, and left the Taylor home with the first real peace it had known in four years.

But it was an uneasy peace for Carolyn Taylor, for despite the pain that Jim brought to those who loved him, she did, nevertheless, love him. He was the child who tugged at her heart the strongest because he was the one who needed her most. Now that Jim was gone, she felt a terrible emptiness inside. Losing her son — and then Chester — was almost more than she could bear. Her nerves had been on edge for weeks; she couldn't sleep or eat or think. And now, the bad feeling came. Jim was in trouble, and she knew it.

Carolyn finished her cup of black coffee and dressed. She intended to find her runaway son and bring him home. Climbing into their blue Ford Granada, her mind raced as she tried to think of places to look for Jim. She decided to begin her search with Mr. Mahler, the elderly grandfather of Walter Frye. She arrived just moments after the sheriff's deputies had taken the boys into custody and driven away toward the Bell County Jail.

Even before Carolyn stood on Mr. Mahler's front porch and asked him about the charges against the boys — before she felt the numbing chill when she heard the word "murder" for the first time — she had known somehow. From the moment she had learned of Chester Brooks' death four weeks earlier, she had suspected Jim's involvement in the savagery. She remembered turning to Von and asking him if he thought Jim did it. "Yes," had come the reply.

But when the Mexican man had been arrested and the evidence against him seemed conclusive, Carolyn had blocked the suspicion and fear from her mind. She had wanted to believe that her son had nothing to do with the death of her dearest friend and that Jim wasn't capable of such a brutal act against anyone, let alone against Chester. But she had always known.

"All right," she said through clenched teeth as she pounded the steering wheel with her fist, wiped the tears from her eyes, and drove home to pick up Von and the two younger children.

117

"Jim thinks he's such a big man; let him get out of this mess all by himself."

And so, Von and Carolyn Taylor had intentionally not been at home when the DA's office tried to reach them. They had driven to their forty acres of farmland near Chester Brooks' store and had spent the afternoon cutting firewood. They had vented their hurt and rage against Jim by hacking, slashing, and sawing section after section of oak logs. Logs like the one atop Aggie Harrison's grave in the New Hope Cemetery.

The Taylors had no way of knowing that their son had become involved in another life-threatening situation, one as potentially deadly as that tombstone accident some five years before. They believed that because Jim was a juvenile, the authorities couldn't question him without one of them being present. They thought if they refused to bail Jim out of trouble immediately, perhaps jail would scare him. Maybe someone could finally teach Jim the lesson that he had refused to learn: accountability for his actions.

They had no way of knowing that their son had already done "the right thing." In their absence, the criminal justice system had taught Jim about accountability, all right, but the lesson wasn't nearly over.

The young outlaw had placed the noose around his own neck. Now all the DA had to do was tighten the rope.

When Jim turned from watching the northbound freight train rattle past the courthouse window, he saw his parents standing just inside the DA's office. He felt a great sense of relief until he noticed their reddened, tear-streaked eyes and saw the hurt and the anger and the disbelief reflected in them. Slowly, like a penitent puppy facing a severe scolding, he walked over to face his parents. Jim placed his arms around Carolyn, pulling her close to him. He felt his mother's body stiffen and recoil at his touch. She did not return his hug.

Jim then turned to embrace his father, something that he had seldom done while growing up. The ex-football player had always seemed too rugged and tough for sissy-stuff like hugs, but Jim reached for his dad without thinking.

"Have you said anything?" Von asked him.

"Yes, sir."

"Well then, son, you've really done it this time."

Frightened by the foreboding in his father's voice, Jim glanced toward his mother, searching for the comfort that he usually found in her eyes. He saw nothing.

"If I were big enough," she said in a voice that Jim did not recognize, "I would kill you with my bare hands."

Jim felt her hatred and contempt and loathing sear him to his very soul. He suddenly wished that he were like Chester Brooks — dead. Then maybe he wouldn't hurt so bad.

"I wouldn't worry about killing your boy, Mrs. Taylor," Dick White's voice intruded. "He and his friends have committed murder, and we intend to see that they're punished to the fullest extent of the law. In Texas, that means the electric chair."

Carolyn felt the blood drain from her face as she turned to confront the assistant DA. Moments before, she had hated Jim and wanted to make him pay for what he had done to Chester Brooks. In anger, she had talked of taking his life, but she hadn't meant it. Now, as images of her sixteen-year-old son being strapped into "Old Smokey" took shape inside her head, she felt a desperation she had never known. If she must choose between loyalty to her dead friend or loyalty to her child, she had no choice but to protect her son. All the rage she had previously felt for Jim was transferred to the sneering man who intended to see her son fry.

Whether or not he sensed Carolyn's animosity or noticed Von's clenched fists, Dick White took his leave of the Taylors, suggesting that they find a lawyer for their son right away. Jim was to be brought before the juvenile court on Monday, where the DA's office would ask that the court retain the boy in custody until a motion could be filed. The DA's office intended to petition the juvenile court to waive its jurisdiction, certify Jim as an adult, and turn him over for criminal prosecution and the death penalty.

Overwhelmed by the gravity of the situation, Jim assured his parents that he hadn't killed Chester Brooks. He had gone to the store to rob the old man, but he had changed his mind and tried to call it off. He had never intended for Chester to be hurt, and he hadn't been present when the blows were struck.

Listening to her son's tearful confession, Carolyn sensed the

119

sincerity of Jim's remorse and the pain in his pleas for forgiveness. She felt relieved, somehow, that Jim hadn't been the one to strike Chester. He was there and he was involved, but he hadn't been the one, thank God. For that she was grateful.

The Taylors spent several moments counseling their son before they walked Jim back down the hall to Sheriff Walker's office. They assured him that they would find a lawyer for Monday's hearing and that, with God's help, they would get through this ordeal together, somehow. Standing in the doorway of the sheriff's office, Jim embraced both of his parents again.

This time, his mother hugged him back.

By the time Von and Carolyn Taylor climbed inside their blue Granada, turned the corner in front of the courthouse, and began the forty-minute drive back to Temple, the lights inside Josie's Restaurant had dimmed. The quiet little town of Groesbeck had nodded off to sleep.

With tomorrow's sunrise, however, things would be different. By then, rumors about the long-haired killers would have spread throughout the community, and the talk inside Josie's would become ugly. The steel-eyed patrons would gulp down swigs of black coffee, grind out Marlboro cigarette butts, and talk about what they'd like to do to those "goddamned boys" if they met up with them on a dark road at night. They'd save the county some time and money.

But for now, the historic little town slept on amid the shadows of Fort Parker, unaware of the uprising that would come with the dawn.

CHAPTER FOURTEEN

Reaping What He Sowed

"Jim's in trouble," Nancy Castro said just seconds before she darted from my homeroom and disappeared into the swirling swarm of ninth-grade students shoving their way through the crowded halls of Temple High School. I could tell by the anxious look in her eyes that she was deeply troubled, that I had touched on something painful, and that she didn't want me to press her further. I didn't.

Nancy, a pretty, petite brunette with large, soulful eyes, had been a member of my homeroom for almost six months, yet I scarcely knew her. She and twenty-nine other ninth graders with last names C-F filed into my room for thirty minutes once a week as part of an innovative "human relations" program initiated by the new principal. During the weekly sessions, teachers were expected to build rapport and "relate" with students, encouraging them to open up and discuss teenage concerns and personal problems. It was an administrative attempt to personalize the campus so that students wouldn't feel lost among the 2,300+ enrollment in grades nine through twelve.

It was a good idea in theory, but, like many educational theories engineered by those outside the classroom, it didn't work in practice. Teachers had not been trained in the art of counseling, nor had they been given specific strategies for "relating" with students. Most faculty members felt ill-at-ease in discussing personal topics, especially with students whom they did not know. The students, in turn, felt the same reluctance to share their innermost thoughts with strangers who had no business intruding in their personal lives. Poorly planned and poorly executed, the homeroom program was doomed for failure. As the school year progressed, most thirty-minute sessions became either study halls or free-for-alls, dreaded by both teachers and students alike. Absenteeism ran high.

That February morning when I approached Nancy to inquire about Jim Taylor was probably the first time we had talked at length, one-on-one. I knew she was a friend of his because I had seen them together on the parking lot several weeks before Jim dropped out of school. He had walked with his arm around Nancy's shoulder, and it was apparent from the sparkle in her eyes that she felt more for him than mere friendship. Nancy Castro was in love with Jim. She, like so many others, had been hopelessly smitten by his boyish charm and his Paul Newman good looks.

And Jim had cared for Nancy, in the beginning, before her parents had gotten in the way of their relationship. He had been invited to the Castro home many times, and Nancy's parents had liked Jim. Then he was arrested for the church burglaries, and everything changed. Nancy's father, a prominent Temple businessman from a fine old Central Texas family, had issued the ultimatum. The young outlaw was never to set foot on Castro soil again.

Like Shakespeare's star-crossed lovers, however, Jim and Nancy had disobeyed her father's edict, stealing forbidden moments whenever they could, at school, at friends' houses, or at football games. Sometimes, Jim even sneaked into Nancy's second-story bedroom window, willing to risk her father's rage — and a loaded shotgun — for a few brief moments of intimacy. Once, Jim had narrowly escaped detection by jumping from Nancy's window, sprinting across her lawn, and hurdling a neighbor's six-foot fence.

The neighbor, watching from her dining room window, had been startled by the black-hatted cowboy, but she soon forgot the incident. It wasn't until five months later, when she was hired to teach English at Temple High School and found the same black-brimmed outlaw sitting in her CVAE classroom, that the neighbor made the connection. Perhaps my encounter with Jim Taylor had been fated from the very beginning, as though we were destined to meet. Maybe that's how I knew to ask Nancy about Jim on that February morning — I could feel that he was in trouble and needed help.

Jim clearly had been on my mind of late, but perhaps it was because of the book we were reading in class, a gang novel by S. E. Hinton called *The Outsiders*. The novel wasn't part of our vocational English curriculum, but I had added the book in a moment of inspiration, or desperation, using it as a last-ditch effort to hang on to the Dozen.

By midterm, a second member of the group had defected, and I felt a keen sense of loss. My disappointment turned to fear when I overheard several of the boys discussing the economic advantages of quitting school and getting a full-time job. Despite my efforts to make the Dozen feel positive about learning, some saw little value in the long-term investment of an education, preferring instead the short-term gratification of a weekly paycheck, albeit minimum wage. And our school administration seemed all too willing to accommodate the Dozen's defection by encouraging these overaged troublemakers to "test out" with a General Equivalency Diploma (GED).

To quell the talk of mutiny, I had introduced *The Outsiders*. This story about a "hood with potential," who decides to stay in school and make something of his life, would provide me with the opportunity to counsel the boys. It was a strategy that I had used often: allowing books to "show" rather than me "tell." I knew that the Dozen hated sermons from teachers, but they usually tolerated what writers had to say. It was worth a shot, anyway.

Reading the S. E. Hinton novel had reminded me of another "outsider" with potential, and my thoughts turned to Jim. I recalled how I had acquired the class set of books in the first place — with the $25 Jim had collected from the Dozen and presented to me as a Christmas present, some three weeks before he dropped out.

Because I was new to the staff and had no budget to purchase materials for students with reading disabilities, I had been buying supplemental books with money from my monthly paychecks. When the boys found out, they seemed touched that someone cared, and they wanted to show their appreciation. Jim had gone from boy to boy, collecting the money and asking for suggestions about an appropriate Christmas gift. Unable to come

123

up with an acceptable suggestion, the boys had decided on a cash contribution. That last Friday before the Christmas holidays — the last day that he stood in my classroom — Jim had handed me the money, grinned sheepishly, and said, "Get whatever you need, Mrs. Post." I had been thrilled by the Dozen's generosity and genuine feeling, despite the fact that the money may have had questionable origins.

Although accepting gifts from students violated school policy, I knew that a rejection of the Dozen's gift would be interpreted as a rejection of them. I'd worked too hard to risk that, so I accepted the money from Jim and thanked the boys for their thoughtfulness. During the Christmas holidays, I used the money to buy a class set of books I thought they would enjoy reading. Fast-action novels about teenage gangs were always popular, so I took a chance on this adolescent book by Ms. Hinton, even though I wasn't familiar with her work at the time. The boys never asked how I spent the money, and I never told them.

While reading *The Outsiders* and counseling the Dozen about staying in school, I became troubled by recurring thoughts of Jim, and so I had approached Nancy Castro during homeroom and asked about him. "Jim's in trouble," I heard her say again and again as I walked down the hallway toward my classroom in the main building, where the Dozen awaited me.

Unsure of how best to reach Jim, I asked the Dozen to do some checking with their sources on the street. Several of them had either seen Jim around or knew of someone who had. It didn't take them long to find out.

The following morning, Robert Scott, nicknamed "Big Rob" by the Dozen because of his massive size, met me outside my classroom door. A gentle giant with a teddy-bear disposition, Big Rob started to say something, paused, then focused his eyes squarely on the floor, as if he dreaded what he was about to tell me. "It's bad, Mrs. Post," he said at last, placing his arm around me protectively. "It's real bad."

Several members of the Dozen began to gather around, their faces solemn and taunt, as Big Rob told the story about drugs and robbery and murder, and a sixteen-year-old boy caught up in a self-made hell. The plot sounded familiar, only this time it wasn't fiction and the character wasn't make-believe. This time it was Jim, the one that I had believed in, and hoped for, and loved.

The boys' faces blurred into a swirl of sparkling lights, and I dropped my head so they wouldn't see me cry. That's the first thing you learn in Education 101: A teacher must always be in control and never show emotion. Professional distance, it's called. Yet I felt my heart splinter into a thousand jagged pieces, just as it had done on that January morning when I stood in this same hall, listening to the thumping of his cowboy boots as he walked away. That fateful January morning, five days before his gang hit Chester Brooks' store and transformed him into a black-hatted fugitive, just like the one I saw running from Nancy Castro's house and springing over my backyard fence.

It was bad, all right. Real bad.

After Assistant DA Dick White had obtained Jim's written confession at the Groesbeck courthouse, he turned the three murder suspects over to Sheriff Walker. Seventeen-year-old Wes Folger, a legal adult under Texas statutes, was taken to the Limestone County Jail, an old, primitive, three-story structure located two blocks west of the courthouse. The deteriorating, red-brick building served as an austere reminder of what Texas jails were like before modern reforms were enacted to improve jail standards.

Standing stern and somber in the shadows of the city's water tower, the T-shaped facility housed the jailer and his wife (who prepared the food for the prisoners), along with as many as twenty-four inmates housed in the half-dozen solitary cells on the first floor or in the open, eight-man dormitory cellblocks on the second and third floors. There, Wes Folger remained until his lawyer petitioned the court to release him on bond.

Sheriff Walker made arrangements for Jim and Walter to be confined at the McLennan County Juvenile Detention Center in Waco, some forty-five minutes west of Groesbeck. Limestone County, in the process of renovating its juvenile facility, could not house the boys overnight because of security problems.

The Groesbeck juvenile center, located on the third floor of the courthouse above Walker's office, hadn't completed renovating a cellblock unit to lock up the alleged murderers at night.

Walker's deputies had, therefore, handcuffed the two boys, loaded them into the back of a squad car, and transported them to Waco, traveling over the same territory where Quanah Parker and his band of Comanche renegades had terrorized the Texas frontier.

By the time the Limestone County sheriff's car pulled into the driveway of the McLennan County Juvenile Detention Center at 1200 Clifton Street in Waco, most of the lights in the former rest home facility were out. The sheriff's deputies deposited their prisoners within a matter of minutes, advising the juvenile staff that they would return on Monday morning to transport Jim and Walter back to Groesbeck for their detention hearing.

Under Texas law, juveniles had to be brought before the juvenile court within three days of their arrest to determine if there was sufficient cause to retain them in custody. At the hearing on Monday, the judge would listen to evidence in the Chester Brooks murder case and would rule in one of two ways. He could release the youths if the State failed to prove that there was probable cause to believe that a crime had been committed and that these boys had committed it. Or, he could order that Jim and Walter be confined to the Waco juvenile center if he believed that the State's evidence supported their commission of a serious crime and if their criminal behavior required intense supervision to protect society.

Juveniles accused of serious crimes in Texas were not eligible to be released on bond, unless they had been certified to stand trial as adults. The statutes did provide, however, that their cases be reviewed by the juvenile court every seven to ten days to determine if there was a change in circumstance to warrant their release from the juvenile detention facility.

After the sheriff's deputies had gone, Jim and Walter were unhandcuffed and led into the cafeteria, where a staff member briefed them on the rules. The juvenile officer then led the boys down a side hall toward their cells, where they were to remain in solitary confinement throughout their stay at the juvenile facility. After the officer confiscated each boy's boots and belt, he slammed the metal doors shut, leaving each boy a prisoner of his own mind.

Jim threw himself down on the twin-sized cot and felt the

126

mattress, paper-thin and plastic, rise up to meet him. With his back braced against the cold concrete wall, he glanced around the stark-white room, an eight-by-ten box resembling the holding cell where he had cracked up just hours before. Despite the sparse furnishings, he had lucked out; at least his room had a toilet. Only two cells in the sixteen-room detention center had plumbing. The other prisoners had to urinate into plastic milk bottles with the tops cut out; or, if they needed to relieve themselves further, the inmates had to knock on the metal doors for the guard to escort them to a restroom down the hall.

And Jim had a window this time, a small one covered by a chain link fence, and a steel plate with fifty-two holes layered on top of the fence. When daylight came, he peered out into the barren yard, across the fence, and toward some houses across the street. He stood there for hours, watching in silence, without a book, a radio, a television, or a human voice to distract him from his solitary vigil.

Cornered and caged, Jim felt rage against the authority figures who had used their cunning to trap him. He had done the "right thing" and cooperated with the assistant DA, and look where it got him. Jim became surly and morose, vowing that he'd never tell anyone anything again. When a court-appointed psychologist came to question him several days later, Jim unleashed his wrath against the system. He railed and raged throughout the doctor's questioning, convincing the psychologist that the boy was dangerous and should be locked away for society's protection.

Without realizing, Jim had entrapped himself further in the snares of criminal prosecution.

The interior of the 77th District Court, which might have been used as a movie set for *Inherit the Wind* or *To Kill a Mockingbird,* seemed more like a museum than anything else. As Jim sat at the scarred, mahogany defense table and waited for the detention hearing to begin, he turned his head ninety degrees to pan the pristine courtroom.

The many rows of wooden theater seats with their ornate, wrought-iron framework stood virtually deserted, except for a handful of somber-faced people seated near the side door. The antiquated ceiling fans suspended from high, wooden beams stood motionless, their metal blades collecting dust until the summer. The semicircular balcony at the rear of the courtroom, with its brass railing reflecting sunlight from the rectangular window below, probably had been marked "colored" in years past, back during the time when the Joe Johnston Confederate veterans had been active in these parts. A musty odor permeated the chamber and, despite a central heating unit added during renovations, the courtroom felt cold and uncomfortable.

Seated to Jim's immediate right was Walter Frye, who sat drumming his fingers on the table and leaving thick fingerprint smudges on the glass top. He turned his head periodically and scanned the faces, watching for his mother, who had not yet arrived from Temple.

Next to Walter sat Don Folger, who had surrendered to authorities earlier that afternoon. Don had gone into hiding at a friend's house when he learned of his brother's arrest, but he had later contacted his parents, and they had persuaded him to turn himself in. In the company of his parents and his lawyer, Jerry Secrest of Temple, Don had arrived in Groesbeck a few hours before the juvenile detention hearing began.

To the right of Don and at the far end of the defense table sat Mr. Secrest, a prominent criminal attorney who had recently defended a boy accused of raping a girl, slitting her throat from ear-to-ear, and leaving her for dead in a deserted field. Secrest occasionally whispered something to his young client, and Don nodded nervously as he stared at the American flag, standing next to the judge's bench immediately in front of him.

Seated to Jim's left was Joe Cannon, a highly respected Groesbeck lawyer who had agreed to defend Jim despite the unpopularity of the case. A slender Southern gentleman in the tradition of Atticus Finch or Ashley Wilkes, Cannon was refined, genteel, and soft-spoken. Educated at the University of Texas and active in Democratic politics, Cannon had been elected by his Limestone County constituents to serve in the Texas legislature from 1959 to 1963, making him the youngest legislator in the history of the county. Folks liked Joe Cannon because he was bright, personable, and hard working; but, more than that, they admired him because he was honest, a trait sometimes rare in Texas politics.

128

Cannon had liked Jim from the moment he met the boy. He was impressed by Jim's polite behavior, his forthrightness, and his genuine remorse. Cannon had been straightforward with Jim, explaining the seriousness of the charges against him and insisting that the boy tell him everything, exactly as it happened. "Don't ever lie to me," Cannon warned him. "I can't help you if you lie, and I won't defend you if I can't trust you."

Cannon had rehearsed Jim for the juvenile detention hearing, explaining that the court's purpose was to determine whether or not there was sufficient cause to retain the boy in custody. The DA would present evidence to demonstrate "probable cause," and at that point Cannon could better determine what kind of a case the State had against Jim.

In addition, Cannon explained that Jim had been charged with violating Section 7.01 of the Texas Penal Code, a recently revised statute known as the "Law of Principals." According to the provisions of this law, a person could bear criminal responsibility for the conduct of another. If a person were present during the commission of a felony and did nothing to stop the crime, that person was guilty of the felony — whether or not he actively participated in the act.

In Texas courts, each man was his brother's keeper. There was no longer any such thing as an "accomplice" or an "accessory" to a crime. In murder cases where there were multiple conspirators, it was too difficult for law enforcement to determine which suspect actually did the killing because felons frequently lied to protect themselves. To streamline the law, simplify prosecution, and clear the overcrowded court dockets, the statute had been amended to eliminate the accessory charge. In the eyes of the law, Jim Taylor bore criminal responsibility for what happened outside Chester Brooks' store because he didn't stop Wes Folger. Legally, there was no difference between what Jim did and what Wes did.

Cannon's explanation to Jim ended when he noticed Judge Clarence Ferguson entering the courtroom from his second-floor chambers next door. Ferguson, a balding, bespectacled, sixty-five-year-old jurist, climbed the red carpeted steps to the elevated platform and seated himself in the high-backed, upholstered chair behind his richly-carved mahogany bench.

Judge Ferguson was something of a local hero in Limestone County, with a long and distinguished career in public office. During the 1930s, with only two years of college behind him, he began his public servant role as the principal of the Mustang Springs school, earning a salary of $80 a month. He then decided to become a lawyer and entered the profession the hard way — without going to law school. Instead, Ferguson had borrowed the detailed college notes of a friend who had attended the University of Texas Law School in Austin, and he had studied for the 1938 state law exam on his own. Few folks were surprised when he passed. Ferguson was known to have a brilliant legal mind.

His career as the Limestone County prosecutor was interrupted, however, when Ferguson was called up with the 36th National Guard Division during World War II. Ferguson distinguished himself in battle, earned numerous decorations, and was promoted to the rank of Army major. The real test of his endurance came when he was captured by the Germans and spent two years in a POW hell-hole. The tough, young Army major displayed the same fortitude as the early settlers at Parker's Fort had shown, refusing to give up despite the odds against him.

Ferguson lived to return to his Central Texas prairies, where he distinguished himself in politics, first as a county judge presiding over the four-member commissioners court and then as the 77th District Judge for Limestone County since 1952. Although Ferguson was not without his political enemies, he was known as a fair-minded man and was regarded with respect, especially by the lawyers who came before his bench.

Judge Ferguson, acting in the capacity of juvenile judge for the detention hearing, began the hour-long proceeding in much the same manner as Cannon had explained to Jim. One unexpected thing did occur, however, when Walter Frye's mother arrived in court without legal counsel for her son. Under questioning by the judge, Mrs. Frye explained that she could not afford an attorney for Walter and wished the court to appoint one for him. When Judge Ferguson asked Mrs. Frye why she had not advised the court of her need for counsel prior to this hearing, she explained that she had not known to do so.

Judge Ferguson, clearly annoyed by the legal interruption, recessed the hearing, rushed across the hallway to the district clerk's office, and nabbed the first lawyer he could find, L. L. Geren. The elderly Geren, a prominent Groesbeck attorney and long-time friend, had administered the oath of office to Ferguson when the war hero was sworn in as district judge some twenty-five years earlier. Ferguson and Geren went back a long way, so the judge believed that he could count on his friend for a legal favor.

Geren, however, vehemently objected to Judge Ferguson's request that he serve as the court-appointed attorney for Walter Frye. Chester Brooks had been a friend of Geren's for many years, and there was no way the lawyer could represent one of his killers. Ferguson urged Geren to reconsider, explaining that he didn't have time to find another attorney. The detention hearing had to be held that afternoon, within the three-day time limit following the juveniles' arrests, or the court would be forced to let the boys go free. Ferguson assured Geren that all he had to do was sit beside Walter Frye during the hearing and protect the boy's legal rights. Afterward, Ferguson promised to allow Geren to resign from the case, if he so desired.

Geren, not wishing the boys to go free on a technicality, reluctantly accepted the court's appointment. The lawyer followed Judge Ferguson down the hallway and into the 77th District courtroom, where he was given several minutes to confer with his client before the hearing reconvened.

With all juveniles now represented by counsel, Judge Ferguson listened to the sworn statements of witnesses and examined the evidence presented by Sheriff Walker's department connecting the boys to the murder of Chester Brooks. Joe Cannon objected twice, insisting that two pieces of evidence should not be admitted. First of all, Cannon pointed out, the bloodstained concrete block introduced as the murder weapon had not been tagged by deputies before they removed it from the murder scene. Because the untagged block had been in the possession of several people before being brought into the courtroom, the "chain of custody" had been broken. Who could say that this block was the actual murder weapon?

And secondly, Cannon insisted, the murder confession of Jim Taylor was inadmissible because the statement had been obtained in violation of his client's civil rights. The boy had not waived his right to have his parents and an attorney present during his questioning by Justice of the Peace Marvin Pruitt. Twice, Jim had requested to speak with Von and Carolyn Taylor, but was told both times that the DA's office couldn't "get ahold of them." Furthermore, Cannon pointed out, the assistant DA and the justice of the peace may have led Jim to believe that his statement would be used "for" him as well as "against" him. According to the proper reading of the juvenile warning—the Miranda rights for juveniles—a statement could only be used "against" the accused. To suggest otherwise constituted coercion, Cannon insisted.

Judge Ferguson overruled Cannon on both objections, declaring that the sheriff's office could, no doubt, trace the chain of custody for the concrete block and link it to the scene of Chester Brooks' murder. Furthermore, Ferguson knew that oral confessions were rarely stricken in pretrial hearings, regardless of the circumstances by which they were obtained. He would let an appeals court handle the coercion allegation.

Based on the evidence presented, Judge Ferguson ruled that the DA, Don Caldwell, had proven "probable cause." He therefore ordered that the three juveniles be held in the McLennan County Detention Center, with their cases to be reviewed by the juvenile court every seven to ten days. Before dismissing the detention hearing, Judge Ferguson instructed the boys and their parents to meet with Limestone County juvenile officers on the third floor of the courthouse, where a family history would be taken.

Joe Cannon gave Jim a few final instructions, shook hands with Von and Carolyn Taylor, and then left for his law office across the street, just north of the courthouse. Jerry Secrest, likewise, advised Don Folger and his parents about what to expect upstairs, then climbed into his car and made the forty-five-minute drive back to Temple. L. L. Geren approached Judge Ferguson and immediately requested to be withdrawn from the case, or so the records of the juvenile court docket indicated. Walter Frye disagreed with the records, however, insisting that they had been "doctored" after the fact.

According to Walter, Geren had sat inside the juvenile office and questioned him for almost an hour while the two juvenile officers were busy talking with the Taylor and Folger families.

During their alleged conversation, Walter insisted that Geren obtained privileged information about Chester Brooks' murder.

Both Mr. and Mrs. Folger later testified that they saw the court-appointed attorney speaking with the boy. Geren, however, denied that such an interview took place and suggested that he may have been confused with a balding juvenile officer who resembled him in appearance.

The controversy over whether or not Geren questioned the boy would have legal significance two months later, for Geren was again to enter the Chester Brooks murder case — but this time on the side of the prosecution.

In compliance with Judge Ferguson's order, the Limestone County juvenile department prepared a detailed "Social History" of each boy's family. After interviewing Jim and his parents, case worker Charles Wilson prepared a summary statement for Judge Ferguson, outlining two important conclusions. First, Wilson perceived that Jim, despite his street-smart exterior, was still very much a child. "There is no indication," Wilson wrote in his report, "that he [Jim] realizes the nature of what he has been charged. He seems to believe that if he ignores the problem, it will go away."

In addition, Wilson made a clinical observation about Jim's homelife, as if trying to explain its effect on Jim's low self-esteem. "The Taylor family seems to be very stable, with no major conflicts other than discipline problems with James." However, Wilson continued, "this could very possibly be a home of discipline and no outward show of love and affection."

No outward show of love and affection. The words troubled me, for I had recently met Jim's mother and observed her to be quite the opposite. Our first encounter came when Carolyn Taylor stopped by my classroom to pick up an audiotape that the Dozen had made for Jim.

The boys had wanted to talk with Jim personally and to offer him their support because several of them had done jail time and knew what it was like to be locked up. However, they had not been allowed to visit Jim at either the McLennan County Detention Center, where he spent eleven days in solitary confinement,

133

or at the Freestone County Jail, where Jim had been transferred after he turned seventeen on February 28, 1977.

Sensing the Dozen's frustration with the legal system and their hostility toward law enforcement, I had suggested that the boys send their best wishes to Jim via a recorded message. I telephoned Mrs. Taylor, and she agreed to take the cassette tape to Jim, who was being held in the Limestone County Jail in Groesbeck following the release of Wes Folger on a $10,000 bond.

I'm not sure what I had expected Jim's mother to be like, but Carolyn Taylor didn't fit the profile I had been taught in education classes. The pert, petite woman with the sparkling eyes and the pixie haircut reminded me of a June Cleaver type, an all-American mom who befriended every kid in the neighborhood, bandaged all the injured dogs, and handled any crisis.

As we sat side-by-side in the classroom desks, talking for more than an hour about her troubled son, I found Carolyn to be warm, personable, and genuine. There was something very remarkable about her — an inner strength I couldn't quite fathom. Despite the heartache Jim had brought his family, she managed a courageous smile and spoke openly of their anguish.

Carolyn shared the toll that Jim's tragedy had taken on her husband who, despite his massive size and phenomenal strength, had spent the first three days in bed. Physically sickened by what his son had done, Von believed he had failed somehow as a father, and he seemed a broken man.

She related the verbal abuse her other children suffered at school after gossip spread about Jim's involvement in the murder. She talked about holding Gena and Glenn and Julie, trying to quiet their heartbroken sobs, yet never allowing herself to cry. She knew Von and the children depended on her to be strong. She wore a stalwart smile and concealed her private pain. But behind the locked bathroom door where no one could see, the tears had come. And with them came the question: Why?

She had first asked that question of Reverend Guinn Williams, her pastor at Immanuel Baptist Church, when he came to minister to the Taylor family shortly after Jim's arrest. "Why would Jim do such a thing?" she asked as she peered into the pensive eyes of her soft-spoken pastor.

Carolyn had turned to Reverend Williams often in the aftermath of Jim's juvenile crime spree. He always brought such comfort and assurance; surely he could help her find some meaning in all of this. Yet, Reverend Williams had seemed at a loss to explain Jim's actions.

The pastor, who had baptized a ten-year-old Jim during a church revival service, recalled the boy as having a "kind and gentle soul." The boy had always been faithful in his church attendance, and the minister believed that Jim had found a personal relationship with God. Reverend Williams could not reconcile Jim's involvement in the murder.

At the request of the Taylors, the Baptist minister had spoken to Jim briefly in the McLennan County detention facility. During a visit to the Taylor home the following day, Reverend Williams shared his conversation with Jim's heartbroken parents. "I think Jim believes in God," Reverend Williams said, sitting in the Taylors' living room and sipping coffee.

As Von and Carolyn listened earnestly, Reverend Williams described how he and Jim had talked for thirty minutes while sitting in the dim dining room of the juvenile facility in Waco. "I asked Jim if he felt he was a Christian. He said he'd done some things he shouldn't have done, but he felt he had a relationship with God."

Carolyn Taylor closed her eyes and breathed a heavy sigh. "Do you think Jim meant that?" she asked.

The middle-aged minister paused a moment to swallow the coffee and consider his answer. "Jim's a very kind young man," he began, "he's not hard or haughty. He's very kind, and I'm sure he wanted to answer the way I wanted him to answer. He had the desire to please. But, at the same time, I think Jim would have told me if we'd been traveling a road he didn't want to go."

Reverend Williams confessed to the Taylors that he had been torn about whether to emphasize God's forgiveness or God's judgment when he spoke with Jim. Finally, he had decided to share both. "God's in the business of forgiving sin," he had told the tormented, guilt-ridden boy as they sat before an opened Bible in the detention center dining room. "The scripture says, 'Call upon Me and I will answer thee and show thee great and mighty things.' "

Reverend Williams recalled how Jim had stared solemnly at

the Bible while the pastor turned to 1 John and read another passage: "If we confess our sins, He is faithful and just to forgive us our sins and to cleanse us from all unrighteousness." The pastor had stressed that Jim's part was simply to confess; that was all he could do. He couldn't forgive; he couldn't right the wrong. He could only confess. But, the minister continued, if Jim were honest with God and honest with himself, God had promised "I'll forgive."

The pastor had then reminded the boy that God was both a God of love and a God of judgment. Reverend Williams had turned in his Bible to Galatians 6:7 and read: "Be not deceived; God is not mocked: for whatsoever a man soweth, that shall he also reap." The pastor's eyes had focused squarely on Jim. "We must reap what we sow, son. You understand that, don't you?" Somber and contrite, Jim had nodded his head in quiet affirmation.

The minister related to the Taylors how he and Jim had then bowed their heads in prayer. Jim had prayed silently, confessing his sin and seeking God's forgiveness. As Reverend Williams concluded his own prayer, he noticed the boy's hands trembling.

Moved by Jim's deep remorse, the minister had sought to comfort him. Reverend Williams shared with Jim one of his favorite verses of Scripture, a passage ending with the words ". . . unto Him who is able to do exceeding abundantly above all that which we ask or think." Reverend Williams had wanted Jim to know that God could do *big* things in his life, seemingly impossible things. "Not only will God do more than we ask for, Jim, but He will do more than we've even thought about asking for." With that promise of hope and a firm embrace, the pastor had left the boy.

After Reverend Williams told the Taylors about his conversation with Jim, he attempted to minister to their needs. Recognizing their feelings of guilt and failure, he counseled them. "Parents must not take the blame for what their children have done," the pastor insisted, "otherwise, parents would stay in trouble all the time." He assured the Taylors that they had done everything they could for Jim. The boy had done fine until he reached the age of fifteen. Then, Jim had made the choices, not them. They weren't responsible.

Reverend Williams also reminded them that Jim needed to face what he had done. "We shouldn't try to minimize his ac-

136

tions," the minister told them. "The Bible teaches that God holds each man accountable." Both parents dropped their eyes, focused on the empty coffee cups, and stared stoically.

Sensing their pain, Reverend Williams had hastened to assure the parents of God's mercy. "Romans 8:28 teaches us that all things work together for good to them that love God and are called according to His purpose." He explained that the Bible didn't say each individual thing was good. Certainly, murder was not good. "But this . . . and this . . . and this, all working together, will produce good for those who love God," he said. "God promised to bring something good from every situation, even this one. And God always honors His Word."

Carolyn Taylor must have found comfort in Reverend Williams' counsel, for she mentioned the Romans passage when she came to pick up the Dozen's tape for Jim. "In a way," she said, "I'm almost glad this happened."

I must have glanced at her in disbelief, for she hastened to explain. "All things work together for good, you know. We had completely lost Jim. There was no hope. And now, we have our son back."

She seemed to take comfort in that. As she placed the Dozen's tape inside her purse and stood to go, I reached out and hugged her. I'm not sure why I did that. We had met only an hour before, yet I felt I had known her for a very long time. Perhaps it was because she was so like Jim. As she returned my embrace, I felt her body tremble. She fought to stay in control; she had to be strong, for all of them.

I liked Carolyn Taylor, right from the very beginning. I marveled at her quiet courage, her firm resolve, and her deep convictions. I wondered whether I, under similar circumstances, could have endured such heartache.

My meeting with Jim's mother had been an emotional one, and tears flooded my eyes as I watched her walk away. Listening to her footsteps on the hollow corridor, I was reminded of a similar sound from weeks before, back when her errant son had first begun his fateful journey. Now the prodigal child had finally returned. Carolyn Taylor had her son back.

But, I wondered, for how long?

CHAPTER FIFTEEN

Intimidating the Witness

*L*imestone County DA Don Caldwell lost no time in tightening the noose around Jim Taylor's neck. On February 21, three days after Jim signed the confession, Caldwell placed a motion before the juvenile court, asking Judge Ferguson to waive jurisdiction and certify Jim to stand trial as an adult.

Caldwell gestured toward the stoical boy who sat with head bowed and pointed out the seriousness of Jim's crime. If the boy were tried and convicted in a juvenile court, he would serve only one year in a reform school before being released on his eighteenth birthday. Such a punishment, the DA argued, was far too lenient for the crime of capital murder.

The juvenile court agreed. Ruling in favor of the DA's motion, Judge Ferguson ordered certification hearings to be held for Jim and his two co-defendants. On March 11, the three juveniles and their lawyers appeared during separate proceedings before the 77th District Juvenile Court in Groesbeck.

Once again, Caldwell presented the evidence linking Jim with the murder of Chester Brooks. In addition, the DA called the court's attention to the incriminating study made by the court-appointed psychologist at the McLennan County Juvenile Detention Center in Waco. Holding the clinical report in his hand, the DA alluded to several passages documenting the boy's belligerent behavior and violent temperament. Jim Taylor was one of the worst cases that the examining psychologist had ever seen.

Joe Cannon rose to his feet and objected to the court's consideration of the psychological report. His client had neither waived his right concerning psychological testing nor voluntarily agreed to participate. As a matter of fact, Cannon argued, Jim had vehemently opposed such questioning, as evidenced by his hostility toward the psychologist. The boy never should have been tested in the first place; such action clearly violated Jim's civil rights.

Cannon saw a sharp flicker in the DA's eyes. The stress that had surfaced since Cannon accepted this controversial case had become more blatant, permeating the courtroom walls and spilling over into his private life. Several folks in Limestone County made it plain that they didn't think the former legislator should do much to defend the Taylor boy.

It would have been easier if Cannon had walked away from this one, but the idealistic young lawyer lived by a code of ethics that wouldn't allow compromise. He had accepted the case because the boy needed help, and, despite the personal or professional risk involved, Cannon intended to defend Jim Taylor.

Relying on the legal acumen that had earned him a name in Central Texas, Cannon made a surprise move. Turning to face the county prosecutor, the determined defense lawyer requested that Judge Ferguson dismiss the juvenile proceedings against James Edward Taylor because the court had no jurisdiction to conduct the certification hearing.

Caldwell's face reddened as Cannon cited Section 54.02 of the Texas Family Code and outlined the district attorney's failure to follow proper procedure. According to law, the State must notify the juvenile of a hearing by serving a summons directly to the child. Failure to serve the summons to the child would deprive the juvenile court of its jurisdiction to conduct hearings or to make orders.

The Family Code was clear, Cannon argued, yet Caldwell had cut corners. The DA had not requested that a summons be served to either Jim or his co-defendants. Such notification might have been unnecessary if Jim's parents, acting in his behalf, had waived the summons in writing. However, such was not the case.

As a result of the legal blunder, the juvenile had been denied due process. Cannon argued that the court had not established jurisdiction over Jim, and without jurisdiction, could neither waive its authority over the boy nor certify him to stand trial as an adult. Cannon moved to dismiss.

Judge Ferguson listened carefully to Cannon's argument, deliberated for a moment, then decided to overrule the motion. Peering down at the blond-haired boy, now clean-cut and neatly dressed, the judge waived the juvenile court's jurisdiction. Judge Ferguson certified Jim to stand trial as an adult for the murder of Chester Brooks and ordered the boy held in the Limestone County Jail on a $10,000 bond.

Jim's face showed little emotion as the deputies led him from the courtroom. He had retreated into himself, blocking out everything, just as the juvenile officer had observed in the "Social History" lying on Judge Ferguson's desk.

Later that morning of March 11, when Judge Ferguson made similar rulings in the certification hearings of Walter Frye and Don Folger, their lawyers gave notice of appeal. Raymond Matkin of Waco, the new court-appointed attorney for Walter Frye, joined forces with Jerry Secrest of Temple, the defense lawyer for Don Folger. Secrest, having recently defended a seventeen-year-old rapist/slasher, knew the intricateness of juvenile law. Working in consultation with one another, the two lawyers prepared their briefs for the Tenth Court of Civil Appeals in Waco, hoping to have the certification judgment overturned because of the summons mix-up.

Joe Cannon, realizing that the Taylor family could not afford the financial expense of such a legal battle, chose not to join his colleagues in their motions for an appeal. Besides, Cannon reasoned, if Matkin and Secrest should succeed in getting Judge Ferguson's ruling reversed, Jim would also benefit from the decision. The result would be the same. Therefore, Cannon opted to hold his cards and keep his ace in reserve.

Pending the outcome of the appeal, the Limestone County district attorney chose to postpone immediate prosecution of the three juveniles. Why spend time and money on a legal action that may be overturned? Caldwell reasoned. Therefore, the DA backed away for the time being, preferring instead to concentrate his efforts on prosecuting seventeen-year-old Wes Folger, the legal adult. There would be plenty of time for the others.

Concern about the DA's handling of the certification hearings spread quickly throughout Groesbeck legal circles, and the talk eventually found its way into the conversation of patrons at

140

Josie's Restaurant across the street. In a town steeped in a tradition of law and order, there was no way folks were going to stand by and let those young outlaws get away with murder because of some legal loophole. Chester Brooks deserved better than that.

Several of Chester's friends approached the county commissioners court and asked it to appoint a special prosecutor who knew the law and would make sure that "them boys got what's comin' to 'em." Yielding to the pressure of the citizens from Coit and Kosse, the commissioners court hired one of the finest legal minds in the county, L. L. Geren.

Geren, a silver-haired fox known for his shrewd maneuvering in the courtroom, had been a personal friend of Chester Brooks, and he welcomed the opportunity to see justice done. Together with his law partner, James Bradley, Geren began to prepare the prosecution case against Wes Folger. Because of the extensive investigative work done by Sheriff Walker and his deputies, it was virtually an open-and-shut case.

In addition to having the murder weapon and Jim Taylor's sworn confession, the sheriff's department had provided another piece of incriminating evidence: the set of old keys. On the day of the boys' arrests, Chief Deputy Bill Fletcher had followed up on information given by the informant, Hank Worley. During a search of Ricky Dominick's house in Belton — the place where Jim and Walter had been staying before and after the Brooks robbery — Fletcher recovered a King Edward cigar box from beneath an attic rafter.

Examining the contents of the box for possible clues, the deputy found several old keys inside. A couple of the keys were marked "YALE," and probably belonged to some sort of generic padlock. Fletcher's suspicions were aroused, however, when he examined two keys with the numbers 232 engraved on them. Following up on a hunch, Fletcher contacted Assistant DA Dick White and attorney P. K. Reiter, the new executor of the Chester Brooks estate. Together, the three men drove out to the First State Bank of Kosse.

There they met Frank Mitchell, the mail carrier who had found the body of Chester Brooks. In addition to working for the U.S. Postal Service in the mornings, Frank also served as president of the local bank in the afternoon. Deputy Fletcher told

Frank his suspicions concerning the keys, and the bank president agreed to cooperate with the investigation.

Frank Mitchell led the three men toward the back of the Kosse First State Bank, which resembled a nostalgic, sepia set from the film *Bonnie and Clyde*. Once inside the vault, Frank inserted a bank key into a lock on a safety deposit box, and Fletcher pushed a key numbered 232 into a second lock on the same box. As Dick White and P. K. Reiter gathered around to watch, they saw the narrow lid to the safety deposit box open.

When Frank Mitchell checked the bank records for the names of deposit box customers, he confirmed the gut feeling that Deputy Fletcher had had all along. The box belonged to one Chester Wade Brooks, deceased. The innocent-looking keys found during the search of Ricky Dominick's house had directly linked Taylor and Frye to the murder victim. A faint smile creased Fletcher's lips, and he nodded his head toward the two Groesbeck attorneys. They had all they needed.

Later, when Jim was questioned about the keys, he couldn't explain why he hadn't taken them with him on that afternoon when they drove out to Cedar Ridge Park to destroy the evidence. He had seen them, all right, but he had intentionally left them behind. What harm could they do? he had asked.

Now that the keys were in the hands of the special prosecutor, he and his three partners were about to find out.

The appointment of L. L. Geren as special prosecutor brought a storm of protests from the covey of defense lawyers. Joe Cannon openly spoke out among his Groesbeck associates, insisting that there was no precedent for such action on the part of the commissioners court. Limestone County rarely required the services of a special prosecutor unless the local district attorney had some conflict of interest in handling a case. When that occurred, a DA from a neighboring county was usually asked to fill in as special prosecutor.

Cannon pointed out that the present Limestone County district attorney had no conflict of interest in handling the Chester Brooks murder case, nor did he have a case load that would prohibit him from carrying out the county's work. Cannon objected to the apparent lynch-mob, vigilante tactics on the part of some "interested parties" within the county.

Raymond Matkin, the defense attorney for Walter Frye, joined Cannon in his outcry. Matkin's vehement objection to L. L. Geren as special prosecutor stemmed from another source, however. Because Geren had served as Walter's court-appointed attorney at the first detention hearing, Matkin alleged a conflict of interest. Matkin insisted that Geren had been privileged to confidential lawyer-client information and that the juvenile's civil rights would be violated if Geren became involved in the prosecution. It was a charge that would be taken all the way to the U.S. Fifth Circuit Court of Appeals before it would finally be resolved five years later.

Even if Geren had obtained information from Walter Frye, as the boy alleged, he wouldn't have needed it to prosecute Wes Folger. Whereas Jim Taylor had placed a noose around his neck by signing a confession, Wes Folger went one step further. He built his own gallows.

Within five weeks of his release on a $10,000 bond, Wes was back inside the Limestone County Jail in Groesbeck. He was rearrested on April 1 because he had, like a proverbial April fool, gone around threatening witnesses. Undoubtedly, Wes had acted out of desperation after he had talked with his lawyer and learned about Old Sparky.

Wes was being represented by James H. Kreimeyer of Belton, a real heavyweight in the criminal law arena. Kreimeyer, a former assistant DA from El Paso, had moved to Bell County to enter private practice. With more than fifteen years of courtroom experience as both prosecutor and defense counsel, the competent and articulate Kreimeyer clearly knew his way around Texas criminal law.

Kreimeyer had gained notoriety in Bell County by prosecuting two teenagers who had sliced open a grandmother's throat and smothered her with a pillow until the gurgling noise stopped. Then, the youths had killed her three-year-old grandchild and stuffed the tiny body down a toilet. Kreimeyer was used to tackling difficult cases, and he wasn't a stranger to blood and gore. The Chester Brooks case almost paled by comparison.

The sharp young defense attorney became involved in the Brooks murder case after he received a phone call from Wes Folger's mother-in-law, advising him that her son-in-law had been taken to the Bell County Jail for questioning. She explained that she had been referred to Kreimeyer by Bob Burleson, a mutual lawyer friend in Temple, and she asked Kreimeyer to meet Wes' family at the jail, where they sat waiting until they could find out something about him.

The Bell County Jail was a couple of blocks down the street from Kreimeyer's office in Belton, so he "went hot-trottin' " over there and got to the boy before they got a statement from him." Actually, when Kreimeyer first arrived at the jail, he was denied access to Wes Folger by Chief Deputy Bill Fletcher of Limestone County. Fletcher explained that they hadn't finished talking with the boy, so the lawyer would have to wait.

At that point Lester Gunn, the Bell County sheriff who was known to be tough-as-nails but fair-as-they-come, intervened in the confrontation. "In my jail," the crusty old sheriff said, "lawyers can talk to their people." With that, the Limestone County deputy had stepped aside.

Kreimeyer spent several minutes in the room with Wes Folger. "I don't know if I'm going to represent you or not on this case," the lawyer said, "but I'll tell you one thing right now. Don't you be talking with these guys. You just shut up."

Wes Folger nodded his head in agreement, and Kreimeyer stepped outside to speak with the mother-in-law, who sat in the waiting room of the Bell County Jail with her tearful daughter, Jill. None of them were aware that Jim Taylor was already standing at the opposite end of the hallway, giving his oral statement to Justice of the Peace Joe Harrison.

After talking with the family, Kreimeyer agreed to accept Wes' case. The lawyer arranged for Wes to be released on bond, and he spent several hours counseling the boy and attempting to prepare a defense. Kreimeyer, in his customary shoot-from-the-hip fashion, leveled with the boy about the weight of evidence against him. In addition to Jim Taylor's incriminating confession, there were also two witnesses whom the State intended to call. Hank Worley, the original informant, would testify concerning what Jim and Walter had told him about Wes' role in the rob-

144

bery/murder. In addition, Ricky Dominick would repeat what he heard Wes say to Jim and Walter while they stood outside the Quality Discount store in Belton: "If the old man is dead, I guess I killed him."

Kreimeyer explained that the Limestone County district attorney intended to make Wes the scapegoat for the Brooks murder because the other three boys were under the age of seventeen when the crime was committed. Under Texas law, the juveniles could receive a sentence of five to ninety-nine years or life imprisonment, but they couldn't be given the death penalty. Seventeen-year-old Wes, on the other hand, was eligible for the same fate as the recently executed Gary Gilmore. "The chances are real good," Kreimeyer said, "that you'll see Old Sparky."

Wes, clearly shaken by the prospect of receiving the electric chair, bolted from his lawyer's office. Acting impulsively and using the same tough-guy tactics he had displayed outside the old man's store in Coit, Wes got into his car later that night and, accompanied by his wife Jill, drove to the Dairy Queen parking lot in Belton. There he found Hank Worley sitting in a two-tone blue, 1975 Chevy van with his girlfriend.

Wes and his wife got out of their car and walked over to the passenger side of the van, where they began speaking to the ashen-faced Worley. Jill leaned against the door with her shoulder and explained that she had read a statement the ex-con made to the Belton police and a Texas Ranger about the Brooks murder. Hank Worley sat motionless inside the van, trying to avoid the mean-eyed gaze of Wes Folger and looking ill at ease until he saw someone approaching. Ricky Dominick walked up to the far side of the van and stood listening.

At that moment, Wes looked Worley squarely in the eyes and spoke in a voice loud enough for Dominick to hear. "My lawyer says I've got a good chance to see Old Sparky." Then, lowering his voice to a cold monotone, Wes continued. "If anyone gives any testimony about me that will hurt me in this case, they'll have something done to them."

With the warning duly delivered, Wes and Jill walked back to their car and disappeared into the darkness. Shortly thereafter, Dominick reported the incident to Limestone County officials, and a warrant was issued for Wes Folger's rearrest.

Brought before the 77th District Court on April 1, Wes was charged with threatening to cause the death or physical harm of the State's witnesses. Judge Ferguson ordered the $10,000 bond revoked and ruled that boy be held in the Limestone County Jail without bail.

Kreimeyer immediately filed a writ of habeas corpus, insisting that the court had acted improperly in denying bail to his client and requesting that a reasonable amount be set. Judge Ferguson considered the defense counsel's writ, but denied the motion for two reasons. First, the judge ruled, the defendant made threats to intimidate witnesses already summoned to testify; such action constituted "a continual, unlawful interference with evidence with the intent to suppress testimony."

Furthermore, the judge pointed out, the evidence against the defendant was such that a Limestone County jury would probably assess the death penalty. Therefore, under Texas law, the court had every right to deny bail.

Kreimeyer gave notice of appeal and filed a brief with the Court of Criminal Appeals in Austin. When the case was finally reviewed in November of that year, the judgment of the trial court was reversed. According to the Court of Criminal Appeals, the evidence in the case was not of sufficient strength to make the death penalty a certainty. Therefore, the court ruled that bail could not be denied to the defendant. Wes Folger was ordered to be released on a $55,000 bond.

But the damage was already done, and most folks at Josie's Restaurant knew about the mean-looking youth who had threatened to kill two witnesses. In addition, a story had circulated about the boy's vow to get even with the Limestone County Sheriff's Department. Back in September, when Chief Deputy Bill Fletcher was inside the county jail preparing to transfer the boy to the Rusk State Hospital for psychoanalysis, Wes had resisted an attempt to have handcuffs placed on him. According to Fletcher's version of the incident, the youth had shouted, "As soon as I get out, I'm gonna come back here and take care of all the sorry bastards that had anything to do with my staying in jail."

The words were spoken in a moment of anger by a young boy clearly frightened for his life. People who knew and loved Wes Folger didn't believe him capable of carrying out a revenge

146

scheme against anyone. James Kreimeyer seemed to share the same opinion, insisting that his client was "basically a good kid."

But Wes Folger seemed to be his own worst enemy. As far as a lot of folks in Limestone County were concerned, Old Sparky would be too good for him.

CHAPTER SIXTEEN

Changes in the Dozen

About the time Wes Folger returned to the Limestone County Jail, stalked into his dingy cell, and heard the barred door slam shut behind him, I was being set free. After months of fighting physical exhaustion from an impossible paperwork load, not to mention mental burnout from the emotional drain of caring about kids and their problems, I had been bailed out. With April came the warming sun, the brilliant Texas bluebonnets, and a much-needed spring break.

With April also came something else — the unexpected telephone call from the Dozen. When the phone rang on that Monday evening, I was standing at my kitchen stove, putting the finishing touches on a fried-chicken dinner for my husband's three children, who were visiting us during spring break.

Joy, LeeAnn, and Neal were a product of Ron's first marriage, which had ended about the same time that the Vietnam War heated up. Helicopter pilots, it seemed, had not only been shot down by the North Vietnamese; they had also sustained heavy casualties on the homefront, and marriages fell apart during their absence.

Ron's two teenage daughters and his eight-year-old son had flown down from their home in Minnesota to bask in the balmy Texas weather, meet their new half-brother, and get reacquainted with their dad. It was the first time we had seen the children since our recent return from Ron's three-year tour of duty in Germany.

"Hey, Mrs. Post," came a robust, cheery voice as I picked up the receiver and balanced it between my chin and shoulder, trying to turn the crispy chicken in the iron skillet at the same time. "This is Robert Scott, and I've got somebody here who wants to talk to you. Hold on a second."

A moment of silence followed while the telephone switched hands, and then came the unmistakable cowboy drawl, "What's going on, lady?"

It was Jim. I motioned for one of the girls to man the iron skillet while I grasped the phone with both hands, straining to hear the familiar voice of the leader of the Dozen. Jim had been released on bond, and he wanted to know if he and Big Rob could stop by later that evening to see me.

Big Rob, it seemed, had already undertaken a role that he would play often during the year Jim was out on bail and awaiting trial: chief bodyguard. Robert, a heavy-set, cowboy-type with baggy Levis, was probably the most sensitive member of the Dozen. With the same "heart of gold" that characterized so many sidekicks in the Louis L'Amour westerns, he responded to a need he saw in Jim.

Without being asked, Big Rob had taken it upon himself to assume responsibility for Jim, driving him from place to place and making sure Jim didn't get a speeding ticket that would give the cops an excuse for throwing him back in jail, as they had done with Wes Folger. In addition, Big Rob saw to it that Jim stayed away from his old doper gang and honored the 10:00 P.M. curfew suggested by Joe Cannon. There would be no slip-ups, not while Big Rob was around.

Although Big Rob and Jim had not been close friends before Jim dropped out of school, I watched a bond develop between them after Jim got into trouble. Robert became very protective of Jim and watched his every move. In a sense, he became his brother's keeper, beginning with that first night when he chaperoned Jim there in my living room. Robert had sat in the brown leather chair next to Jim, swigging a Dr Pepper, making small talk with Ron's daughters, and trying to keep the conversation lighthearted.

With the girls present, I didn't press Jim for details about his arrest, and that was probably best. He seemed preoccupied by the attention he was receiving from the pretty, young female audience. Within moments of their meeting, the girls had been

149

smitten by the black-hatted cowboy with the impish grin and the piercing blue eyes. Whatever power he had over women, I wished I could bottle it.

Although Jim had tried to project his usual devil-may-care, tough-guy image that night, I sensed he was covering his emotions. Jail had changed the leader of the Dozen. He didn't smile as often as before, and when the famous grin did come, it seemed phony and forced. He looked older, seemed quieter and more stoic. Despite his attempts to block out what had happened, he must have wondered about the price yet to be paid.

There had to be moments when he peered through the cell bars and wondered about his fate, just as Gary Gilmore had done during those predawn hours in a Utah prison while he waited for a target to be pinned to his black T-shirt. Certainly there were times during solitary confinement when Jim wondered what was coming next, like Jesse James had done right before the bullet from Bob Ford's gun had ended his waiting.

Jail had changed Jim, all right. As he leaned over to hug me goodbye, I noticed a frightened look mirrored in his eyes. An empty, hollow look, as if he had gone far away, deep within himself, and couldn't find his way back.

Perhaps Big Rob noticed it, too, and felt compelled to reach out to Jim. "You could tell he wanted to change," Robert said later. "He knew he'd gone too far, and it scared him. Jim needed someone to help him."

Robert Scott's devotion to the Dozen's outlaw leader should have come as no surprise to me, for it was a role that he had been destined to play. History books recorded that on April 6, 1882, a heavy-set Missouri man had served as pallbearer in a funeral procession at the Baptist church in Kearny. Inside the metallic casket that he shouldered was the body of his boyhood friend, fatally shot in the back of the head by a "dirty little coward" seeking reward money.

Supported in death, as he had been in life, was the outlaw Jesse James, carried to his final resting place on the shoulders of a friend surnamed Scott.

Despite Robert Scott's attempt to ride roughshod over Jim, the young outlaw managed to get himself in trouble when he was

150

left alone one night at Stillhouse Hollow Lake. Trying to crowd a lifetime of living and loving into one last summer, Jim had gotten his fifteen-year-old girlfriend pregnant.

While Big Rob was out of town, Jim had driven to the home of Donna Burns, a pretty little brunette whom he had dated off and on for several months before his arrest. Donna had been one of the many girls who dropped by Ricky Dominick's house, competing for the attentions of the blue-eyed cowboy who changed women as often as he changed shirts.

But the feisty little Belton High School freshman was different from the rest of the harem, at least in the beginning, and that's probably what attracted Jim to her. For three months, she had resisted his sexual advances, refusing to give in despite his line that he would love her forever. "I want to get married in white," Donna told him each time he pressed her for sex. Her resistance had made her something of a challenge, and Jim enjoyed a good chase. He lost interest when girls gave in too easily, dumping most of them within two or three months.

Nevertheless, Donna had finally given in. After Jim was released on bond, she drove to his parents' home, stood outside in the driveway, and told him that she missed him. While he kissed her lips and nuzzled her ear, she whispered that she loved him and wanted him back. She would do whatever it took.

Jim had used the same ploy on her that had worked so often with the others: "Make them want you, then threaten to drop them if they don't come around." She had come around all right, just as he knew she would.

And so, he had made love to Donna that night at the lake without using any sort of precaution. Why bother? He had always beaten the odds before. The lucky ones never got caught.

Behaving wildly and recklessly, he had yielded to a moment of passion, responding to his own immature need for immediate sexual gratification and blocking out all thought of the long-term consequences. But this time, his luck had run out.

He knew Donna was pregnant even before she told him that she had missed her period; he could feel it, somehow, with that uncanny sixth sense of his. A visit to the doctor confirmed Jim's suspicions, and he felt the full impact of what he had done. He was scared.

151

Jim broke the news to his parents and told them that he intended to marry Donna. Tears welled in the eyes of Carolyn Taylor as she listened to Jim's latest crisis. Reacting out of fear and desperation, Carolyn "threw a fit" when Jim suggested marriage. She reminded Jim that he was seventeen years old and was probably on his way to prison. How did he intend to support a family? Carolyn demanded to know. "I'm not going to raise your baby while you're in the penitentiary," she said emphatically.

Donna's mother had reacted in much the same manner. Why should her fifteen-year-old daughter ruin her life by having a baby who had been fathered by a teenage murderer? Insisting that she knew what was best for her daughter, Mrs. Burns rejected any suggestion of marriage. There was only one solution: abortion.

When Donna broke the news to Jim over the telephone, he begged her not to listen to her mother. Despite his renegade behavior, Jim held traditional values when it came to things like home and family. He equated abortion with murder, and he couldn't kill his child, no matter what. He pleaded with Donna to reconsider.

But Mrs. Burns remained firm in her resolve. Not only did she insist that Jim stay away from Donna, but she telephoned Carolyn Taylor, urging her to persuade Jim about the abortion. Too emotionally distraught to think clearly, Carolyn telephoned Joe Cannon for legal advice.

The defense attorney counseled Jim, suggesting that he go along with the abortion decision and not make trouble; otherwise, Mrs. Burns could accuse Jim of statutory rape, have him rearrested, and add another felony to the charges against him. With the trouble he was in already, Jim couldn't afford to take the risk, Cannon advised. He had no choice.

No choice. Jim's eyes blurred with tears as he dialed Donna's telephone number. When the familiar voice answered, Jim told her he would pay half of the doctor's fee. He'd been saving the money he earned as a maintenance worker at a local hospital, trying to assist his parents with his legal expenses.

Later that afternoon, Jim handed the $150 to Donna, choked back the tears as he drove away, and felt the best part of himself die with the tiny fetus the following morning.

In the months that followed, Jim lay awake at night, wondering about the baby — what it might have looked like, what it might have become. He hated himself. In his own mind, he was now a murderer.

Not of Chester Brooks, for he hadn't killed that old man, regardless of what the law said. His conscience told him that he had murdered his own child. He had allowed a doctor to destroy it, much as the infant son of Rachel Plummer had been destroyed at the hands of a Comanche war party some hundred years before.

Big Rob's attempt to run interference for Jim continued into the next school year. When classes began in September, Robert lagged behind that first morning while the rest of the Dozen bolted through the door at the sound of the dismissal bell. I could tell from the deep furrow creasing his round, whiskered face that something was bothering him. He shoved his paper on my desk and waited to speak with me.

Robert and eight of the original Dozen had been assigned to my first-period English class for a second year, along with two "low-achievers" whom the coaches hoped to keep eligible by enrolling in the class. Unlike the Dozen, the two athletes hadn't actually qualified for the CVAE program because they weren't a grade level behind and they didn't work off campus in the afternoons — major prerequisites for the work/study program. However, no one enforced the guidelines. Successful kids were what counted, and the alternative program was producing results.

By the end of that first year, I saw a marked change in the Dozen. Not only had their reading and writing skills risen two grade levels, but their behavior problems had decreased and their attitudes toward school had improved. Through this new work/study program, the boys had begun to feel better about themselves. They felt successful in the classroom, catching up on many of the credits they had lost and learning basic survival skills that would help them in the workplace. In addition, they felt useful on their afternoon jobs, becoming productive employees and making money — the legal way. For the first time in many years, they didn't see themselves as "losers."

Working with the Dirty Dozen had been difficult, frustrating, and heartbreaking at times, but it had also been challenging

153

and rewarding. Through the vocational English program, I had been given an opportunity to impact a change — to make a real difference — and that was exciting. A little selfishly, perhaps, I wanted to keep the Dozen for another year and continue what we had started.

I couldn't bear the thought of turning the boys over to someone else, someone who might consider them "hopeless" and simply "mark time" until they dropped out of school or wound up in jail. They had worked too hard and come too far for that. The Dirty Dozen deserved better.

Marching into the principal's office with my old missionary fervor, I had asked to have my teaching schedule changed for the following year. I requested to move up one grade level with the Dozen so that we might "assure a continuity in the academic component of the program." CVAE was still new, I explained, and we needed additional time "to modify our English curriculum and make sure that we address the basic survival skills that students need in the workplace."

My carefully rehearsed rationale proved unnecessary, for the principal was more than willing to grant my request. Few faculty members had the desire or the training to teach throwaway kids with emotional problems and learning disabilities. And so, by acclamation I became the eleventh-grade vocational English teacher, and the process of salvaging the Dozen began again.

"It's Jim," Robert said as he shoved his notebook under his burly right arm and waited for me at my desk.

"Is he all right?"

"Yes, ma'am. It's just that, well, I think he oughta be in school."

"Does he want to come back?"

"He wants to, but not his mother. She's afraid he'll get in trouble at school. She wants him working out at the hospital, where she can keep an eye on him."

"She could be right, you know."

"Yes, ma'am. But Jim's changed a lot. I don't think he'd do anything now. And I'd be around to make sure."

As the tardy bell sounded, Robert hurried to explain that he needed my help in executing a plan to get Jim back in school. He intended to talk with Carolyn Taylor and convince her that school would look good on Jim's record when his trial came up. In the meantime, Robert wanted me to speak with the principal and use my "influence" to have Jim readmitted. Because of the murder charge against Jim, Robert feared a problem with the administrators or the teachers. He was right.

Several members of the faculty voiced "concern" about having a suspected murderer on campus. Their fear stemmed largely from the bombardment of newspaper articles about David Berkowitz, the "Son of Sam" killer who had been arrested three weeks before school started.

Berkowitz had first begun terrorizing New York State two years earlier, when he approached two young women with a hunting knife in separate incidents. Berkowitz had repeatedly plunged the knife blade into the back of his first victim, then watched her stagger away. Moments later, he had stalked a second solitary victim as she crossed a bridge, using the knife first to puncture the back of her skull and then to slash her body. All the while that he was stabbing and slicing, he claimed that demonic voices inside his head screamed, "Get her, get her. She has to be sacrificed."

Berkowitz had failed to kill either victim, however, and the demonic voices continued to hound him for a blood sacrifice. Possessed by the archfiend "Sam" and his hoard of demons, Berkowitz became the "Son of Sam" and purchased a .44-caliber pistol, an instrument better suited for what he had to do. Concealing the weapon in a paper bag, Berkowitz stalked the New York streets, randomly selecting his victims. Usually, they were pretty young women with long, dark hair.

During his two-year carnage, the killer's m. o. was always the same. He appeared suddenly, crouched, fired, and then fled the scene without molesting or robbing his victims. Before his reign of terror ended, Berkowitz had blown apart the heads and chests of six people, in addition to crippling, blinding, and maiming nine other "sacrifices."

As the saga of this serial killer continued to attract media attention, several staff members protested the re-enrollment of Jim at Temple High School. They insisted that violent criminals should be kept in jail, not allowed to roam loose on the streets — and certainly not allowed to sit inside classrooms.

But the principal, who had taught vocational students in the past and knew about their potential, hadn't listened to the fears of the faculty soothsayers. "Sometimes young people need a second chance," he said as I sat in his office, assuring him that Jim Taylor hadn't done the killing and would pose no threat to the school. Staring out his office window, as if reflecting on a faraway place and time, the principal said hoarsely, "We'll take a chance on him and see what happens."

Two days later, Jim Taylor walked into my English class, sat at the same desk he had occupied the year before, and began reading. We had one final chance with the young outlaw. Could we make a difference in time?

CHAPTER SEVENTEEN

The First Verdict

Jim learned about the Folger trial verdict quite by accident as he walked through his half-darkened living room on that drizzling Tuesday night of January 31. He felt bone-tired after a long stint of maintenance work at the hospital, and he looked forward to crashing until the metallic ringing of his alarm clock rousted him out for school the next morning.

His mother, sitting in a rocking chair next to the lamp table, had started to say something to him as he passed through the room, but the TV reporter on the ten o'clock news interrupted her bantering in midsentence.

"Next up on Newswatch: Temple Man Convicted in Groesbeck Murder Trial. But first, this." The Waco station had then broken for a two-minute commercial spot that neither Jim nor Carolyn remembered seeing.

Jim stood transfixed, leaning against the wobbly back of his mother's chair and watching the meaningless images flicker across the twenty-four-inch screen with the red-tinted glow. Until that moment, he hadn't known about Wes Folger's trial; he had no idea that the drama was being played out in an archaic courtroom forty miles away. He had just presumed that nothing would ever happen and that people would forget. It had been more than a year since the murder.

Jim saw the muscles in his mother's hands grow tense as she clutched the rocker's worn arms, her whitened knuckles standing out in stark contrast to the dark-grained wood. He felt her chair move with her uneven breathing as she sat there waiting, waiting for a verdict that would irreparably impact all of their lives.

*   *   *   *   *

The trial had begun eight days earlier with the tedious process of jury selection. Defense counsel James Kreimeyer had
placed a change-of-venue motion before the 77th District Court
of Judge Clarence Ferguson. Kreimeyer alleged that his client
could not receive a fair and impartial trial in Limestone County
because extensive pretrial publicity had inflamed and prejudiced
the community.

The Limestone County district attorney, Don Caldwell, had
countered the venue move by placing a motion before the court,
requesting that the sheriff be instructed to summon 250 prospective jurors — more than three times the usual number. With such
an extensive juror pool from which to choose, the State had every
reason to believe that a panel of twelve impartial jurors could be
found.

Judge Ferguson had concurred with the DA and issued an
order for special venire, instructing Sheriff Dennis Walker to
summon the 250 persons whose names appeared on the five-
page list. On the morning of January 23, most of those summoned appeared on the second floor of the Groesbeck courthouse to begin voir dire examination.

After three and a half days of screening prospective jurors,
one at a time and out of the hearing of other jurors so as to insure
complete fairness to the defendant, a twelve-member panel was
selected. The jury was composed of nine women and three men,
most of whom were old enough to have children the age of Wes
Folger. Eight members came from the town of Mexia, in the
northern part of Limestone County, and hadn't known Chester
Brooks. The three panel members from Groesbeck insisted that
they hadn't been prejudiced by pretrial publicity and could judge
the case on the merits of the evidence presented.

The only member of the jury panel who stood out in
Kreimeyer's mind was a large, heavy-set woman whose husband
was a game warden. She was a strong, grandmotherly type in the
tradition of the pioneer women who had tamed Central Texas,
and Kreimeyer knew she would make a good juror *if* she were on
his side. If she felt the slightest bit of empathy for Wes Folger, she
could hang the jury.

On the rainy, bitter-cold afternoon of January 26, the jury was selected, sworn, and impaneled at 1:30 P.M. in the 77th District Court of Limestone County. With both the prosecution and the defense announcing "Ready, Your Honor," the trial of *State vs. Folger* began.

District Attorney Don Caldwell, acting in conjunction with special prosecutors L. L. Geren and James Bradley, began the criminal proceedings by reading the indictment to the jury. Facing the elevated, red-carpeted jury box to the right of Judge Ferguson's bench, Caldwell read slowly and with deliberate emphasis. "Wes Folger, on the seventeenth day of January in the County of Limestone and State of Texas, did then and there unlawfully and intentionally cause the death of Chester Wade Brooks by striking him with a shotgun and by dropping a concrete block on the said Chester Wade Brooks."

When Judge Ferguson leaned forward and asked the husky, seventeen-year-old defendant for his plea, the baritone voice of Wes Folger reverberated throughout the hushed courtroom. "Guilty, Your Honor."

Two members of the jury looked confused, for they had anticipated a bloody legal battle lasting several days, with the defense and prosecution snarling at one another's throats, as in the movies. But Kreimeyer had headed off any such showdown days before by striking a deal with the prosecution.

The burly defense lawyer had driven over to Groesbeck and negotiated with Special Prosecutor Geren and District Attorney Caldwell, laying his cards on the table like an old-fashioned poker player. "I'll tell you what I'll do," Kreimeyer said as he leaned back in his chair and stared at the musty ceiling of the DA's office. "I think the jury will probably give him (Wes) the death penalty, but I don't think it will stand up on appeal."

Kreimeyer paused a moment to look at Geren and Caldwell, trying to read their faces and see if they understood his meaning. They did. The Court of Criminal Appeals had said as much when it ruled against the county earlier that year on the denial of Folger's bond. There wasn't enough evidence to assure the death penalty, the high court had said in its ruling, and ordered the trial court to set bond at $55,000.

"Rather than go through this two or three times," Kreimeyer

159

continued, "why don't I plead him guilty to murder and you waive the death penalty and let the jury decide the punishment? They can give him five years probated or life in the penitentiary, whichever it is."

Geren and Caldwell weighed the offer carefully and considered their options. Their case against Wes Folger, although a strong one, had been weakened considerably because none of the juveniles would take the stand and testify against him, as the prosecution had initially believed would happen.

Furthermore, the sworn confession of Jim Taylor was inadmissible because it was an "accomplice testimony." According to Article 38.14 of the Texas Criminal Code, such testimony could not be used for conviction unless it was corroborated by other evidence connecting the defendant with the murder. Because the defense would have no opportunity to cross-examine Jim Taylor and determine the veracity of his statement, the sworn confession could not be used in court.

And finally, Wes Folger was a seventeen-year-old kid with no prior convictions. There was no guarantee that the jury would assess the death penalty. To do so, the jury would have to answer "yes" to two questions: Do you believe, beyond a reasonable doubt, that the defendant deliberately killed the deceased? And secondly, do you believe that the defendant will commit future acts of criminal violence and be a continuing threat to society? The last question could go either way during jury deliberations.

Facing three impending trials against the juveniles, the special prosecutor had neither the time nor the money to draw out the criminal proceedings and risk the appeals court overturning the verdict. Therefore, he and the district attorney had agreed to accept Folger's guilty plea on a lesser charge of murder. The indictment was reduced from "capital murder," punishable by the death penalty, to "murder," punishable by probation, by five to ninety-nine years, or by a maximum of life imprisonment in the Texas Department of Corrections. The jury would decide.

After the deal had been negotiated and the judge had been advised, Kreimeyer walked out of the DA's office and down the courthouse stairs with a lighter step. His primary concern had been keeping Wes Folger off death row, where the macabre room with Old Sparky had surely awaited him.

160

*   *   *   *   *

Judge Ferguson accepted Wes Folger's plea of guilty, and instructed the jury that the murder trial would move into the punishment phase. The State would call witnesses and produce evidence to support the guilty plea, and from said corroborating information, the jury would decide the appropriate punishment for the defendant.

The State began by calling Bill Fletcher. The tall, big-boned deputy mounted the steps to the witness stand, his heavy boot heels crushing the red carpet piles beneath his tread. After the wild-eyed officer was duly sworn, Special Prosecutor Geren began direct examination.

"State your name, your occupation, and residence address."

"Billy A. Fletcher, chief deputy sheriff of Limestone County, Texas, 818 West State Street, Groesbeck."

"Mr. Fletcher, were you so employed on January 17?"

"Yes, sir."

"And did you have an occasion around 9:00 on January 17 to make a call at the Coit community?"

"Yes, sir."

"And what was the purpose of your call down there?"

"To investigate the murder of Chester Brooks." Fletcher shifted slightly in the hard-backed chair and scanned the courtroom. The spectators were scattered throughout the room, with several onlookers peering from their perch in the balcony at the back.

Although the defense attorney had feared the presence of an unruly crowd and had filed a motion to prevent a "carnival" atmosphere from developing, the move had proven unnecessary. More than a year had passed since the brutal murder, and tempers had settled down considerably. Most of Chester Brooks' friends were farmers who lived in the southern part of the county. The bad weather and icy roads had prevented many of them from making the drive to attend the proceedings. Only three or four dozen came, and they sat with iron-clenched jaws, listening to the deputy sheriff recall the events of that dismal day when they had stood outside the old man's store, shaking their heads in disbelief.

161

"When you arrived at this location, what did you find as to Chester Brooks?" Geren inquired.

"I found Mr. Brooks dead. His grocery store had also been broken into, and paper, debris, and money were scattered around the floor of the store."

"And could you, by observing the body — in your experience as a peace officer — could you tell what the cause of death was?"

"Yes, sir. Mr. Brooks had been beaten severely about the head."

"And did you see anything in the area of the body that could have been used to perpetrate this crime?"

"Yes, sir. I found this concrete block in front of me here," Fletcher said, gesturing with his right hand toward the prosecution table as the jury's eyes followed him and focused on the bloody, twenty-five-pound block.

"Was there any other item in the area that you found that might have been used?"

"Yes, sir. Several pieces of a .410 shotgun."

At that point, DA Caldwell interrupted. "Marked State's Exhibit No. 1, Your Honor," he said, indicating the broken shotgun stock and barrel, "and State's Exhibit No. 2," he continued, motioning toward the slate gray building stone lying on the corner of the prosecution table.

Geren continued his questioning. "Mr. Fletcher, I show you this particular concrete block right here. Would you step down, please sir, and come around so you can get a closer look at it?"

As instructed, the deputy sheriff left the stand to examine the alleged murder weapon. "This item," explained Geren, "has been marked State's Exhibit No. 2. Can you identify that block?"

"Yes, sir. This is the block that was used to kill Mr. Brooks."

"Objection," Kreimeyer called from the defense table on the judge's left, rising halfway from his chair.

"Yes, sir," Judge Ferguson responded, "the objection will be sustained and the court will not consider the answer."

Caldwell rose to assist Geren with the direct examination of the deputy sheriff. "Mr. Fletcher, you have identified the block. Where have you seen this block before?"

"On Mr. Brooks' property," the officer responded as he

turned sideways and glanced toward Kreimeyer, as if half expecting some objection. There was none.

"And how do you identify it?" Caldwell asked. "By what means do you identify the block?"

"By the bloody fingerprints inside the block here," Fletcher said, indicating the dark smears on the porous inner surface of the concrete stone.

"In other words," Caldwell said as he pressed to make his point, "you are telling the court you saw this particular block and those particular handprints on the morning of January 17, is that correct?"

"Yes, sir," the deputy sheriff affirmed, nodding his head decisively as he stared at State's Exhibit No. 2.

"And you identify the interior fingerprints today as being the same?"

"Yes, sir," Fletcher said in a firm, authoritative voice directed toward the jury.

Caldwell offered the shotgun pieces and the block into evidence, but Kreimeyer objected and asked to take the witness on voir dire. He, like the defense counsels for the three juveniles, hammered away at the same point of law: The block had not been tagged at the murder scene and the chain of custody had been broken as the unmarked evidence was transferred back and forth between the sheriff's property room, the crime lab, and the pretrial hearings. How could the sheriff's department say for sure that this was the same block?

"Well, if it's not," came the reply, "it's a reasonable Republican of it." Judge Ferguson smiled, allowing the political commentary to pass without official notice.

Fletcher returned to the witness box, where Caldwell pursued another line of questioning. "Mr. Fletcher, on or about February nineteenth, did you have occasion to make a trip to Bell County?"

"Yes, sir."

"And what was the purpose of your trip?" Caldwell asked, his voice skipping across the words like a stone skimming water.

"To meet some officers at the sheriff's office in Belton, Texas, in reference to further investigation of the Chester Brooks murder case."

"From there did you go to any residence?" the DA asked as he turned to face the jury.

"Yes, sir. I went to 609 North Wall."

"And who was staying at that house?"

"Jim Taylor and Walter Frye."

"And did you have permission to search those premises?"

"Yes, sir."

"Who gave you permission to search them?"

"Ricky Dominick. He owned the property."

"All right," Caldwell said as he referred to his notes before continuing. "And when you searched this particular house, what did you find?"

"I found several coins — commemorative-type new coins in collector's envelopes, folders. I found two cigar boxes full of those. I found some keys." As if on cue, the special prosecutor produced the props Fletcher had mentioned, preparing to introduce them into evidence.

"In connection with the keys," Caldwell said slowly, enunciating the words to attract the jury's attention, "what type keys did you find?"

"They were safety deposit box keys."

"Mr. Fletcher," Caldwell continued as he picked up two shiny objects from the prosecution table, "I show you for identification two keys marked State's Exhibit No. 2-B. Can you identify these?"

"Yes, sir."

"Where did you first see these keys?"

"609 North Wall, Belton, Texas, in the attic in a cigar box."

"Did you take these keys at that time and did you have occasion to investigate these keys in any way?"

"Yes, sir. I brought the keys back to Limestone County and made calls to various banks in the area, and I found the bank these keys belonged to."

"And did you prove that up?"

"Yes, sir. I went to the bank and —"

"Which bank?" Caldwell asked, interrupting the witness and breaking his concentration for a moment.

"First State Bank of Kosse."

"And did you carry these keys with you?"

"Yes, sir."

As if he anticipated Kreimeyer's objection to the untagged evidence, Caldwell asked, "How do you identify these keys?"

"The number on the front and back of each key," Fletcher said. "Number 232."

Caldwell half-smiled and nodded his head in acceptance of the explanation. He'd headed off any question about the admissibility of this evidence. "And when you got to the bank, who were you with?"

"Mr. Frank Mitchell, president of the bank."

"And what did you do there?" Caldwell asked.

Fletcher closed his eyes for a moment, as if visualizing the scene in his mind. "I opened the safety deposit box. I told Mr. Mitchell what I had, referring to the keys. He took the bank key and opened one lock on the box, and I took those keys and opened the other lock."

"And did you determine whose lock box that was?" Caldwell asked as he pivoted slightly toward the jury, surveying the expressions on their faces as Fletcher paused for dramatic effect before answering the DA's question.

"Yes, sir. Mr. Chester — Wade — Brooks."

The DA continued to question the deputy sheriff for several minutes more, asking Fletcher to relate the circumstances surrounding his visit to Lake Belton on February 19 with Jim Taylor. Fletcher described how the boy had led him and Ranger Jim Ray to a campfire site some 150 yards into the brush overlooking the bluff at Cedar Ridge. There they found several articles that had been partially burned, items that Jim Taylor had identified as coins, charred clothes, and the remnants of a ski mask.

When Caldwell passed the witness for cross-examination, James Kreimeyer sat at the prosecution table for several seconds before rising slowly to approach the witness stand. Staring the sizable deputy sheriff squarely in the eye, the defense attorney zeroed in on the legality of the search at the Dominick house in Belton, where the incriminating safety deposit keys had been found.

Kreimeyer questioned whether or not Ricky Dominick had the legal right to authorize a search of the house on Wall Street. Dominick had not resided there for several weeks after Jim Taylor and Walter Frye had taken up residence as tenants. Since the boys "did custom farm work" for Dominick and received housing as part of their financial compensation, Taylor and Frye should have been the ones to authorize the search. Kreimeyer, like his juvenile defense counterparts, suggested that the keys may have been obtained through an illegal search-and-seizure, and he objected to their admission as evidence. Without the keys, there was nothing concrete to link his client or the juveniles to Chester Brooks.

Furthermore, Kreimeyer insisted, his client had not lived at the house in Belton with Taylor and Frye. There was nothing to connect Wes Folger with the evidence found there except a statement by Jim Taylor and the "guilt by association" premise, both of which should be disregarded from consideration.

Noting the defense attorney's objections, the court accepted the State's evidence corroborating the testimony of Chief Deputy Bill Fletcher, and the officer was dismissed from the witness stand.

For the remainder of that afternoon and continuing through the next morning of January 27, the State conducted the direct examination of three more witnesses. Frank Mitchell, the rural mail carrier and bank president, testified about finding the frozen body of his childhood friend next to the bloodied concrete block and the broken shotgun pieces. In addition, the slow-speaking, deep-voiced Mitchell corroborated Deputy Fletcher's account of keys No. 232 fitting the victim's safety deposit box at the Kosse bank. Mitchell seemed relieved when Kreimeyer said, "No questions, Your Honor," and allowed him to leave the stand. The recounting of that dreadful day and the reliving of the nightmare, in hearing after hearing after hearing, had taken its toll on the elderly mail carrier. He was tired and sick unto death.

When Dr. K. P. Witstruck, a Waco pathologist, was called to testify, Kreimeyer heaved a heavy sigh. The moment he dreaded had come. Dr. Witstruck testified that, based upon an autopsy of the victim's body conducted at the Mexia funeral home on the following morning, the official cause of death was severe lacerations to the scalp and a crushed skull. Under direct examination by Geren, the pathologist went on to speculate that the shotgun could have caused the lacerations to the scalp and the concrete

166

block could have caused the crushed skull. The pathologist's testimony about the cause of death gave the State an opportunity to introduce the bloody pictures of Chester Brooks.

After being entered into evidence, the graphic color photographs were passed from juror to juror for closer examination. Kreimeyer watched the twelve middle-aged faces for their reactions, focusing primarily on the game warden's wife, the litmus-paper member of the jury. Her face remained expressionless as she made a cold, clinical assessment of the evidence. Several spectators sitting close by craned their necks to see the gory pictures, but few of the curious onlookers caught a glimpse of the battered old man.

Passing the pathologist's photographs to the woman seated next to her, the game warden's wife focused her eyes on Wes Folger, as if studying the boy under a microscope. Wes sat with shoulders slightly slouched, his hands folded together on the defense table, as passive as a stone.

The boy's expression changed only slightly when the State called its final witness: Ricky Dominick. Wes' lips curled into a slight smirk as he watched the nervous Dominick, sitting rigidly in the witness box and avoiding eye contact. During direct examination by the special prosecutor, Dominick tied Wes to the murder by repeating what Jim and Walter had told him when they came to his trailer house the night of the robbery.

"Going back to January 16," Special Prosecutor Geren began, "I will ask you whether or not you had occasion to see Jim Taylor and Walter Frye out near Lake Belton?"

"Yes, sir," Dominick said. "About 9:30. They wanted to get — they had some gloves, cigarettes, and a pair of bolt cutters, they thought, in my Ford pickup."

"Did they work for you?"

"Yes, sir."

"What kind of work do you do?"

"Custom farm work."

"And they were working for you. What was your arrangement for them staying in the house?"

"I let them stay there in kind of paying for their help at that time because there wasn't that much work to do." Dominick

167

shifted slightly in his chair, following the movements of Geren as the special prosecutor moved closer toward the jury.

"And on this occasion when they were out at your place on Lake Belton, did they, so far as you know, get any bolt cutters?"

"Not to my knowledge, no, sir," Dominick answered as his eyes dropped down and focused squarely on the railing in front of him.

The special prosecutor continued. "Did they discuss with you about wanting to borrow a shotgun?"

"Yes, sir."

"Did they tell you what they were going to do?"

"Yes, sir. They said they were going to Marlin to rob an old friend."

Geren paused a moment, letting the implication of Dominick's words have full impact on the jury. "What kind of car were they in?"

"A gold-colored Cougar."

"And was anybody else in the car with them?"

Dominick nodded his head slightly. "There were two other people."

"Did they tell you who it was?"

"Not at the time. They told me later."

"Who did they tell you it was?"

"Wes Folger and his brother."

"Your Honor," protested a stern-faced Kreimeyer as he rose from his chair beside the stoic Wes Folger. "I object to the hearsay answer and ask that it be stricken. He said they told him who it was."

"Counsel, what exception to the hearsay rule does this fall within?" Judge Ferguson asked, shifting the glasses on his nose and waiting for Kreimeyer's response.

Kreimeyer took several steps toward the bench, explaining that the testimony of co-conspirators to a third party was only admissible under one of two conditions. First, if said statements were made in the presence of the accused, or secondly, if said statements were made before the alleged conspiracy had terminated.

Kreimeyer insisted that Dominick's testimony failed to qualify on either count. Folger was not present during the alleged conversation between Dominick and the co-conspirators, and the defendant's identity was not known until after the robbery had occurred, thus ending any conspiracy, if indeed there was one. To admit Dominick's testimony constituted rank hearsay, and Kreimeyer insisted that the court strike it.

Judge Ferguson overruled the defense attorney's motion, explaining that the court chose to believe that a conspiracy still existed when Dominick learned the names of the occupants in the yellow Cougar. Taylor and Frye had not yet split up the robbery loot with the Folger brothers; thus, the conspiracy had not been terminated. "Accomplice statements" as to Folger's presence in the car were admissible.

The court also accepted Dominick's account of how Wes Folger had come to his house in Belton to divide up the loot and to dispose of a garbage bag full of papers and junk from the robbery. In addition, Dominick related what happened that night when he drove to the Quality Discount store in downtown Belton with Jim Taylor and Walter Frye.

"Wes Folger came up," he recalled as he drummed his thumb nervously against the right thigh of his blue jeans and stared straight ahead toward the balcony. "The discussion was over the robbery. They were discussing if anyone had been hurt. Wes told them it wasn't — Wes made the statement if the old man had been hurt or killed, that he was the one that did it."

The game warden's wife shifted her focus from the man on the witness stand to the acne-pocked face of Wes Folger, still expressionless except for the occasional blinking of his hard-looking eyes.

"Why didn't you report all this to the authorities?" Geren asked as his slow, resonant voice brought attention back to the twenty-two-year-old man pressed against the back of the witness chair.

"Well, I heard of a robbery up in an area where a man had been killed," Dominick explained, "and I asked Jim and Walter if anyone was hurt in the robbery that they did, and they said there hadn't been. But talking with them, I wasn't sure about it, and so I was scared my life might be in danger if they were the ones that did the robbery."

Satisfied with the performance of the State's star witness, Geren passed Dominick for cross-examination. Kreimeyer zeroed in on the key points that he had attempted to raise all morning, hoping that Dominick would slip up and give him ground to subtly pursue the points that the court had overruled. Did Dominick have the right to authorize the search of the house that he had "rented" to Taylor and Frye as part of their wages? Did Dominick have firsthand knowledge that Wes Folger was in the yellow Cougar the night of the robbery? If Dominick had accepted a cut of the robbery money, as he had admitted doing, didn't that compromise his veracity as a reliable witness?

Kreimeyer hammered away, but the slow-speaking witness failed to fall prey to the defense counsel's maneuvering. When Kreimeyer concluded his cross-examination with "Nothing further, Your Honor," Judge Ferguson dismissed the witness. Glancing at his watch and gazing toward the frost-covered windows at the left of the courtroom, the judge adjourned the 77th District Court for the day at 11:30 A.M.

Kreimeyer suspected that the early adjournment stemmed from the cold spell that had set in. Before court had convened that morning, he had overheard the judge and the special prosecutor discussing the bad weather as they sat around the open space heater inside the district clerk's office, leaned back in the rocking chairs, and sipped cups of steaming black coffee. Both men were worried about the effect the bitter cold was having on their cattle and needed to get home before dark so they could ride over their pastures and check on their livestock. The trial of *State vs. Folger* would have to wait until the following morning, it seemed, when Kreimeyer's twelve character witnesses took the stand in behalf of the young defendant.

Choosing not to put Wes Folger on the stand, Kreimeyer began his defense by attempting to discredit the testimony of Ricky Dominick, the State's star witness. Terry Whitley, a licensed private investigator from Belton, testified that Dominick had a bad reputation for truth and veracity, a polite way of saying that the man was a born liar. Kreimeyer hoped that if the jury had cause to question Dominick's testimony, perhaps it would give Wes Folger the benefit of the doubt when it came to sentencing him.

After the PI left the stand, Kreimeyer introduced twelve character witnesses, hoping that these respected, upstanding citizens could further persuade the jury to consider leniency for his client. In Texas courts, character witnesses fell into two categories: those who testified concerning the defendant's character traits and those who testified about the defendant's reputation for being a peaceful, law-abiding citizen. Kreimeyer presented testimony from both types, realizing that the reputation witnesses would be cross-examined by the special prosecutor with "have you heard" questions challenging Wes Folger's character.

First, the jury had listened to testimony from Wes' neighbors, Little League coaches, teacher, and counselor, who described the boy as being kind, responsible, cooperative, and a bright student with excellent potential for college. After the boy's character traits had been established, Kreimeyer called Wes' parents, former pastor, and Sunday school teacher to testify concerning Wes' good reputation in the community.

Mr. Folger described his oldest son as being a hard worker, explaining that the boy often helped him with the family's bricklaying business. Mrs. Folger added that her son held high moral standards, and insisted that Wes could not have been inside the yellow Cougar at Ricky Dominick's house at 9:30 P.M. on the night of the robbery/murder. Wes had spent the evening with his family at his grandfather's birthday party, and he and Jill hadn't left until almost 10:30 P.M.

Gene Shoemake, the former pastor of the Eastside Baptist Church where Wes and his family attended, testified that the boy was a peaceful, law-abiding, Christian citizen. Wanda Rhodes, who had been Wes' Sunday school teacher and had known him since she first began babysitting him at age six, agreed with the minister's high opinion of the boy.

It was Mrs. Rhodes' testimony that brought special prosecutor Geren out of his chair, attempting to discredit the picture of Wes Folger as an all-American boy, a la Beaver Cleaver. Geren began hammering away with the "have you heard" questions, designed to test the witness' knowledge about the defendant's reputation.

"Now then," Geren said as he paced before the witness stand where Wanda Rhodes sat, "I will ask if you have heard that, since he (Wes) was released on bond for the murder of Chester Wade Brooks, that he saw Hank Worley and Ricky Dominick at the Dairy Queen in Belton?"

171

"Yes, sir," Mrs. Rhodes replied in a voice barely audible to the sprinkling of spectators seated in the balcony.

"And I will ask you if you heard that he told Hank Worley that if he gave any testimony against him that would hurt him in this case, he (Wes) would have something done about it?"

"Yes."

"And have you heard that on that occasion, he did threaten anybody who gives testimony against him that would hurt him — said he would have something done to the witnesses — have you heard of these threats?"

Kreimeyer drummed the pencil on the table. "Your Honor, we object."

"Yes, sir," Judge Ferguson said in a firm voice reminiscent of his officer days, "you may have your exception on all of this."

"All right, sir," the defense attorney said as he leaned back in his chair, continuing to drum one thumb on the wooden arm while he listened.

Kreimeyer knew that the special prosecutor was walking a legal tightrope with his line of questioning, tottering on a precipice that could send him tumbling into an abyss of appeals litigation if he made one mistake. The law was clear about the proper method for the State's cross-examination of a reputation witness.

Back in 1972, the Court of Criminal Appeals had ruled in *Brown vs. State* that the prosecuting attorney must phrase his "have you heard" questions in such a way so as not to imply guilt on the part of the defendant. If a question were phrased in a way that suggested the act was actually committed, then the prosecutor's question was improper. Kreimeyer watched his legal adversary like a chicken snake in a hen house, waiting for the culprit to strike. He didn't wait long.

Geren narrowed his eyes on Mrs. Rhodes and resumed his questioning about Wes Folger's alleged threats. "Have you heard of that?"

"I haven't heard of all of it."

"Well, you have heard of some of it? You have heard of some of it?" he pushed.

"Some of it," Mrs. Rhodes conceded, "but that doesn't change my opinion."

172

"Even though he has made these threats, it still doesn't change your opinion?"

"No, sir, it does not."

"You think he is entitled to threaten witnesses, do you?"

Mrs. Rhodes gripped her hands tighter and raised her voice an octave. "It does not change my opinion how —"

"I am asking you to answer my question 'yes' or 'no.' *Do you think he is entitled to threaten witnesses?*"

Geren had crossed the line, and Kreimeyer knew it. "Now, Your Honor," the defense lawyer protested, "on that question he is assuming it to be true, and we object to the form of that question."

"I'm going to overrule the objection," Judge Ferguson said. "I will let you answer the question," he said to Mrs. Rhodes, who had been momentarily rattled by the rapid-fire hammering of the special prosecutor.

Mrs. Rhodes nodded, quickly regained her composure, and answered that she didn't think anyone had the right to threaten witnesses, if indeed the boy had done so. However, she stood steadfast in her assessment of Wes Folger as a fine, peace-loving, law-abiding citizen. He had never been in trouble before, posed no threat to anyone, and should be shown mercy so that he might continue his role as husband, father, and a productive member of society.

The game warden's wife leaned forward and listened to the impassioned pleas of the Sunday school teacher as she spoke of the boy sitting at the defense table, the "good" boy who had never done anything "bad" before. The boy she had helped raise, had taught Bible scripture, and had loved. The solemn, silent boy who sat staring straight ahead into nothingness while his lawyer pronounced the benediction. "The defense rests, Your Honor."

At 9:00 A.M. on that overcast morning of January 31, jury foreman-to-be Eugene A. Branch and his eleven panelists focused their eyes squarely on Judge Clarence Ferguson and listened to his reading of the court's charge to the jury. They concentrated on every word spoken, just as they had done the preceding afternoon as they listened to rebuttal testimony from Sheriff Dennis Walker, called to the stand to confirm that Wes Folger had a "bad" reputation among the deputies at the Limestone County jail. They listened to the judge's charge much as they had listened to the final arguments of Kreimeyer and Geren, before weighing the merits of each lawyer's summation against their own standards of right and wrong and reasonable doubt.

Judge Ferguson propped his forearms against the edge of the rich mahogany bench, revealing his stiff, starched, white cuffs beneath the folds of his black robe. Reading in a voice loud enough to be heard by the dozen or more balcony spectators, the judge began his charge to the jury. "The defendant, Wes Folger, stands charged with the offense of murder, alleged to have been committed in Limestone County, Texas, on or about the seventeenth day of January. To this charge, the defendant has entered his plea of guilty.

"He has persisted in entering his plea of guilty, notwithstanding that the court, as required by law, has admonished him of the consequences. It plainly appears to the court that the defendant is sane, and that he is not influenced to make said plea by any consideration of fear, persuasion, or any illusive hope for pardon prompting him to confess his guilt. His plea is by the court received."

Wes sat staring at the plastic water pitcher sitting on the table in front of him, the muscles in his throat tightening and shrinking as he listened to the judge's words snap with a military cadence.

"You are instructed to find the defendant guilty as charged and assess his punishment as provided by law. The punishment for murder is by confinement in the Texas Department of Corrections for life, or for any term of years not less than five nor more than ninety-nine. You will, therefore, assess his punishment at confinement in the Texas Department of Corrections for life or for any number of years not less than five nor more than ninety-nine."

The boy raised his head for a moment to focus on the words mouthed by the solemn-faced judge, then returned to his solitary vigil over the black-and-gold-colored water pitcher. The judge droned on.

"In arriving at your verdict, it will not be proper to fix the same by lot, chance, or any other method than by a full, fair, and

174

free exercise of the opinion of the individual jurors under the evidence admitted before you."

Kreimeyer glanced toward the pensive jury, wondering if his case had been strong enough to make a difference. Had he said something to change the mind of one free-thinking soul who would hold out against the others and wear them down? Had someone, like the gray-haired grandmother or the balding man, listened to the Sunday school teacher's story and believed that Wes Folger was a "good boy" who deserved a lighter prison sentence, if not probation? He hoped so.

Kreimeyer cast a sideward glance toward his stoical client as he listened to Judge Ferguson read the court's final admonishment of the jury. They were not to discuss the possibility of parole or how long the defendant would be required to serve a sentence, if any. In addition, Judge Ferguson instructed the jury to base their decision solely on testimony presented in court, to weigh the credibility of each witness, and to reach a unanimous vote concerning sentencing. Furthermore, the jury was to disregard all questions related to the alleged threatening of witnesses by the defendant, and it must not assume any wrongdoing on the defendant's part because he had declined the privilege of testifying. Finally, the judge advised the jury of the defendant's request for probation, and instructed them that they must assess a sentence of less than ten years for probation to be granted.

At 10:44 A.M. the jury of nine women and three men filed out of the courtroom to begin their deliberation. At noon, they took a brief recess and followed a sheriff's deputy across the street to Josie's Restaurant, where they ate a hot plate lunch at the county's expense. An hour later, they were back inside the jury room on the second floor of the Groesbeck courthouse, carrying out each provision of the judge's charge to them. Within twenty-five minutes, they had reached a decision.

The jury had taken longer than Kreimeyer expected, so perhaps one of them had held out until the hard-liners had compromised on a lesser sentence. Kreimeyer tried to read their faces as they filed back in and took their places, but they wore a facade as expressionless as his client's.

Within moments, foreman Eugene A. Branch stood to read. "We, the jury, find the defendant, Wes Folger, guilty of murder and assess his punishment at confinement in the Texas Department of Corrections for life."

Wes Folger dropped his chin toward his chest as his wife's scream rent the courtroom. His mother slumped into his father's arms, crying silently as her body jerked with each heart-wrenching sob. The spectators, including several of the old grocer's Coit neighbors, murmured in muffled tones as the impact of the foreman's words set in. The jury had given the seventeen-year-old defendant the maximum sentence allowed by law. Chester Brooks' death would be avenged.

The television reporter read the news story about the Folger verdict in a routine, matter-of-fact tone, then turned to the station's meteorologist for an update on the severe weather crippling Central Texas.

Jim mumbled, "Night, Mama," to the rigid form seated in the rocking chair, and walked down the narrow hallway to the bedroom he shared with his younger brother. There was no point in talking about it. Not now, anyway.

He dropped his dirty flannel shirt and blue jeans at the foot of the bed and climbed beneath the cold covers, pulling the blanket up over his ears and wadding his pillow into a hard ball.

The next thing he knew, his mother was sitting on the edge of his bed and shaking him, telling him to wake up and stop screaming. He had had the nightmare again, the one that had started after he was released on bond — the one he couldn't remember afterwards, no matter how hard he tried.

For two years, the same nightmare would stalk him, interrupting his sleep at irregular intervals when he least expected and making him thrash in his bed until he was awakened by his own screams. Finally, he would be able to recall the details.

The dream was always the same. He was inside the old man's store, slumped on his knees in the dirt, with his hands bound behind him. When he turned his head to the left, he saw the other three boys, kneeling next to him in a straight line in front of the wooden counter. Their hands were bound behind them with rope, and they were watching for something over by the red-and-white Coke machine. Then he saw fear on the other boys'

176

faces as a shadowy form appeared out of the darkness, carrying a double-bladed axe and slicing the air with pendulum movements.

The black figure reached the first boy and raised the rusted blade high above Wes Folger's head. As the axe began to slice downward toward the screaming boy's skull, Jim clenched his eyes shut and waited for the sound that he knew would come. *Thump.*

He heard a shuffling of heavy feet as the dark figure moved down the row two steps and stood in front of Don Folger. A swishing of the air, followed by *thump.*

Two steps more and the sinister form had stopped at the boy next to him. Jim heard Walter's frantic breathing and muffled crying as the axe rent the air for a third time. *Thump.*

Jim opened his eyes and focused on the unlaced, hightop shoes standing in front of him. Slowly, he lifted his eyes along the gray khaki trouser legs, past the bulging stomach, and up toward the red baseball cap. A toothless grin was pasted across the ashen face as it lifted the axe one final time. Jim watched the blade falling, falling, falling . . .

And then, a scream. It was over, until the next time.

Several days after the Folger verdict had been delivered, three jury members contacted Judge Clarence Ferguson at his chambers in the Groesbeck courthouse. Each wanted to know why the jury had not been allowed to assess the death penalty to the young killer.

Judge Ferguson later related the jurors' comments to defense attorney James Kreimeyer when the two men met to discuss Folger's formal sentencing scheduled for February 15. "You were smart to plead your client guilty," the judge said. Kreimeyer nodded his head in agreement, realizing that he had succeeded in keeping the boy away from Old Sparky, despite Mrs. Folger's allegation that Kreimeyer had sold Wes out by letting him take the rap.

Mrs. Folger wasn't the only mother to question the jury's verdict. Despite Wes' guilty plea to a reduced charge of murder, Carolyn Taylor wasn't convinced that the boy had struck the fatal blow that killed Chester Brooks.

What if someone else came to the store that night after the yellow Cougar had sped away? Someone whom the sheriff had arrested, but then turned loose after the boys were implicated by an informant. Someone named Luis Torres.

Suppose the Mexican had hidden in the darkness on that January night, watching as the boys jumped Chester, knocked him unconscious, and broke into the store. Might Torres' movements have been the noise that frightened Wes Folger as the boy stood in the doorway of the dirt-bottom store, listening to the sounds in the darkness?

And suppose Torres came out of hiding after the boys left and began searching Chester's front shirt pocket for money he knew the grocer kept there. What if, as Torres was removing the blood-stained bills from the pocket — the bills that the Mexican later cashed at Rand's Food Store in Groesbeck — what if the old man regained consciousness and recognized Torres? Fearful of being caught, could the Mexican have picked up the concrete block and finished the job that Wes Folger started? How else could you explain why the victim's body lay in a different place and in a different position than when the boys left it?

And what about Torres' failed polygraph test? Or the can of pennies crusted with dirt from the old man's store that the Mexican cashed in at the bank? Or the traces of hair and blood inside Torres' vehicle, traces which matched the same type as the victim's? Didn't the evidence indicate that the Mexican man could have been there that night?

And who could say for certain when the old man died? she asked. The funeral home had embalmed the victim's body before an autopsy could be performed to determine the hour of death. What if Chester Brooks had been alive when the boys left, as Jim had contended? Could Torres be ruled out as a suspect — beyond a "reasonable doubt"?

If two cars run over the same pedestrian, who can say which vehicle inflicted the fatal injuries? It was the same thing with a stone block.

Carolyn Taylor didn't buy the Folger verdict, not beyond a reasonable doubt. Perhaps the gnawing suspicion inside her was nothing more than a mother's attempt to protect her child — a futile attempt to cling to some desperate hope concerning his innocence. And yet, she wondered. There were too many questions left unanswered.

178

CHAPTER EIGHTEEN

Love: A Common Denominator

"**S**he's armed those hoods," came a colleague's disparaging whisper as she scurried down the north hall in Paul Revere fashion, sounding the alarm to the half-dozen or so teachers standing outside their doorways during the changing of classes. A weathered old relic from the history department stuck her head out into the crowded hallway, raised her scruffy gray eyebrow to a forty-five-degree arch, and shook her head from side to side as she stared toward my classroom at the opposite end of the hall. What now? she wondered.

I had created a disruption earlier that semester when I sent the Dozen out, en masse, to fetch typewriters from the offices of secretaries, counselors, and aides. Hoping to make my English curriculum relevant to the boys' needs, I had decided to teach the Dozen how to type their spelling words. By using a little innovation in my classroom, I could combine an instructional goal with a saleable job skill, thereby better preparing the boys for the real world. The typing project sounded like a good idea when I approached the principal for his approval.

But whereas the principal had adjusted to my unorthodox teaching methods, several colleagues had not. They seemed mortified by the thundering herd of delinquents I had turned loose in their hallowed hallways. Prone to be boisterous and rambunctious when excited, the Dozen had reenacted the Oklahoma land stampede, complete with war whoops and chase scenes. The old crones stood outside their classrooms and wagged their heads in horror. Why couldn't the English department stick to teaching gerunds and participles? they asked.

179

News traveled quickly about my latest project: western wood-carving. I had placed knives in the hands of the Dozen, and the boys were seen brandishing the weapons about the classroom. No one was safe in the halls of Temple High School, especially not with that murderer back on campus.

I had opted to teach the boys the craft of whittling as an enrichment activity following their study of western literature. Many of the Dozen were talented with their hands, and I had hoped that this activity would not only bolster their self-esteem but also stimulate their creativity. In addition, it would give me a chance to interact with the boys as they sat around in a circle and carved something other than notches on their guns.

After handing out the X-Acto knives and the eight-inch pine plaques I had purchased at a local craft store, I showed the boys several patterns they could choose to carve in relief, from birds to animals to words. Despite their varied backgrounds and interests, they all chose the same pattern for their plaques: the word "LOVE."

That choice spoke volumes about them. The Dozen's need for love was the common denominator that united them, whether they came from middle-class homes like Jim Taylor's or from drug abuse homes or housing project slums. Love, with its unconditional acceptance, was the one thing that they desperately sought, yet seldom found. It always seemed to allude them, no matter how hard they tried.

Early on, I had recognized the Dozen's need for love, especially parental love. From the beginning of my first year with them, I had tried to provide a surrogate support system in my classroom that would substitute for the one they lacked at home. I had looked for ways to teach the boys basic coping skills, especially how to handle their feelings of frustration and anger and inadequacy. Time after time, I had invited them to open up and share their concerns, believing that they trusted me enough to know I would never betray them.

Yet, despite my noble intentions, several members of the Dozen, including Jim, seemed reluctant to talk about themselves or their problems. Through their years of academic failure and emotional scarring, they had built protective walls around themselves as a self-defense mechanism. No one could get through to hurt them because they wouldn't allow themselves to feel.

Recognizing that they were always "on guard," I had opted to try the whittling circle during our last year together. Although I told the boys that this was an enrichment activity for our Old West unit, I had intended to use the week-long woodcarving session for much more.

I remembered from my Child Psychology 101 class that doctors often used non-threatening, game-playing sessions to get children to open up. By sitting down informally with a child, the psychologist could ask all sorts of questions while they laughed and played a game together. The unsuspecting child, engrossed in the fun, often revealed attitudes or values that he might not share with a stranger otherwise. I hoped our whittling circle would serve the same purpose, providing me with an opportunity to delve into each boy's dark world and to counsel him in a non-threatening way. Sitting beside a different one each day, I laughed and joked and talked with them as we carved out "LOVE." I reminded them that they were important to our school and that our class wouldn't be the same without them. They made a difference.

But mostly, I listened to them. It was surprising how much I learned after I stopped talking and started listening. I learned which ones came from broken homes, and who resented the upheaval of divorce or the intrusion of stepparents.

I learned which ones survived from week to week on food stamps, and who had little chance of breaking the poverty cycle because welfare had existed in the family for generations and education was "a waste of time."

I learned which ones had been abused, emotionally and physically, by alcoholic parents during drunken stupors. And whose belongings had been stolen after a prostitute mother brought a john home to turn a trick and shack up for a few weeks.

I learned which ones had gotten their girlfriends pregnant, paid for the abortion, and considered themselves murderers. And which ones were thinking about dropping out of school because they couldn't stand the beatings at home any longer and had to work full-time to pay for an apartment and bills.

I learned, all right. I learned about their hurt and pain and disappointment, learned more than I ever wanted to know about what adults can do to kids and themselves in the name of love. The whittling circle taught me a lot, and somehow gerunds and participles didn't seem so important after that.

I decided that maybe John Ruskin had been right when he wrote, "Education is not teaching students what they do not know; it is teaching them to behave as they do not behave."

I weighed the wisdom of Ruskin's words and wrote them across my lesson plan book so I wouldn't forget. "Teaching them to behave as they do not behave" so they can survive in the real world. That's what public schools ought to be doing, I decided — teaching the whole child, and not just his mind. Students were more than mathematical averages or letters on report cards, or bluebirds and redbirds. Much more.

In a nation where parents, churches, and communities had abdicated responsibility for the young, public schools, I realized, had a mandate to impact the physical, spiritual, and emotional needs of children. In addition to teaching the "basics" of reading and writing and arithmetic, we had an obligation to teach such things as life skills, interpersonal relationships, self-esteem, moral ethics, and creative expression. Or, so it seemed to me at the time.

Given the flexibility to deviate from a prescribed English curriculum, I resolved to put John Ruskin's maxim to use in my classroom.

When one of the Dozen nicked his finger with an X-Acto knife and uttered a volley of expletives, we talked about tolerance and how to control our impulses and frustrations. We also talked about a broader definition of the word, like how to handle people who were different, and how to deal with authority figures at school and home.

We discussed the value of staying in school versus the consequences of leaving, and about how the CVAE program would allow them to catch up academically by granting them credit for their work experience. We talked about the reasons why some students fail to achieve in academic classrooms and about the need for alternative classes that accommodate different learning styles.

We talked about the high expectations that the work/study

program had for them, and how they were expected to give it their best shot whether at school or on the job. I reminded them that there were many teachers who cared about them, who believed in them, and who wanted them to succeed. But only they themselves could make it happen.

And we discussed alternative remedies to problems that might cause them to want to drop out, or abuse drugs, or commit suicide. There were always alternatives in every situation, and they had the power to choose.

The power of personal choice was a message that I pounded into the Dozen during our last year together. Teaching them to use good judgment and to make responsible decisions were the life skills that I emphasized in lesson after lesson, book after book.

I used literature to open up dialogue and facilitate communication in discussing things like personal values and ethics. Assuming the role of amateur psychologists, we focused on the behaviors of the literary characters that we studied, many of whom were plagued by the same problems confronting the boys.

We considered the characters' alternatives, analyzed their choices, and examined the consequences of their actions. Through this subtle technique, the Dozen gained practice in the art of responsible decision-making. I hoped that the boys would somehow transfer the process into their own lives.

I had especially wanted Jim Taylor to make this connection, and my efforts focused on counseling him during the last three months before his trial. I wished that Temple High School had a crisis intervention program with a professional psychologist to work with troubled kids, but, like many public schools, we couldn't afford such budget "frills." So, I was on my own.

In desperation, I took a real gamble. I brought a book into the classroom that directly paralleled Jim's tragic story. *That Was Then, This is Now,* a street-gang book by S. E. Hinton, focused on the fate of a violent juvenile offender. The central character, like Jim, had pushed drugs, committed a felony, and behaved recklessly, believing he could get away with things because he was sixteen. "Nothing bad ever happens to you when you're young," the character insisted.

And like Jim, the central character had witnessed the brutal murder of a man, standing by and doing nothing to prevent it.

Unfeeling, unthinking, and out of control, the teenage hood in the book faced the same fate as the young outlaw in my classroom: the state prison, or worse.

I chose to confront Jim head-on by using our discussion of this book as an "intervention" session. As we sat in a circle and talked, I asked the Dozen to focus on the character's decision-making skills. What did the author want us to think about the character's choices?

"I don't think he was very smart," Big Rob said.

"Why not? He had a good time," I said, baiting him.

"Yeah, but look where he wound up."

"Did he have any other alternatives?" I pressed.

"Sure," shouted a couple of voices in unison. At this point, two more of the Dozen chimed in; they liked controversy and the discussion had begun to heat up.

I let them rattle on for several minutes before I interrupted their discussion and did something that I rarely did: preach.

"We *are* accountable for our actions," I said, holding the book in my right hand and waving it back and forth for emphasis. "We *must* think about others and behave responsibly. We must consider the consequences *before* we act, and ask ourselves: 'What if something goes wrong?' We can't expect society to let us off the hook because we're young. It doesn't work that way, gentlemen."

I saw a look of recognition flash through Jim's piercing blue eyes, and he stared at me through endless seconds of time. Several members of the Dozen dropped their heads as the deafening silence filled the void, and I felt a terrible awkwardness blanket the room. I had stepped over the line, and the Dozen knew it.

Afraid that I'd gone too far, I laid the book on my desk and looked away. When I finally found the courage to glance toward Jim and survey the damage I'd done, his fathomless eyes were still focused on mine, as if he were trying to make a choice. Finally, without saying a word or changing the expression on his face, he closed his book and pounded the cover with a silent fist. Then came the nod of acceptance.

I looked in his eyes and I knew. S. E. Hinton's book had accomplished what no one else had been able to do — get through to Jim Taylor. At that moment, Jesse James bit the dust.

* * * * *

From that day until his trial in early June, the Dozen formed a peer support group for Jim, making sure that he didn't suffer a relapse while he was "getting his head together." With Big Rob acting as overseer, the other boys took turns in monitoring Jim's activities: where he went, who he went with, and how late he stayed out.

Streetwise boys who had never cared about rules or behavior learned to think responsibly and to consider the consequences *before* they acted. In the process of helping Jim stay straight, the Dozen learned to stay straight themselves.

The salvaging of an outlaw kid by a class of delinquents made for good fiction, but it seldom happened in real life. Yet, I had watched the heart-wrenching climax transpire, and, like a detached narrator in a Fitzgerald novel, I had been caught up by the tragic tale of a young boy's journey to hell and back.

Jim and the Dozen had come a long way during the two years we spent together. I had watched the metamorphosis take place, and I marveled at the change in the boys. My experiment in behavior modification had finally paid off.

Of course, the Dozen's constant vigil over Jim was not without its occasional drawback. Like the March morning when I arrived at my classroom and found Big Rob and Donny standing guard outside the door.

"You can't go in just yet," Big Rob said, bracing his burly body against the doorknob.

"Why not?" I asked.

"Jim's inside," Donny said, rolling his eyes toward Big Rob and smiling a knowing look.

"Great," I said. "It's almost time for the bell. Let's all go inside, turn the lights on, and get started."

"No, ma'am," said Big Rob, "you don't understand."

"Jim's not alone," Donny said, "he's with a girl."

"In the dark?" I asked as I reached out and grabbed Big Rob's left bicep, motioning for him to end the tomfoolery and step aside.

As I reached for the doorknob, I remembered the last poor girl who had been trapped inside a classroom with the Dozen.

Lori had entered the CVAE program shortly before midterm, and she had lasted for about three weeks, until we reached the western literature unit and read *Little Big Man.*

Thomas Berger's brilliant satire of the Old West taught the Dozen many things about the frontier, including the price of prostitution during the 1880s, when the going rate was a dollar a poke. The boys were amazed that supply-and-demand (a term they had recently picked up in their government/economics class) had greatly inflated prices since then and created a real scarcity of the commodity.

After they left my classroom with their newfound knowledge, the Dozen tried to simulate the economics of the Old West during their second-period math class. When the teacher stepped outside the room to handle an interruption from the office, the boys pulled out their wallets, fingered crisp dollar bills, and waved them toward Lori.

The Dozen seemed downright disappointed when she buried her face in her hands, shook her blonde head vehemently, and refused to take advantage of the free enterprise system (another term they had learned). Not only did she rebuff their frontier money-making scheme, but she also had her schedule changed that very day. I never saw Lori again.

Visions of Lori filled my mind as I brushed Big Rob and Donny aside, opened the door to my classroom, and turned on the lights with a ceremonious thrust. "What's going on in here?" I asked in my official teacher voice.

While I waited for an explanation, Big Rob and Donny scurried into the room behind me. They nudged at my elbows and peered over my shoulders, trying to signal a "we're sorry" to the black-hatted cowboy across the room.

Jim stood over in the corner by the yellow filing cabinet, with his back to the door and his head tilted to one side. When he finished what he was doing, he turned around casually and flashed a sheepish grin. Then he took someone by the hand, strolled over toward me matter of factly, and said, "This is Lisa."

Lisa. A dark-eyed, long-haired brunette with a dazzling smile and an inner glow reminiscent of those wholesome, all-American girls parading across an Atlantic City stage in the Miss America beauty pageant.

Lisa. Bright and vivacious and alive. Something right off the cover of *Seventeen* magazine, she was truly breath-taking.

Jim had met her several weeks earlier when he and Big Rob had driven out to Action World, a local bowling alley/pool hall hangout for bored Temple teenagers looking for action. Jim had just finished his pool shot when he glanced across the room and saw her watching him. From the first moment he looked into her innocent, fawn-like eyes, he felt seared to his very soul. Jim knew that this girl was something special. She was a lady.

Wanting to impress her, yet feeling ill at ease, Jim began to grandstand. He took his pool cue, pretended to strum it like a guitar, and nodded for her to come over. Lisa, misinterpreting Jim's gyrations, thought he was making obscene gestures, so she shook her head with an emphatic *no*, turned abruptly on her heels, and walked away.

Jim followed her with his eyes, sizing up the beautiful brunette as she and her girlfriend seated themselves at a small table and ordered Cokes, waiting their turn for a bowling lane to open. She was proud and spirited and had a mind of her own. Jim liked that in a girl. And he clearly liked Lisa, right from the first snub of her turned-up nose.

Never one to take *no* for an answer, Jim finished his pool game, motioned for Big Rob to follow him, and strutted over to Lisa's table like a bantam rooster in pursuit of a prize hen. Above the din of clattering pins, crashing balls, and blaring music, Jim introduced himself, sat down in the chair next to Lisa, and asked if he could treat the girls to a game of doubles, using Big Rob's money, of course.

Lisa seemed hesitant, although she later admitted thinking that the black-hatted cowboy was "a real cutie." Jim turned on the Paul Newman charm, staring deeply into Lisa's eyes until she felt something "magical" between them. They talked for more than two hours, and Lisa was impressed by Jim's openness and his attentiveness. By the time the doubles match had ended and the final pin had fallen, so had the pretty little brunette. Jim had Lisa's address, her phone number, and a promise that she would come to his eighteenth birthday party the following week.

That's when he told her about the trouble he was in, when he drove her home from the party and they were alone for the first

187

time. With her head pressed against his shoulder, Jim felt his heart hammering as he described the events of that night a thousand years ago. He told her about the robbery at the dirt bottom store and about the old grocer who had died. Swallowing hard, he told her that he would go on trial as soon as school was out.

He didn't tell her about the probability of prison, for he had blocked that thought from his mind. He wouldn't allow himself to think about it, not during his last few weeks of freedom, and certainly not when he was with her.

Jim waited for Lisa to say something, but she didn't. He heard her slow, soft breathing as she gripped his hand tightly and nestled her head deeper into the folds of his jean jacket. Her touch warmed him inside, and he felt her all the way through him. It had been so long since he had felt anything.

Jim listened to the irregular whacking of the wipers across his rain-pelted windshield. He reached for a well-worn tape on the dash and shoved it into the stereo tapedeck. Moments later, the hard rock sounds of Bad Company blared from the front and back speakers, drowning out the droning of the blades with the lyrics "I'm ready for love, I'm ready for love." And he was.

Jim drove in silence, wondering if he had done the right thing in telling Lisa about his past. He could have kept the truth from her until they had dated longer, until she had fallen hopelessly in love with him, like all the others, and couldn't have turned back even if she wanted to. But Lisa deserved better than that, and he didn't want her under false pretenses. He owed her his honesty, even if it meant losing her.

And it almost did. When Lisa told her parents about the charges against Jim, they forbade her to date him. Even though Mr. and Mrs. Bannick had met Jim and liked him right away, they insisted that their fourteen-year-old daughter was too young to get involved with an eighteen-year-old boy, especially one on his way to prison. Jim Taylor was "bad" for Lisa, they insisted, and would only bring her heartache. They loved her, and they weren't about to let Jim ruin her life. She was to stay away from him. Period.

But Lisa stood her ground, defying her parents' ultimatum. She told them that she loved them and had always tried to obey them, but she had every intention of seeing Jim — with or without their permission. They could either allow him to come to their home, or she would find another way to be with Jim. After an ugly scene in the living room, the Bannicks reluctantly relented.

Except for the four or five times that Lisa "slipped around" and met Jim at the movies or at the bowling alley, their courtship was confined to school or to the Bannick living room, where they sat on the couch holding hands and watching television under the stern supervision of her family. The atmosphere was strained, at best, but the star-crossed lovers seemed grateful for whatever moments they had together.

And that's why the Dozen had stood guard outside my darkened classroom, trying to run interference for Jim while he stole a few precious, private moments with Lisa. Moments when he could hold her in his arms and kiss her, and not worry about her parents, or prison, or anything.

Big Rob and Donny had already recognized what I soon came to know: Lisa was very special. She was the girl Jim had looked for, longed for, and yet, somehow never believed he would find. She was the one that his mother had told him to wait for, during one of her long lectures about dating "nice" girls instead of whores. But he hadn't wanted nice girls. Until now.

This time it was different. With all of the others, he had just gone through the motions, sweet talking them into bed by the third date, taking what he wanted for two or three months, and then hitting the road. No commitments, no strings. But not with her.

Lisa had touched something deep inside him — feelings that he hadn't known existed — and there was no walking away from her, of that he was sure. Like some knight out of a forgotten storybook, he wanted to protect her, to shield her and love her and lay down his life for her, if need be. He wanted to make sure that he did everything just right — lived up to her high opinion of him — so he wouldn't disappoint her or hurt her.

And there would be no game-playing with her. No pressure for sex. As badly as he wanted to make love to her, he would wait, if she asked him to. With Lisa, it had to be "right."

The beautiful, spirited Lisa Bannick was the real catalyst in changing the direction of Jim's life. My behavior modification strategy had made a small inroad, and the Dozen had done their part in keeping him on the straight-and-narrow, but it was Lisa who touched his heart and worked the miracle. She brought out the best in him and made him believe in himself once again. "You've got to stand up to life," she told him, "and never settle for less than the best."

Standing with Lisa in his arms while they gazed at the stars and dreamed of tomorrow, Jim felt at peace with himself for the first time. Feeling safe and loved, he allowed his gentleness and his sensitivity to surface. He found a quiet confidence in himself, a contentment replacing the anger that had kept him restless. Through Lisa's love and encouragement and support, Jim found both the strength and the will to turn his life around.

There had been many before her, and there would be others after her, but he would never love anyone as he loved Lisa. If only he had met her before that night. Before he'd put the price on his head.

CHAPTER NINETEEN

"Whatever you want, Mama"

Joe Cannon sat waiting, listening to the rhythmical *bong-bong-bong* of the Westminster chimes emanating from the wall clock opposite his desk. Almost 11:00 A.M. The Taylors would be there shortly for a briefing on Jim's second certification hearing, scheduled for later that afternoon.

The boyish-looking Cannon, sporting a Beatles-style haircut with thick bangs covering his high forehead, rose from his leather chair and walked to the doorway of his Groesbeck law office, richly furnished with paintings of Texas longhorn steers and other memorabilia from his University of Texas law school days. In a smooth, baritone voice flavored with a tinge of Southern drawl, the former state legislator called to his secretary. "Miss Shirley, ma'am, hand me the Taylor boy's file."

Seated once again behind his massive mahogany desk, with the photos of his wife and two young children featured prominently, Cannon plopped a piece of hard candy into his mouth and leafed through his notes on the Taylor case, reviewing the records of recent proceedings. Shuffling through the papers, he found a Xerox copy of an article published recently in the *Texas Bar Journal*. He skimmed the title: "The Child Savers of Texas: The Progeny of *Gault* and *Kent.*"

Nodding his head in affirmation, Cannon returned the article to the folder and laid the Taylor file aside. He leaned back in his chair, folded his hands behind his head, and smiled. He had found a way to get Jim off.

The Limestone County legal battle had begun to heat up by

191

early March. Two weeks after Judge Ferguson had sentenced Wes Folger to life imprisonment in the Texas Department of Corrections, the lawyers for Don Folger and Walter Frye had received good news about their appeals. Because of the DA's failure to issue summonses to the juveniles, the Texas Court of Criminal Appeals had overturned Judge Ferguson's rulings at the certification hearings.

The State's high court ruled that the juvenile court had no jurisdiction to conduct such hearings because the DA had not followed "due process" as outlined by the Texas Family Code. Therefore, Don Folger and Walter Frye retained their juvenile status, the Court of Criminal Appeals stated, and neither juvenile could be turned over for criminal prosecution unless they were recertified to stand trial as adults.

Although Cannon had not filed an appeal for Jim, he knew that the Court of Criminal Appeal's ruling would impact his client's certification as well. Within days of the high court's decision, the Limestone County DA's office had ordered a summons delivered to each juvenile. The three youths were requested to reappear at separate times before the 77th District Juvenile Court on March 15 for their second certification hearings.

Joe Cannon met briefly with the Taylors in his office before he and Jim walked across the street and climbed the gray granite steps to the drafty courtroom on the second floor. Walking across the red carpet with a brisk step, the defense attorney took his place beside Jim at the defense table and waited for the second certification hearing to convene. Cannon was about to make a surprise move, reminiscent of a Perry Mason maneuver against an outfoxed District Attorney Berger.

Actually, Cannon had borrowed his strategy from the *Texas Bar Journal* article. He knew the legal implications of the *Kent* (1966) and *Gault* (1967) cases mentioned in "The Texas Child Savers" article, and he hoped that these precedent-setting U.S. Supreme Court decisions would give him the legal edge he needed in the Taylor case.

Within moments, the stoop-shouldered bailiff entered the courtroom, followed by Judge Tate McCain, one of the best-loved and most respected jurists in those parts. The huge, crusty old East Texas judge, known for his forthrightness in "calling a spade a spade" and for his occasional use of profanity from the bench, was presiding over Jim's juvenile hearing in the absence of Judge Ferguson.

Judge McCain had been a close friend of Cannon's for many years, and the young lawyer half-smiled when he saw the crotchety old jurist take his place behind the bench, shove his bifocals up to the bridge of his bulbous, Santa Claus-shaped nose, and peer out over the near-empty courtroom. Nodding his head toward the defense and prosecution tables, the judge began the proceedings with "Hidy, neighbors."

Despite Tate McCain's country-boy mannerisms and his down-home persona, Cannon knew that the judge was a smart man and a shrewd judge of character. More importantly, McCain believed in doing what was right, no matter what it took. The colorful old judge had proven that in his own courtroom, and his reputation for law-and-order had spread throughout neighboring counties. Especially after the time he took his six-shooter to Dallas and taught those big-city boys a lesson.

A Dallas judge who had been through a difficult divorce case didn't feel like presiding over "Runaway Daddy's Day" and had asked Judge McCain to come up and listen to the sob stories of delinquent fathers who hadn't paid their child support. Judge McCain, wanting to make a real impression on the culprits and teach them to do "what was right," opted for the dramatics.

The six-foot, 300-pound jurist entered the packed courtroom, chunked his coat on the bailiff's table, loosened his tie, and pulled out a revolver. Slamming the gun on the bench, the judge asked, "What's up first, Mr. Bailiff?"

"Failure to pay child support," the bailiff responded.

"Well, bring the sorry sons-of-bitches up here before me. If there's anything I can't stand, it's some bastard who won't take care of his kids."

As the first defendant warily approached the bench, Judge McCain greeted him with a gruff, "Hidy, neighbor. Why haven't you been paying your child support?"

"Don't have the money."

Judge McCain studied the man through his black, owl-rimmed glasses, narrowing his eyes as he asked, "Workin'?"

"Yeah."

"Well, I see you've got cigarettes."

"Yeah."

"You probably drink some beer, too, don't you?"

"Yeah."

"Then there's no reason you couldn't be paying something; you haven't paid a damn penny in so long." The judge fingered the revolver lying on the bench, turning the barrel slightly toward the wide-eyed man. "You sit your ass down in the hall out there," McCain said as he gestured toward the door, "and I'll give you a tour of the Dallas County Jail this weekend. You can spend some time there while you think about why you haven't paid your child support."

With that pronouncement, the other fathers in the courtroom broke like a covey of quail and raced to the phones in the hallway. For the rest of that day, each father who came before Judge McCain and his revolver managed to scrape up some money for his kids. Even the first delinquent daddy had raised more than $500 toward "doing what was right" by the time the crusty old judge recessed for lunch. All of which proved that the six-gun still had its place in keeping law and order.

A man always knew where he stood with Tate McCain, and Cannon felt relieved to see his old friend sitting on the bench for Jim's second certification hearing. Not only would Jim receive a fair proceeding, but he'd get every break the judge could give him. Cannon knew that Judge McCain took a special interest in kids and would go the extra mile in trying to salvage one.

Once the judge's preliminary remarks were out of the way, Cannon rose to his feet. "Your honor," he said, "I'd like to request that this hearing be dismissed. This juvenile court has no jurisdiction over my client."

Judge McCain, clearly puzzled by the young lawyer's motion, asked for clarification. "Now, Joe, I think you better explain that one to me."

Cannon proceeded to do so, using the argument outlined in the *Texas Bar Journal* article. During the year that the DA's office had postponed prosecution of the juveniles pending the outcome of the summons appeal, Jim Taylor had turned eighteen. As a legal adult, he no longer fell under the jurisdiction of the juvenile justice system. Therefore, Cannon pointed out, the court had no authority to conduct this second certification hearing, nor did it have the jurisdiction to turn Jim over to a criminal court for prosecution in the murder of Chester Brooks.

And, because Jim was sixteen at the time of the Brooks murder, the criminal court had no authority to prosecute the eighteen-year-old for something he did as a child. Cannon moved that the charges against his client be dismissed since Jim fell under the jurisdiction of neither court.

"Well, Joe, that's mighty interesting," the old judge said as he shifted his bifocals and studied the motion for dismissal. "Yes, sir, mighty interesting. But I'm gonna overrule you on that one."

Judge McCain went on to explain that he interpreted the law differently. The Limestone County juvenile court, he claimed, had authority to hear the Taylor case because the DA's office had begun prosecution while the boy was still a juvenile.

"But, Your Honor," Cannon protested, "that proceeding was thrown out by the Texas Court of Criminal Appeals. For all practical purposes, it never happened. The juvenile court failed to establish its jurisdiction . . ."

"Now, Joe," the slow-talking jurist said, "I'm gonna let you have your exception on this point, but we're still gonna go ahead with this hearing. Mr. Prosecutor, call your first witness."

Despite Cannon's protests, Jim's second certification hearing proceeded in much the same manner as the first, with the outcome unchanged. After listening to the evidence against the eighteen-year-old defendant, Judge McCain recertified Jim as an adult and ordered him turned over to the 77th District Criminal Court for prosecution. There he would be tried for the murder of Chester Wade Brooks, along with Walter Frye and Don Folger, who had been recertified as adults earlier that morning.

Cannon gave notice of his intent to appeal, confident that the Texas Court of Criminal Appeals would overturn Tate McCain's ruling. The legal precedent was clearly there: *Gault, Kent,* and *R.E.M. vs. State.* Perry Mason couldn't hope for better odds.

"The court has violated *Kent* and *In re Gault,*" Cannon explained to the Taylors as they sat in his office following the hearing. He gestured toward the copy of the *Texas Bar Journal* lying atop his cluttered desk as Jim and his parents focused their eyes on the cover, looking mystified by the lawyer's legal mumbo-gumbo.

Recognizing their confusion, Cannon switched to layman's language as he explained the two landmark U.S. Supreme Court decisions handed down in 1966 and 1967. According to *Kent* and *Gault,* the high court established "due process" for juveniles facing criminal prosecution, ensuring them the same constitutional rights as guaranteed to their adult counterparts. The Court ruled that "juvenile proceedings which may lead to commitment in state institutions must meet constitutional standards of due process as to notice, right to counsel, the privilege against self-incrimination, and the right to confront and cross-examine sworn witnesses."

Because the 77th District Juvenile Court had failed to properly notify Jim about the first certification hearing, it had violated the due process procedure outlined by *Gault.* The court had not only disregarded the boy's civil rights, Cannon argued, but it had also failed to establish jurisdiction over Jim while he was a juvenile. By the time a summons was finally served, Jim had turned eighteen and had attained legal adult status.

Cannon went on to tell the Taylors about a third precedent-setting case mentioned in the *Texas Bar Journal* article. The Texas Court of Civil Appeals had recently heard a case called *R.E.M vs. State,* where a juvenile burglary offender had evaded arrest until after his eighteenth birthday. The appeals court ruled that the defendant was not a juvenile at the time of his arrest and, therefore, did not fall under the jurisdiction of the juvenile court system.

Using the *R.E.M.* decision in conjunction with the *Kent* and *Gault* cases, Cannon believed that he had the legal precedent to win an appeal and throw out the murder charge against Jim. The defense attorney estimated that his chances for walking the boy were seventy-five percent or better.

As Cannon laid his cards on the table for the Taylors, he became excited by the prospect of arguing Jim's case before the Court of Criminal Appeals. This appeal, he knew, would set legal precedent in Texas by helping to revise the State's juvenile laws and bring them in line with federal rulings. Cannon believed that

Taylor vs. State would be a landmark decision. A case of this magnitude rarely came along in a lawyer's career, and he was excited by his good fortune. He could win his client's freedom and revise the law at the same time.

Cannon's elation subsided, however, when he looked across his desk into the eyes of Carolyn Taylor. He had expected her to be overjoyed by the legal loophole that would free her son, yet she sat there as stoical as a stone madonna. She wasn't buying any of this.

Suspecting that her reluctance stemmed from financial hardship, he told the Taylors not to worry about the cost of the appeal. They could pay him whatever they could afford, whenever they could afford it, and he would do the rest for free.

"We'll have to think about it," Carolyn said as she and Von led Jim down the narrow hallway of Cannon's law office and out the front door of the small red-brick building across the street from the courthouse. "We'll let you know."

Cannon stood watching as the Taylors' blue sedan drove around the town square, past Josie's Restaurant, and then disappeared beyond the town's one red light. He was completely mystified by Carolyn's response. He had told her that he could keep her eighteen-year-old son out of a Texas hell-hole. What was there to think about?

Carolyn Taylor sat on her Early American sofa, both feet propped against its overstuffed cushions as she sipped meditatively from a glass of iced Lipton tea. She heard Von and Jim's muffled voices in the hallway, bantering about some ballgame.

Drumming her fingers in a quiet cadence against the frosted glass, Carolyn focused on the row of scratched K-Mart picture frames sitting atop the antique credenza on the opposite wall. There, spread across the scarred top of the old cabinet that Chester Brooks had given her, were the school portraits of her four picture-perfect children. Not so perfect, it would seem.

One by one, she studied the innocent, silent faces that stared back at her through broad, beaming smiles reminiscent of happier times. Times when gleeful laughter, excited screams, and rambunctious roughhousing had filled her home with chaotic merriment.

197

Closing her reddened eyes, she could almost picture Jim and Gena on their shiny blue bicycles, zooming by at Indy 500 speeds while preschooler Glenn squealed with delight and toddler Julie gave a pat-a-cake ovation. Such happy, carefree times filled with Halloween jack-o'-lanterns and Christmas stockings and Easter baskets. Perhaps if she listened harder, she might hear the echoes of their excited childhood voices, still lingering somewhere in a playful game of hide-and-seek. Come out, come out, wherever you are . . .

She opened her eyes and stared at the picture of Jim. He had been the rascally one, always hiding from her, always sneaking off and getting himself into mischief. She had never known a moment's peace with Jim around.

No, that wasn't exactly true. There had been moments, long ago. Fleeting moments when she had held him in her arms as they stood beneath the blackened night sky, inspecting shimmering stars and glittering galaxies far beyond them. Moments when his pudgy baby fingers had extended heavenward in sheer delight, pointing out the wonder of some mystical, magical phenomenon, like a half-crescent moon or a falling star or a gaggle of geese migrating south across the distant horizons.

Even when the years had distanced him — when he would no longer allow her to hold him or to touch him — she would sometimes catch him standing out in the backyard, looking up at the silent heavens and preserving the nighttime ritual of two old stargazers, lost in time and space as they dreamed of worlds far away. There had been moments. Long ago.

Lifting the iced tea glass to her lips, Carolyn saw the framed faces of her other three children. They peered at her from across the room in silent protest, accusing her of loving Jim best. And perhaps she had, once. But the years had taken their toll, and Carolyn Taylor was tired.

She was tired of the guilt she felt for neglecting her other children as she anguished over Jim. Tired of robbing them of the stable, supportive homelife that they desperately needed. She knew that Gena showed signs of emotional distress and that Glenn displayed behavioral problems. Even little Julie, the pigtailed ten-year-old, cried herself to sleep at nights. Carolyn knew that she had to do something. For the well-being of her family, she had to do something.

Carolyn had sat at the kitchen table the night before, discussing Cannon's proposal for an appeal with Von and Jim. Jim had leaned back, propped his chair against the wall, and listened to what his parents had to say, without interruption or argument. She and Von had adopted a "toughlove" policy with their son since his release from jail. "We refuse to live with a rebellious son," she had told him, "and we won't tolerate that behavior any longer."

Carolyn and Von had then set limits, taken a stand, and held Jim accountable for his actions. Whenever a crisis presented itself (for example, Donna's pregnancy), they handed the problem back to Jim for resolution. They provided "selective support," but they insisted that Jim assume self-responsibility for his life. For almost a year now, he had submitted to their authority and abided by the rules they set down for him, except for one time when he missed his 10:00 P.M. curfew and incurred his mother's lengthy lecture about "bottom lines."

As they tried to come to terms with the life-altering decision that would impact Jim's future, Carolyn had turned to him and asked, "What do you think, son?"

Jim had looked into his mother's troubled eyes and felt the weight of their anguish. He shrugged his shoulders and shook his head. "Whatever you want, Mama," he said as he lowered his eyes, stared solemnly at the table, and fingered the half-empty glass of Dr Pepper. "I've already put you and Daddy through enough," he said.

Sitting there beside him, she had reflected on the pain of those last four years, the living hell of Jim's defiance and drug addiction and lawlessness, followed by the death of her beloved Chester. Despite the recent "miracle" that had altered Jim's behavior — despite the love and trust and understanding that they had begun to reestablish as a family — she knew that they couldn't absolve Jim from his wrongdoing. That wouldn't be right.

Even though Jim hadn't killed Chester Brooks, he had been there that night and he had committed a crime. She had tried to instill in her children a fear of God and a respect for law-and-order. Jim had rebelled against those values, and now he had to accept the responsibility for his choices. If he were allowed to get away with his lawlessness — if he were allowed to go free on some legal technicality — there would be no stopping him, and she knew it.

"Whatever you want, Mama." Jim's words echoed in her ears as she sat in the living room and listened to her husband's and son's voices in the hallway. Tears filled her eyes, and she blinked back the wetness to focus on the photograph of the beautiful, blond-haired boy with the dancing blue eyes. Her reckless, devil-may-care star-gazer. Her perpetual player of hide-and-seek.

She knew Jim's childhood game was over and that she couldn't allow him to hide any longer. She recalled Reverend Williams' words about God holding each man accountable. Clinging to her belief that "all things work together for good," she closed her eyes in submission and made the choice.

There would be no appeal to the Texas Court of Criminal Appeals. No landmark decision impacting the state's juvenile justice system. No *Kent* or *Gault* or *R.E.M.* or any other legal loophole to get Jim off.

Her son would go to prison.

CHAPTER TWENTY

A Lesson of Quiet Hope

On June 5, one day after school had ended, the case of the *State vs. Taylor* came before the 77th District Court of the Honorable Clarence Ferguson. Seated next to his co-defendants and flanked by his attorney, Jim Taylor tuned out most of the proceedings. There was no need to listen. He already knew the outcome of the game, like reading a scoreboard that had been lighted before either team took the field. Twenty-five to nothing.

His lawyer had agreed to a plea-bargain arrangement with the district attorney's office after Carolyn Taylor had nixed all hope of a Texas Criminal Court appeal. Plea bargaining was a legal maneuver often used by State prosecutors in crowded court dockets to expedite justice and save the county money. Cannon had agreed to plead Jim guilty to the murder of Chester Brooks; in return, the DA would recommend that the court sentence the boy to twenty-five years in the Texas Department of Corrections.

Cannon had urged Jim to take the deal rather than risk a jury trial, where the DA would introduce the gory pictures of the old man's battered head and the blood-stained block. "You'd be a fool to walk into a courtroom of Chester Brooks' friends and risk a life sentence like Wes Folger," Cannon advised him. "Besides," the lawyer said, "you can do twenty-five years standing on your head."

Jim had, therefore, agreed to go along with whatever the lawyer and his parents thought best. He signed the half-dozen court documents placed before him, not bothering to read any of them. He scribbled his signature and swore that he killed Chester

Brooks by striking the old man with a shotgun and by dropping a concrete block on his head.

Nudged to his feet by Cannon as the 77th District Court convened, Jim stood solemnly and listened to the judge's formal intonation. "James Edward Taylor," said the black-robed Ferguson as he peered down on the good-looking, clean-cut boy in the starched white shirt and navy dress pants. "You have been charged with the murder of Chester Wade Brooks. How do you plead?"

Jim pressed whitened knuckles against the defense table, steadied himself, and cleared his throat. When he spoke, his voice sounded hesitant and hollow. "Guilty, Your Honor."

For the rest of the afternoon, he sat staring out the second-story window of the courthouse while the DA presented evidence against him. First came the testimony of Deputy Bill Fletcher, then Frank Mitchell, followed by Ricky Dominick and all the rest. Despite Jim's plea of guilty, the court was required by law to examine evidence verifying his guilt before the judge could pass sentence.

When the testimonies ended late that afternoon, Jim stood expressionless as Ferguson's voice pronounced the benediction. "James Edward Taylor, you have been adjudged to be guilty of murder. It is the judgment of the court that you be confined in the state penitentiary for twenty-five years, and that you immediately be delivered by the sheriff of Limestone County to the director of the Texas Department of Corrections, where you shall be confined for a term of not less than five nor more than twenty-five years in accordance with the law governing the penitentiaries and the Texas Department of Corrections." The gavel sounded: *Thump. Thump. Thump.*

Sheriff Dennis Walker moved forward to take custody of the boy who stood behind the defense table, embracing his teary-eyed mother. Like the X's and O's on a football game plan, Jim had been moved through plays he didn't call, toward a goal he didn't want, in a game he couldn't win.

We had talked about football that last evening he came to my house, on the day before his trial. Football, Jim insisted, had been the make-or-break situation in his life. He went "bad" the after-

202

noon he walked off the field. From that moment on, he was off-sides in a game filled with penalty after penalty. He kept fumbling through life, unable to recover what he had lost.

"I should have never quit the team," Jim said, reflecting on a season that had passed all-too-quickly, on a childhood that was lost forever. "That's where I went wrong," he said. "Quitting football, then dropping out of school."

I nodded, recalling the lesson I had tried to impress on the Dozen about the "beginning of loss." There had been so many values I had tried to teach the boys during the past two years. I wondered how much Jim actually remembered, and whether any of it would make a difference.

As Jim sat in my living room that last evening, the "teacher" part of me felt a need to inspire him with some sort of extemporaneous pep-talk. Given my knowledge of literature, surely I could recite some philosophical maxim to comfort Jim and strengthen him for what lay ahead during the next twenty-five years.

What literary work could I use to prepare Jim for the hellish nightmare of a Texas prison, where he would be forced to fight three times that first day to survive? White boys who didn't fight back were used as women; cellblock pimps hauled them out of their beds each night and auctioned them off for a pack of cigarettes or a box of cookies. He would watch more than eighty percent of the white boys in his unit become "little girls."

What words could I recall to help him cope with seeing inmates die of heat exhaustion as they groveled in the cotton fields under 103-degree temperatures, or with watching a black man knifed in the shower room as racial tensions flared? What could I say to shield him from the gang wars, the extortion rings, the dope dealers, and the crooked guards who abused their authority?

"Turn the other cheek" and "do unto others" didn't seem relevant, and I found myself at a loss to say anything. I suspect that Jim understood my dilemma, for he tried to ease my icy silence by changing the subject.

Jim talked about the past, laughing as he reminisced about funny things that had happened during the school year. He recalled the time the Dozen had played a trick on Donny and sent a "mushy" love note to an unattractive girl who liked him. The girl had written Donny a reply, and he had become furious. His ears turned red.

Jim also recalled the time they had rebelled against their new math teacher's edict to "stay in your seats and raise your hands if you want to sharpen your pencils." Twelve pencil leads had snapped in unison as the Dozen's defiant hands shot into the air. The math teacher had burst into tears.

And he laughed about the time he brought a Dr Pepper bottle to class, wrapped it in a brown paper bag, and set it on my desk. The Dozen had then summoned the school photographer and asked him to take a picture documenting "Mrs. Post's drinking problem." My face had turned the color of cranberries, and the boys had delighted in the merriment of my new "wino" image.

Jim talked about so many insignificant things that last evening, silly things from the past that had no real meaning or relevancy. He avoided talking about the future, about his trial and prison. I think he wanted to spare me that.

As Jim finally stood to go, I reached out and hugged him, just as I had done on that January morning so long ago. With my arms wrapped around him, I wanted to hold onto him and protect him from what I feared would come. Despite my lectures to the Dozen about personal choices and accepting responsibility for one's actions, I wondered whether I, like Carolyn Taylor, could have sent my son to prison. I marveled at the strength of her convictions.

I felt Jim's body tremble as he fought to stay in control. The time for tears had passed; he could never allow himself to cry again. His voice, when he finally spoke, sounded hoarse and choked. "If anybody wants to quit school," he began, then paused for a moment to reflect, "don't sign those papers. Okay, Mrs. Post?"

"Okay," I whispered as images of a hallway scene from the year before flashed through my mind. Whether or not the Dozen ever understood my lecture about the "beginning of loss," I knew that Jim had learned it well. I gave him a final squeeze, dropped my arms to my sides, and took a step back. "Take care," I said. And then, breaking every rule in my Education 101 manual, I added a final line. "I love you, Jim."

I blinked back the tears, forced a half-smile, and stared into the fathomless blue eyes framed beneath the brim of his black cowboy hat. I wanted him to remember me smiling.

As he opened the door and walked outside, Jim flashed the mischievous Cool Hand Luke grin, already playing the part of the classic Newman character whose spirit could not be broken by prison guards, or solitary confinement, or death. Jim would do hard time, but unlike the fictional Luke, he would be all right.

We had been given another year to reach him, and that had made a difference. With the help of the Dozen and our alternative class, as well as Lisa's love and his parents' support, Jim Taylor had been rehabilitated before he set foot inside a Texas prison. He would never ride the outlaw trail again.

Without turning to look back or wave goodbye, he climbed into the pickup and drove west, headed toward his last free-world sunset. It would be many years before he saw another.

At 9:00 A.M. on June 6, Groesbeck deputies took Jim Taylor and Don Folger from their second-floor jail cell, shackled them with handcuffs and legs irons, and placed them in the back seat of a waiting Limestone County sheriff's car. Walter Frye had opted to remain behind and complete his personal affairs before being transported to the Texas Department of Corrections, where he would begin serving the twenty-five-year sentence assessed to him and his fellow conspirators.

A stocky, dark-haired deputy slid into the driver's seat, slammed the car door, and glanced in his rearview mirror at the two passengers in back. "Are you boys ready?" he asked.

Jim nodded and replied, "Let's do it." It was a response that he had given often as he sat on the back of a Brahman bull and waited for the chute gate to open. It was also the response given by another black-hooded, convicted murderer just moments before three bullets tore through a paper target and ripped open his black T-shirt.

The deputy turned right at the first corner, and the car passed in front of the Limestone County courthouse, where Judge Clarence Ferguson had passed sentence on Chester Brooks' killers just hours before. Ferguson — it was a name that Jim would remember often, for it not only belonged to the trial judge but also to the prison unit where he would spend the first three years of his twenty-five-year sentence. The Ferguson unit of the Texas Department of Corrections incarcerated some 2,000 prisoners; most of them, like Jim, were under the age of twenty-one.

As the sheriff's car headed east and sped along the near-deserted State Highway 164, Jim noticed the road sign to Palestine, a small East Texas community which housed another TDC prison facility. The Palestine unit would soon become the workplace of a young coach hired to supervise the inmates' exercise program — the same coach who had inspired a fourteen-year-old football player to give his best as he wore the maroon-and-gold colors of the Lamar Bearcats. "Belong to something," Coach Hoppers had told him. "Don't just be a number."

Yet that was precisely what Jim Taylor was about to become. His white prison uniform would bear the number 280665 stenciled in black ink, the same numbers as those pressed into the license plates of two old trucks at Chester Brooks' farmhouse, sitting there in the shadows of the Navasota River.

The Navasota River, a favorite watering hole for Quanah Parker and his Comanches, stretched southeastward from Limestone County to Madison County and joined the mouth of the Brazos River near Houston. Had Jim studied a map of Texas, he might have discovered that the river's course matched that of his own. Beginning on the Central Texas prairies near Chester Brooks' store, the placid river meandered more than a hundred miles before it came within a stone's throw of the towns of Madisonville and Navasota. Both of these communities were sites of prison farms where Jim would be incarcerated for the old man's death. From that night he stood outside the Coit farmhouse, listening to the smashing of a stone block, the young outlaw had merely followed the river's edge to his own tragic destiny.

Four hours after the journey began, the sheriff's deputy exited Interstate 45 and drove his young prisoners toward the East Texas town of Huntsville, headquarters for the Texas Department of Corrections. There Jim would be in-processed at a prison facility nicknamed "The Walls." The unit bore the same name as the street in Belton where he and Walter had lived while they worked for Ricky Dominick. Wall Street, where the deputies found the old keys that Jim had almost thrown away — the only piece of physical evidence that linked him to the crime.

In looking back over this young outlaw's life, I marveled at the many unexplained coincidences that stalked Jim Taylor — the recurring names and numbers and places, as well as the four prophetic tombstones in New Hope Cemetery and the eerie connection with Jesse James, the Old West badman who believed in time travel and out-of-body experiences. It almost seemed as if Jim's destiny had been determined by mystical forces of another time and place. And yet, I ruled out the notion of fate or karma. I believed each man's destiny was charted by choice and not by chance.

Jim apparently agreed. "I don't want anyone to feel sorry for me," he once told me. "Nobody is to blame for any of this — not you or my parents or my friends. Nobody. I made the choices."

Jim had come to accept the truth that Reverend Williams had shared with him months before in the dining hall of the McLennan County Juvenile Detention Center: "Be not deceived. God is not mocked. For whatsoever a man soweth, that shall he also reap."

For the fair-haired boy entering the guarded walls of a Texas prison, the season of reaping had come at last.

CHAPTER TWENTY-ONE

Hard Times in Huntsville

Many times during the next seven years, I walked beyond the guard towers and the barbed wire and the electronic gates of the Texas Department of Corrections. Although my pilgrimage behind bars never became easy, the first visit was the hardest.

The massive Ferguson Unit had stood out, stark and somber, against the fertile cotton fields of rural southeastern Texas as our car wound along the narrow blacktop road. The austere, red-brick building served as a reminder of an antiquated penal system dating back to the days of slavery. I felt my heart pounding as Carolyn Taylor pulled the car to a stop. I stepped out onto the gravel parking lot, and a voice inside my head told me I didn't want to see this.

I preferred to believe Texas prisons resembled Holiday Inns, where inmates lounged in air-conditioned comfort and watched TV. I'd formulated that idea during my somewhat sanctimonious get-tough-on-crime days. Newspapers and television broadcasts had portrayed inmates as leading a "soft life," and my pseudo-John Birch blood had boiled at the very idea of freeloading felons. "What about the victims?" I had railed with an air of righteous indignation.

But on that first humid August morning, as I accompanied Carolyn Taylor on her bimonthly visit to see Jim, all notions about "easy living" in a Texas prison were dispelled. Those were the days before inmate David Ruiz filed his landmark civil rights suit and toppled the Texas Department of Corrections. During the late 1970s, when Jim and his three conspirators did "hard time," conditions inside Texas prisons were bad. Very bad. Between its brutality and bestiality, the TDC was a man-made hell.

"I'll lock your purse in the trunk of the car," Carolyn said, interrupting my trancelike stare at the four guard towers overlooking the sprawling prison complex. She explained that I couldn't take anything inside except my wallet and driver's license. I needed the latter to verify my identity on Jim's official visitation list, she said.

The list consisted of ten preapproved names. According to TDC rules, Jim was allowed a two-hour visit with two people, twice a month. Jim's elderly grandmother could no longer make the four-hour drive from Coit, so Carolyn had asked me to fill Grandma Garrett's slot. (I continued to do so at three-month intervals for the next six years.)

Without speaking further, Carolyn led me to the guard station outside the two chain-link fences surrounding the prison's perimeter. We presented our identifications to a guard in reflecting sunglasses, who then threw a switch and opened the heavy electronic gate. With apprehension, I followed Carolyn through the prison portal and beyond the two towering chain-link fences with the barbed wire coils. I felt my shoulders flinch when, several seconds later, the heavy metal bars snapped shut behind us.

The atmosphere seemed portentous and oppressive. I felt overwhelmed by a strange eeriness, as if I'd been there before. Shards of a jagged image took shape inside my head, and a melancholy coldness numbed me. Then I remembered.

During a tour of southern Germany, my Army major husband had taken me and our infant son inside another place of incarceration. Stark, somber, and foreboding, it, too, had warehoused the human refuse of a failed society. The Germans had called it Dachau.

Carolyn showed no sign of uneasiness as we walked along the well-maintained walkway, past the weeded flower beds, and into the waiting room. She had been there often during the fourteen months that Jim had been incarcerated. Each time he was permitted a visitor, she had come. Her devotion to Jim remained steadfast throughout those difficult, lengthy years of imprisonment. Through her sacrifice and example, I came to learn the meaning of the term "unconditional love."

I dismissed the dismal memory of Dachau as Carolyn and I stood among the throng of visitors in the sweltering waiting area. Almost a year and a half had passed since I'd seen Jim, and I wanted our first visit to be cheerful. I'd written him several letters of encouragement. I knew if he were going to survive in that environment, he had to keep a positive attitude, so I tried to sound upbeat in my letters.

I mustered a pleasant smile when, a half-hour later, the young guard in the starched gray uniform called "Taylor." We followed him down an immaculate, waxed corridor and into the visitation room.

The rectangular-shaped room, filled mostly with young women and small children, appeared noisy, smoky, and crowded. A scarred, wooden countertop divided the room into a U-shape, with visitors seated in folding chairs along the outer three sides of the partition.

To maximize security, a wire screen extended from the countertop to the ceiling, forming a "cage" in the center of the room. The inmates sat within this area. The TDC restricted all physical contact except for one day each year: Mother's Day. On that day, Carolyn Taylor was allowed to attend chapel services with Jim and touch her son.

The young guard seated us in two chairs on the far side of the room, with our backs to the row of windows that spanned the length of the wall. Light filtering in from the outside world cast a glare on the three-foot plexiglas plate that had been added to the wire partition. This additional barrier was designed to prevent visitors from passing drugs through the holes in the wire mesh. Such a precaution, however, proved an exercise in futility. According to Jim, drugs were readily available in prison. Some were even brought in by the guards.

I looked around for the telephones. Movies always showed visitors using telephones to speak with prisoners behind partitions. But there were no phones. Instead, visitors raised their voices to make themselves heard through the plexiglas. With people seated elbow-to-elbow along the countertop, there was no possibility of having a private conversation. Through the noisy din in the room, I heard the woman seated next to me say,

"Mama will get you some drugs when you get out, son, if that's what you want." I winced.

We waited for more than fifteen minutes, and I glanced at the young inmate seated nearby. Despite his clean-cut looks and crisp white uniform, he unnerved me. His eyes appeared hard and cold and cruel. God help us, I thought, when he gets out.

According to statistics, some eighty percent of the paroled inmates returned to the TDC after committing other crimes. With no real psychological counseling or rehabilitation programs, most inmates changed little. The prison system was funded to punish, nothing more. Crime continued to soar, despite Texas' leading the nation in the number of inmates on death row awaiting execution.

I had been so preoccupied with my thoughts about that "lost" young man that I hadn't seen the other inmate approach until the guard seated him in the chair opposite me. "Hey, lady," came the familiar voice.

The glare on the plexiglas obscured his face at first, though I doubt I would have recognized it anyway. The face appeared thin and angular and pale. The hair was cropped short, with highlights of gray beginning to show at the temples. The young body that had once exuded an air of cockiness and confidence now seemed passive and deferential. But the eyes hadn't changed. They were unmistakable.

Carolyn handed some coins to the guard, who walked to the vending machine and purchased a Dr Pepper for Jim. The guard removed the can's pull-tab before handing Jim the soft drink. Inmates couldn't be trusted with a piece of sharp metal.

Carolyn did most of the talking during the first visit, and, for that, I was grateful. I'd rehearsed a number of things to say to Jim, but I forgot most of them. The surroundings bothered me, and it took every ounce of energy within me to maintain a smile and appear cheerful.

Carolyn updated Jim on news of home and family members. His older sister had a new job and was adjusting well. His younger brother was playing Wildcat football and looked very promising, in the Taylor tradition. Jim listened carefully as he sipped from the Dr Pepper can.

Collecting my thoughts, I extended best wishes from several

211

members of the Dozen. The boys had telephoned me during the summer, updating me on their latest antics. When I told them I was going to see Jim in August, each one had sent a personal anecdote for me to share with him. Jim listened with an amused smile on his face.

Seven of the original twelve had graduated in the spring, I told him, and he seemed pleased. He, himself, had enrolled in classes at the prison and had recently completed his GED certificate.

Jim talked about his plans to enroll in two trade programs, welding and electricity. "I'm going to 'use' my time rather than 'serve' time," he told me. Jim realized that to make it on the outside, he had to have a marketable skill. He'd already learned that most inmates who returned to prison did so because they lacked the skills to find a job; they had reverted to stealing or pushing drugs to make a fast buck. "When I get out," he said with a determined smile, "I'm never coming back to this place."

I told him I was proud of him for the choices he'd made. He seemed to have his head together. I should have stopped with that, but I went one step further and asked, "How are you, Jim? Really?"

He seemed caught off-guard by my question. The muscles in his face suddenly tightened, the winsome grin disappeared, and a watery film clouded his eyes. He stared at me for a long time, as if he were deciding whether to tell me something. Then, deciding against it, he merely said, "It's hard here, Mrs. Post. Real hard." He dropped his head, focused on the countertop, and fingered the empty soft drink can.

I felt my heart splinter into a thousand pieces as I stared at him through the plexiglas barrier. I wanted to ask him to explain, to tell me what had happened. But, at the same time, I was afraid he might.

What if my worst nightmares had been realized? What if Jim had been through the same brutality and abuse that I'd seen portrayed on television and in movies? How could I live with that? How could Carolyn Taylor live with that? I glanced away, avoiding his eyes, then changed the subject.

I chattered, instead, about the Wildcats' upcoming bid for the state title in football. Ranked in the top ten, Bob McQueen's team was considered a real contender. Jim knew several players on the team, for he'd played beside them in middle school. "If only I hadn't quit football," he said in reflection. A touch of melancholy tinged his voice.

We continued to make small talk after that, much as we had done on that last night he came to see me, before being sentenced to Ferguson. Now, like then, he wanted to spare me from the terrible truth. Perhaps he knew I couldn't handle it.

The two-hour visit passed quickly. I remember the look in Jim's eyes when the guard walked up, checked his clipboard, and said, "Time's up, Taylor." It was a look of dread, of deep personal anguish.

Jim stood to go. As he straightened, I watched him visibly change character, as if he were an actor playing a part. He flashed the old Cool Hand Luke grin as he shoved his chair under the countertop and said goodbye to his mother. He couldn't allow anyone to see his vulnerability, not if he wanted to survive in that world to which he was about to return.

I, too, forced a smile as I stood to face him. I always wanted Jim to remember me smiling. "Take care," I said as I placed my outstretched hand on the wire partition above the plexiglas plate. Jim hesitated, glanced at the guard for a moment, then did the same.

It was a farewell ritual we repeated often during the long years of his imprisonment. Hand touching hand, reaching across the wire chasm that separated our worlds.

The following morning, while Jim attended chapel services at Ferguson prison, I sat in Pat Brownlee's Sunday school class at Immanuel Baptist Church. When Pat asked for prayer requests, I felt my clammy hand slip halfway into the air.

Although my religious faith had always been a personal matter and I rarely shared my spiritual needs with others, I felt deeply troubled that morning. I told the class about my visit to the prison and asked the ladies to remember Jim in prayer. They promised to do so, for many of them knew and loved the Taylor family. Then someone suggested we turn to Psalm 91:9–12 and read aloud:

> Because thou hast made the Lord thy habitation,
> there shall no evil befall thee.

For He shall give His angels charge over thee,
to keep thee in thy ways.

They shall bear thee up in their hands,
lest thou dash thy foot against a stone.

When we finished reading the passage, a gray-haired member of the class said, "What Jim needs is a guardian angel inside that prison. Let's ask God to send one."

The other ladies quickly concurred and bowed their heads in prayer. At the time, I felt uncomfortable. I didn't know what to think about guardian angels. I knew the Bible spoke of their existence, yet my mind had problems in accepting that aspect of the supernatural. As an educated intellectual, I remained skeptical.

Within days, however, I received a letter from Jim that began to change my mind. Jim wrote about a surly prison guard who had started harassing him, trying to provoke him into a fight. Just when Jim thought he couldn't hold his temper any longer, a fair-minded guard appeared on the scene and overheard the verbal abuse. This gray-uniformed "guardian angel" intervened on Jim's behalf and told the warden. The first guard was reprimanded, and the harassment ended without further incident.

Through the years, other guardian angels took over to protect Jim, especially after the violence escalated among the inmates. The warden, for example, assigned Jim a nighttime job in the boiler room. This job kept him out of the dormitory area in the evenings and away from the gangs which raped and pillaged and murdered almost at will.

When Jim turned twenty-one and was transferred from Ferguson to the Pack II unit, a new "boss" interceded. Jim was, once again, assigned a job away from the hard-core inmates. This time he worked with the horses used by the guards to supervise inmates in the cotton fields. Jim not only did the horseshoeing of the animals, but also rode them across the open fields. It was almost like being free again.

Jim gained additional privileges when he impressed the major at Pack II and advanced to trusty much quicker than the other inmates. He was even allowed once to drive a prison truck into the town of Navasota without supervision.

And my worst fears were never realized. Although Jim had a

number of fistfights while in prison, he was never sexually abused. A Chicano gang ran interference for him. These violent, hard-core criminals watched out for him because they liked his spunk. (They even taught him how to cook Mexican food.)

Some people might have said that Jim was just lucky, but he suspected differently. He said as much in one of his letters, after I'd told him about our request for a guardian angel:

Dear Mrs. Post,

I'm sure glad that you and everyone else are praying for me. Let me tell you, He's doing what you're asking Him to do.

The Lord has really been watching over me these past few months. I've had some really hard times to pull through, but a lot of good things have been happening to me that I couldn't even start to explain.

I want to thank you for your prayers because I've needed them. I can just imagine how hard it would be if I didn't have faith in God.

While I may have doubted the existence of guardian angels, Jim Taylor did not. He'd seen them in action.

Through the years, Jim himself took on the role of a guardian angel. Time and again, he ministered to the needs of my students. Whenever a troubled kid was assigned to my class, I often consulted Jim for advice, especially when I'd reached a dead-end. Like the time I'd tried to reach Ben and had gotten nowhere.

Ben was a bright, popular, all-American kid from a good family. But, like Jim, he had somehow managed to lose himself. Although a talented athlete, Ben began to run with the wrong crowd and to use hard drugs. Troubled and out of control, he was jeopardizing his chance to play college football.

Jim responded to my appeal for advice in his next letter, allowing the voice of experience to speak:

Dear Mrs. Post,

From the way you describe Ben, he seems like a good kid caught between right and wrong. He knows what is right and what he should do, but he wants to be in with the crowd. In other words, he's got to maintain his image in front of his friends. How well do I know that feeling.

You think you've got to be the one who can drink the

most, smoke the most pot, etc., just to keep up that personal image of yourself, but deep down inside you're scared to death of what you're doing.

Then, after a while, you overpower the fear and fool yourself by thinking there's nothing that can hurt you. That's when you're really bad off. You're sliding downhill to such hurt and pain that you'll wish you'd never been born.

If Ben keeps on doing drugs, it will happen to him. He'll fool around and lose his chance to play college ball, and that will cut him deep. Then he'll blame other people for his lost chance, and never see that the problem is himself and what he's doing.

After that, he can go one of two ways. He can straighten up or he can go all the way downhill. It's up to him. You can only try to get him to stop and look at himself. The rest is up to him.

I hope he's smart enough to see what he's headed for. If he can see, I hope he has the guts to make the changes.

Those were hard words, but I shared them with Ben as I told him about Jim and his life behind bars because of drug abuse. I often used Jim as an object lesson when I counseled troubled students. They always seemed to identify with him, as if he somehow knew their pain.

And Jim truly cared about them, all those faceless students whose names I mentioned in letters or during visits. He always listened with compassion and understanding, offering to write to them, if I thought he could help.

"This might be one of the reasons for my coming here," Jim said. "I mean, me being able to help you and the young people you teach."

How ironic that he could see some benefit in his own personal tragedy. Perhaps he, like his mother, had come to believe that "all things work together for good."

Year after year, Jim allowed me to use his story as an example for others. "I want you to tell your students about me," he said. "If I can prevent just one kid from coming here, then all of this will be worth it."

My students weren't the only ones to profit from Jim's counsel. In a strange way, he became my guardian angel as well.

By the winter of 1979, almost eleven years after entering the teaching profession, I had finally reached "burnout." I was tired

216

of getting up at 4:00 A.M. to grade endless stacks of essays. I was tired of ambitious administrators implementing program after program to keep us on the "cutting edge." I was tired of outsiders clamoring for educational reform, especially since none of them had bothered to set foot inside a public school and had no idea what was going on. I was tired.

Believing that there was an easier and more lucrative way to earn a living, I decided to leave the classroom. I made application for a supervisory position at Texas Instruments, and was offered an entry-level salary that would have almost doubled my teacher's pay.

That's when the letter came.

Dear Mrs. Post,

I remember the first day I walked into your class. As soon as I was in, I felt at ease because of the atmosphere in the room. You made us young people feel like we were something more than just kids. Like adults.

If you were to ever leave teaching (I feel I can say this without contradiction), you would be missed. If you could work around young people and help them like you did our class, I think it would be better. You have a way with people, and you lead them in the right direction . . .

The print began to blur as I folded Jim's letter and laid it aside. Images of the Dirty Dozen took shape inside my head.

I recalled those twelve hard-looking boys who swaggered into my classroom that first morning — loud, lawless, lost. I remembered the looks in their eyes as they unlocked the world of language and discovered the magic of reading for the first time. I remembered their sense of wonder as they discovered something worthwhile in themselves and in others, and their looks of accomplishment as they walked across the stage to shake the superintendent's hand and accept their diplomas.

I remembered Robert and Donny and Jim and all the rest. Twelve rascally boys who taught me what was important and what was not. I remembered.

Later that afternoon, I telephoned the personnel director at Texas Instruments and withdrew my application for employment. In the years that have followed, I've never regretted that decision. Despite the long hours, low pay, and lack of confidence in public education, my passion is still teaching. I get butterflies in my stomach with each new September, and there's no place I'd rather be than with my students.

I'm grateful that, at a time in my life when I needed guidance, Jim became my guardian angel and led me in "the right direction."

During those remaining years of his incarceration, Jim chose to stay out of trouble, work hard, and keep to himself. He refused to use the illegal drugs that were readily available from the network inside the prison. While he was often forced to fight in self-defense, he would leave prison with a perfect record. And he would leave it "clean."

He chose to accept his punishment, forgive himself, and get on with his life. He refused to become calloused and hardened like those around him who vowed to "get even" with society when they got out. He chose to believe in his dignity and self-worth, and he hoped for a time when he would become a productive member of society.

Jim's model behavior did not go unnoticed. A veteran guard, long accustomed to the hard-core criminal element at the TDC, approached Carolyn Taylor with a puzzled look one morning. After introducing himself, the guard asked her privately, "What's your boy done, Mrs. Taylor? He doesn't belong here."

In February of 1984, the Texas Board of Pardons and Paroles finally concurred with the guard's assessment. After serving seven years in the Ferguson and Pack II units of the Texas Department of Corrections, Jim stood before a parole panel for the third time and petitioned the State for his freedom. The board reviewed his exemplary record, commended him for his good behavior, and granted his request.

Several days later, Jim walked through the electronic gates of "The Walls," leaving behind the guilt and shame and pain. He had accepted the responsibility for his actions, lived with the tragic consequences, and paid the debt he owed. The nightmare that began so long ago in the shadows of that country store had finally ended. He was free.

An older, graying, twenty-four-year-old man followed the Navasota River as it wound northwestward toward his hometown of Temple. He returned to the parents who had loved him enough to hold him accountable for his wrongdoing. Von and Carolyn Taylor continued to stand by Jim, just as they had done throughout his lengthy incarceration.

With the support and encouragement of family and friends, Jim assumed responsibility for himself. He found steady employment at a local construction company, and he began to rebuild his life.

He had missed out on much. He would never know special moments such as proms or graduation or other ritualistic milestones that marked the "coming of age." As if he had been trapped within some time warp, Jim found that his youth was lost, and nothing could bring it back or fill the empty chasm of his memory.

Just as nothing could recall his lost dreams, or recapture his first love. Despite his hope of returning home to marry the girl who had given meaning to his life, Jim could not reclaim the beautiful Lisa. Time had placed too many obstacles between them, and, contrary to the romantic notions of poets, love rarely conquered all. Jim was forced to relinquish his "happily ever after" dream, and the loss of Lisa proved a far greater punishment than anything inflicted on him by the Texas Department of Corrections. From that painful heartache, there would be no parole.

But, in time, Jim learned to feel again. He married and came to know a joy that he had not thought possible — the birth of his baby daughter, Savanna. Holding that tiny one in his arms as he stood beneath the Central Texas heavens, he continued the ritual of two star-gazers, lost in time and space as they searched for glittering galaxies far beyond them. The magic of his daughter's laughter and the wonder in her brilliant-blue eyes filled the void within him and compensated for all that he had lost, or thrown away.

Jim managed to do what Jesse James and Gary Gilmore never did: hang up his guns and live in peace with himself and others. Sometimes, despite the odds, Shane can come back.

Epilogue

On January 17, 1987, I stood with Jim Taylor on the back porch of Chester Brooks' deserted farmhouse in Coit. It was the tenth anniversary of the old man's death, and I'd asked Jim to help me retrace the events of that day so I could better visualize them.

This was the first time Jim had been back since the night of the murder, and I wasn't sure how he would react to being there again. He described the events of that day calmly and methodically, as if they had happened to someone else. Perhaps they had.

The place had changed considerably. The Fairview Presbyterian Church had been torn down years ago, not long after the death of Miss Ruth's husband. The congregation had dwindled, making Sunday services financially impractical.

Chester's old dirt-bottom store was gone, with no trace of its ever having existed. For months after the robbery, neighbors had avoided driving past that intersection, taking different routes to work or town or home. The memory of Chester's death was still too painful for them; there was no sense in opening old wounds, they said. Finally, the man who bought the property had the store torn down so that the healing process might begin.

The walls of Chester's back bedroom, as well as the car shed where he died, had been torn from the house. Six months after our visit, the old house itself would be gone, and the town of Coit would virtually disappear. Chester Brooks had been the heart and soul of that rural community. Once he was gone, there was no point in remembering.

We stood in what had been the old man's bedroom, and Jim showed me where the furniture had been and where he had stood the night of the robbery, waiting in the darkness for Chester Brooks to come inside. I asked Jim what he thought Chester might say to him if he were there now. Jim turned, focused his eyes on the spot where the old man's bed had been, and reflected for several moments before answering. "I think he'd say, 'I forgive you, son.' "

I hadn't known Chester Brooks, but based on what his friends told me about the compassionate old grocer, I suspected Jim was right. Chester's heart would have been big enough for that. I nodded at Jim in affirmation, and he smiled.

In silence, we walked the short distance to Jim's blue Chevy truck, climbed inside, and drove away. I watched in the rearview mirror as the decaying old house, standing resolute on the barren Texas prairie, disappeared in the distance. A deep sense of sadness enveloped me. At the time, I didn't know why.

I felt a similar sadness several months later when I stood at Chester Brooks' gravesite. I couldn't explain why I'd felt the need to visit that rural cemetery in Thornton, Texas. I'd merely seen a road sign, remembered the connection, and turned my car in that direction. Several minutes later, I found myself among hundreds of graves, searching for a man I'd never known.

I walked methodically, row by row, from the far back corner of the tree-lined cemetery and toward the front gate. I had no idea where Chester Brooks was buried, and I didn't want to overlook his grave. When I finally located the gray granite marker, I glanced up to locate my car and get my bearings. Unknowingly, I had parked beside the same row where he lay.

Standing before his modest tombstone, I read aloud the name and date of birth, and for the first time, Chester Brooks became real to me. Real and alive and vital, just as Carol Fairbairn and Frank Mitchell had described him. I recalled their words of admiration as they related favorite anecdotes about the beloved old grocer, pausing at intervals to stifle a laugh or to wipe a tear. How they had loved him.

I read the date of death, and images of that tragic January night took shape inside my head. I saw the four shadowy figures, the stone block, the blood-splattered car shed wall. From the depth of my memory I heard the raspy voice calling out, choking on the words, "Please, please, don't hit me anymore . . ."

221

I felt a strange sense of loss as I knelt before the grave. Noticing a small weed growing near his headstone, I uprooted it and tossed it aside. Then, without warning, the tears came. "I'm sorry, Mr. Brooks," I heard myself whisper at length. "I'm so sorry."

And I was.

Whenever I read a newspaper headline about violent juvenile crime, I remember the sense of loss I felt kneeling at the grave of Chester Brooks. Whenever I hear a newscast about overcrowded prisons, I remember the heartache of seeing Jim Taylor behind the plexiglas partition, fighting back the tears as he whispered, "It's hard here, Mrs. Post."

Whenever I read a report blaming public schools for the increase in juvenile rapes and robberies and murders, I know it's time. It's time for this nation's teachers to write in bold letters across their curriculum guides the same words I wrote across mine in 1978: EDUCATION IS NOT TEACHING STUDENTS WHAT THEY DO NOT KNOW. IT IS TEACHING THEM TO BEHAVE AS THEY DO NOT BEHAVE.

It's time for educators to focus on what more than eighty percent of the parents surveyed in a recent Gallup Poll expect us to teach: moral ethics.

I can hear the objections of my colleagues in teachers' lounges across the nation. "Teach ethics? We tried that back in the 1970s. You remember the 'values clarification' fad, don't you?"

"Yeah, that was a real can of worms. And just whose ethics are we supposed to teach, anyway? Socrates', Buddha's, Christ's, or Madalyn Murray O'Hair's?"

"I get enough flack trying to teach sex education. Leave moral education where it belongs — in the home and in the church."

"Right. It's their job, not ours. Let's just stick with back-to-the-basics."

But the simple truth is that eighty percent of the American parents believe that teaching *character* is as "basic" as teaching *curriculum,* and that — rightly or wrongly — both disciplines fall within the domain of the public school. Like it or not, the public expects this nation's educators to address the problems of juvenile crime, drug addiction, teenage pregnancy, and adolescent suicide. In short, they expect us to fill the moral vacuum of the 1980s by teaching ethical behavior to their children.

Given this task, what ethics do we teach to avoid the "values clarification" fiasco of the 1970s? To begin with, we focus on those principles found within the U.S. Constitution and the Bill of Rights: namely, respect for people and respect for property.

Teachers of language arts and the social sciences have ready-made opportunities to teach conduct codes acceptable in a democratic society — without altering current curriculum. We merely use opportunities in classroom discussions to assist our students in developing the skills necessary to determine right from wrong, to understand consequences, and to make appropriate choices. By showing them how to apply self-discipline and rational processes, we enable them to live constructively and ethically in a pluralistic society.

What does this look like in the classroom? First, we focus on teaching our students to respect other people. Educators may do this in two ways. We may begin by personally role-modeling this behavior in our classrooms. Ralph Waldo Emerson stated that "the secret of education lies in respecting the pupil." By treating our students with respect and by accepting individual differences, we assist them in learning to value themselves and others. When I called the Dozen "gentlemen" and treated them with courtesy, they reciprocated by behaving respectfully toward me and toward each other. By treating students with respect, we build their self-esteem and affirm their worth as members of society.

In addition to modeling respect for our students, we may also create a learning environment that builds a sense of community and fosters cooperation. We begin by utilizing classroom activities that enable students to know one another as individuals, to care about one another, and to feel a sense of membership in and accountability to the group. For example, my allowing the Dozen to collaborate on their classwork not only improved their language/reading skills, but also developed a spirit of cooperation and solidified a positive group feeling. As the boys came to know one another and trust one another, our classroom community provided a supportive "surrogate family" that met important emotional needs not being met at home or in a gang.

Teaching our students to live successfully in a democratic

223

society also means assisting them in learning to make ethical choices. We may begin by allowing time for moral reflection in our classroom. While our students usually know the "right" thing to do, they do not always choose accordingly. Why not? What gets in the way? Self-interest, peer pressure, anger, anxiety, low self-esteem? By examining these factors and reflecting on their implications, we increase our students' awareness of the complex social system to which they belong.

Language arts teachers may incorporate moral reflection in the study of literature. For example, I ask students to analyze the traits which make Atticus Finch the "hero" of *To Kill a Mockingbird* — honesty, integrity, compassion, courage. What makes Bob Ewell the villain — his bigotry, ignorance, violence? Which traits are valued most by the citizens of a democratic society?

Or, I ask students to consider the consequences of a character's choice, thereby giving them valuable practice in ethical decision-making. For example, should John Proctor have lied to the Salem witchcraft court and saved himself from hanging in *The Crucible*? Should George Milton have been tried for murder after shooting his mentally retarded friend in *Of Mice and Men*? Should Huck Finn have violated the Fugitive Slave Law by helping Jim escape? Such moral reflection requires students to think both logically and ethically.

Social studies teachers may also use moral reflection by asking students to focus on historical incidents or current events, determining the correlation between choice and consequence. Psychology teachers and humanities teachers may use current films or popular music to consider the moral implications of acceptable or unacceptable conduct codes in a democratic society. Opportunities for teaching ethical decision-making are abundant in our classrooms; we must merely raise our consciousness and focus our efforts.

To counter the rise in juvenile violence, we must also teach our students "conflict resolution" strategies. Most adolescents don't know how to handle conflicts; they regard personal disagreements as "contests" with winners and losers. If we can teach students to resolve conflicts in such a way that there are no "losers," we help them minimize the need for violence as an expression of hostility. We must equip students with legitimate ways to settle disputes short of drive-by shootings.

Language arts and social science teachers may help their students examine the dynamics of conflict by using fictional or real-life models. We can promote an understanding of what causes conflicts and why individuals respond differently. In addition, we can explain how basic psychological needs must be met in order to resolve individual differences.

Students may then be trained to use specific "verbal negotiation" skills to communicate needs, mediate problems, and resolve differences. Communication and mediation are important life skills that may be practiced in the classroom through simulated activities related to curriculum. Fictional or historical characters may be role-played as students learn to mediate conflict in such a way as to assure a win-win resolution.

The increase of violence in public schools may also require a change in the way disruptive students are disciplined. Traditionally, schools have dealt with conflict through the detention, suspension, or expulsion of an offending student. The effectiveness of after-the-fact punitive measures is now being questioned. A pro-active prevention program which empowers students and increases their self-esteem may produce better results in reducing the incidence of violence and vandalism.

The word "discipline" means "to teach," not merely "to punish." Perhaps it's time for modern educators to follow a course of instruction as old as the McGuffey's reader: the teaching of moral ethics in conjunction with academic curriculum. While our grandfathers were learning to read stories and poems in McGuffey's, their teachers were also indoctrinating them with subtle doses of American values. The poem "Lazy Ned," for example, encouraged fourth-grade students to set goals and to work hard if they wished to succeed. Yesterday's children learned that a democratic society values responsible citizens with a work ethic. McGuffey's reader taught moral conduct and character development, as well as vocabulary skills and reading comprehension.

Perhaps it's time to go "back to the future" and emulate the McGuffey model. Television, movies, and music have bombarded our children with negative messages; a counterbalance is sorely needed. America's educators, K-12, have the power to ex-

225

ert a positive influence on children if we focus our efforts on teaching moral truths as well as textbook facts.

"What good will all that do?" I hear my colleagues recite in unison. "You're being far too idealistic. Surely you don't think we're going to stop juvenile rapes and robberies and murders with a few moralistic platitudes."

Perhaps not. But when I'm tempted to succumb to the nay-sayers, I repeat a ten-word maxim I learned early in my teaching career: IF IT IS TO BE, IT IS UP TO ME.

Idealistic or not, I believe teachers can make a difference in the lives of their students. I believe educators have the power to impact the moral behavior of our future nation. I believe we can effectively intervene in the lives of troubled teenagers and can salvage juvenile offenders. I believe because Jim Taylor and the Dirty Dozen taught me to believe.

Two of the Dozen went on to serve proudly in the United States military. They had learned well the lessons about accepting responsibility, respecting others, and being committed to society.

Two boys became foremen at construction companies. Daily, they utilized the cooperation and negotiation skills we had practiced as they supervised workers and managed materials.

One boy became a youth minister, another a member of the Masonic Lodge. Both made ethical and moral choices, just like the fictional characters we analyzed in class. The seeds I had sown so many years before finally found fruition.

"*But,*" the nay-sayers will likely interject, "one became a child molester, one an armed robber, and one a convicted murderer. What about them?"

Seeds on stony ground.

Jim and the other two boys taught me an important lesson about seeds: they're not all alike. I'm reminded of that truth each spring when the barren Texas prairies are miraculously transformed into a brilliant patchwork of wildflowers. The reds and yellows and blues give testament to Nature's handiwork, both in the fertile fields and on the stony ground.

My favorite wildflower is the Texas bluebonnet, perhaps because it is the early harbinger of spring. Standing tall and stately

226

with its slender stalk reaching toward heaven, the bluebonnet is truly breathtaking.

Because of my fondness for this flower, I'd tried to grow bluebonnets a number of times, but without success. Despite my painstaking efforts to follow the directions on the package, planting at the optimum time and with the best soil conditions, my efforts had failed to produce a single plant. In my frustration, I had finally consulted a Temple High School colleague, who was a gardener as well as a biology teacher.

"Did you rough up the seed coats before you sowed them?" he asked.

"Did I what?"

"Did you take a piece of sandpaper and rough up the outside of the seeds?" He went on to explain that scratching the seed coat with sandpaper allowed bacteria to enter the interior and begin germination. Without the roughing-up process, bluebonnet seeds could lie in the ground for years without producing a plant, he said.

It later occurred to me that, just as there was a secret in growing stubborn bluebonnets, there was also a secret in growing rebellious children: the seeds had to be roughed up. And as painful as that was to watch, sometimes there was no other way.

I suspected that was true in Jim Taylor's life. He had hardened his heart, and there was no other choice than to rough up the seed coat. Perhaps it took tragedy and prison for the seeds of moral ethics to find fruition in Jim's life.

And as difficult as that was for me to watch, I saw good come from that situation. Even though my heart ached for Von and Carolyn Taylor as they struggled with their errant child, I learned from them a lesson in faith. Those courageous parents made the tough choices, believing that someday their son would be restored to them. And he was.

Behavior modification, positive reinforcement, cooperative learning, self-responsibility, ethical decision-making, conflict resolution — these were the instructional seeds that finally found fruition in the lives of Jim and the Dozen. Each of these intervention strategies enabled me to help them find what Jim Taylor called "the right direction."

* * * * *

Fifteen Septembers have passed since the Dozen last sat in my classroom, yet I think of them often. Each fall as I skim a new roster of faceless names and contemplate the awesome responsibility that is mine, I sense the presence of those twelve rascally boys lurking somewhere behind the walls. I can almost hear their boisterous voices and rowdy banter as they intrude on my thoughts.

Sometimes I glance at the desk on the last row, remembering the black-hatted outlaw who sat there, and I smile. For it's then that I recall the parable of seeds on stony ground and the lesson Jim Taylor taught me about throwaway kids and juvenile offenders.

It's a lesson of quiet hope — a lesson the writer George Eliot must have learned more than a hundred years ago when she wrote: "It's never too late to be what you might have been."

Chester Brooks' dirt-bottom store served as a gathering place in Coit, Texas.
Courtesy of Carol Fairbairn

Chester Brooks, the victim, stands inside his rural store.
Courtesy of Carol Fairbairn

The murderers gained entrance through the back door of the store.

Courtesy of Carol Fairbairn

Chester Brooks stands outside his store with two young customers. Brooks' house sits a stone's throw to the west.

Courtesy of Carol Fairbairn

230

Chester's antique car with the prophetic license plate sits adjacent to his house.
Courtesy of Carol Fairbairn

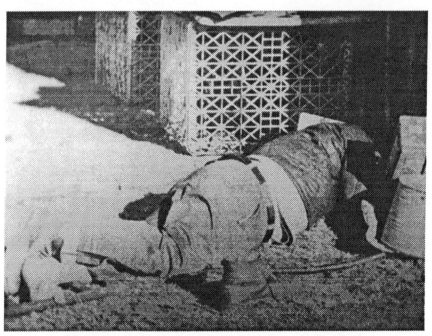

Chester Brooks' battered body lies beside the car shed wall.
Courtesy of Sheriff Dennis Walker

The Fairview Presbyterian Church sits west of the crime scene. Blood was discovered on a nearby fence.

Courtesy of Sheriff Dennis Walker

A young mourner sits beside the Brooks grave in Thornton, Texas.

Courtesy of Carol Fairbairn

The Limestone County jail sits in the shadows of the water tower in Groesbeck, Texas.

Courtesy Author's Collection

Exterior of the Limestone County courthouse in Groesbeck, Texas.

Courtesy Author's Collection

Interior of the 77th District Court in Groesbeck, Texas.
Courtesy Author's Collection

The Honorable Clarence Ferguson of the 77th District Court.
Courtesy of Judge Clarence Ferguson

Joe Cannon, defense attorney for Jim Taylor.

Jim Taylor stands at Cedar Ridge Park, ten years after murder evidence was dumped at the site.

Courtesy Author's Collection

The Brooks store was torn down to ease the pain of neighbors. Only a barren spot remains.

Courtesy Author's Collection

Ten years after the murder, Chester Brooks' house sits deserted. It, too, would be torn down, and the town of Coit, Texas, would disappear.

Courtesy Author's Collection

Aggie Harrison's tombstone in the New Hope Cemetery may have linked Jim Taylor with his boyhood hero, Jesse James.

Courtesy Author's Collection

ABOUT THE AUTHOR

Linda Williams Post is a veteran educator with more than 25 years in the teaching profession. She has been named "Educator of the Year," has been honored by CBS television for her innovative classroom instruction, and has been commended by the Texas Senate for her outstanding contribution to public education.

She teaches Honors English at Temple High School, where her program has been recognized as a Center of Excellence by the National Council of Teachers of English. With such national recognition, she has traveled extensively, lecturing to educators and presenting workshops at state and national conferences.

Linda has won the English Journal Writing Award, presented by the National Council of Teachers of English. Her other publication credits include articles in professional journals such as English in Texas and Teaching English in the Two-year College.

Her first book, *STONY GROUND: One Teacher's Fight Against Juvenile Crime,* has been honored regionally, wining nonfiction awards at the Dallas Writers' Conference and the Beaumont Writers' Conference.

Linda was selected to attend the prestigious Bread Loaf Writers' Conference, a writing school founded by poet Robert Frost in Middlebury, Vermont. While there, she studied nonfiction writing with Ron Powers, the Pulitzer prize-winning journalist and former media critic for CBS News.

She received her B.A. degree from the University of Texas at Arlington in 1968. Linda lives in Temple, Texas, with her husband and teenage son.